A Family's Guide to the Military

FOR

DUMMIES®

A Family's Guide to the Military

FOR DUMMIES®

by Sheryl Garrett and Sue Hoppin

Foreword By Tanya Biank
Author of *Army Wives*

WILEY

Wiley Publishing, Inc.

A Family's Guide to the Military For Dummies®

Published by
Wiley Publishing, Inc.
111 River St.
Hoboken, NJ 07030-5774
www.wiley.com

Copyright © 2009 by Wiley Publishing, Inc., Indianapolis, Indiana

Published simultaneously in Canada

For general information on our other products and services, please contact our Customer Care Department within the U.S. at 800-762-2974, outside the U.S. at 317-572-3993, or fax 317-572-4002.

For technical support, please visit www.wiley.com/techsupport.

Wiley also publishes its books in a variety of electronic formats. Some content that appears in print may not be available in electronic books.

Library of Congress Control Number: 2008936637

ISBN: 978-0-470-38697-2

Manufactured in the United States of America

10 9 8 7 6 5 4 3 2 1

WILEY

About the Authors

Sheryl Garrett, CFP and founder of The Garrett Planning Network, Inc., has been dubbed "The All-American Planner," possibly because of her zealous mission to "help make competent, objective financial advice accessible to all people." Sheryl's fresh approach as a financial advisor working with clients on an hourly, as-needed, fee-only basis has evolved into an international network of financial advisors, the Garrett Planning Network.

As a consumer advocate, Sheryl has been honored to work with the House Subcommittee on Financial Services regarding predatory lending regulation, financial literacy and Social Security reform. She also works as an expert witness in lawsuits against financial advisors who rendered inappropriate financial advice.

She has authored or served as a technical editor on over a dozen books and a couple of monthly magazine columns. These books include *Garrett's Guide to Financial Planning* (National Underwriter), *Just Give Me the Answer$* (Dearborn Trade), *Money Without Matrimony* (Dearborn Trade), *Personal Finance Workbook For Dummies* (Wiley), *Investing in an Uncertain Economy For Dummies* (Wiley), as well as this book, *A Family's Guide to the Military For Dummies* (Wiley).

As vocal advocate for financial education, Sheryl has been frequently interviewed on CNNfn, Bloomberg, ABC World News Now, Fox-TV; NPR's *All Things Considered* and *Marketplace;* and in *Business Week, Newsweek, Time, Forbes, Kiplinger Personal Finance, Money, Smart Money, MarketWatch, U.S. News & World Repor*t, the *New York Times*, *USA Today* and the *Wall Street Journal.* For four straight years Sheryl was recognized by Investment Advisor magazine as "One of the Top 25 Most Influential People in Financial Planning" and was honored by the National Association of Personal Financial Advisors (NAPFA) honored Garrett with the prestigious *Robert J. Underwood Distinguished Service Award* for her contributions to the development of the financial planning profession.

Sue Hoppin is passionate about quality of life issues for military families because she lives and understands the challenges of the military lifestyle. Elements of her story are shared by any number of other military spouses. She met her husband when he was attending the United States Air Force Academy and finished school while he attended undergraduate pilot training. The couple married shortly thereafter and a son followed. Their transient life-style, deployment schedules and other demands kept Sue at home with their son while her husband deployed around the world.

Although she holds multiple degrees, it wasn't until recently that Sue was able to enter the work force. Before then, she served the military community as a volunteer. Her responsibilities ranged from squadron fundraiser and spouse club membership chair to the presidency of both the Kadena Officers' Spouses' Club and of the Ramstein Elementary School PTA. She currently serves as the 2008–2009 President of the Air Force Officers Wives Club at Bolling AFB. Sue was recognized for her volunteer efforts with awards as Volunteer of the Year at McConnell AFB (1999) and as the 76th Airlift Squadron Spouse of the Year (2002).

She joined the Benefits Information Department staff of Military Officers Association of America in 2005 and quickly established herself as an expert in military spouse issues. In 2006, Sue was selected to be MOAA's first assistant director for spouse outreach. In 2007, Military Spouse Magazine named Sue on their 2007 Who's Who of Military Spouses list recognizing 12 spouses who have made significant contributions in the military community for all military spouses.

A tireless advocate for improving the lives of military spouses and families, Sue is the consummate connector — bringing together government, corporate, and nonprofit organizations to meet spouses where they live and work. She is the driving force behind the annual Spouse Symposium held in Norfolk, VA that brings key legislative, spouse, community, and DoD leaders together in an interactive forum to achieve real change for military spouses.

In addition to her work at MOAA, she writes a monthly column for Military Spouse Magazine and serves as a member of the Board of Advisors for the Military Spouse and Family Legacy Association.

Sue holds a bachelor's degree in international studies from the University of Denver and a master's degree in international relations from the University of Oklahoma.

Dedication

This book is dedicated to all of our military families. Your support and devotion are essential to the mission, and we all know too well the sacrifices you make.

Our heartfelt thanks to you and your military member for your service to our nation.

Authors' Acknowledgments

From Sheryl: Because of the love and devotion of my family, staff , and colleagues in the Garrett Planning Network, I have the freedom and support to carry out the mission of my life's work, which involves helping to make competent, objective personal financial advice accessible to all people. But I have a special place in my heart for military families and veterans. I am honored to have been given the opportunity to do a little for those who do so much in service to our country.

This project would not have been possible without the amazing talent and devotion of my co-author, Sue Hoppin. She taught me a lot more than she meant to, I'm sure. I wouldn't have got to know Sue without the most perfect introduction from the energizer bunny himself, Phil Dyer, CFP, RLP. This book required the talents of a lot of people. Sue and I needed one another and both of us relied on Phil as our Technical Reviewer extraordinaire. We also had great support from the folks at Wiley, specifically Mike Baker and Jennifer Connolly. Thanks for your faith in us and for recognizing the need for this book.

From Sue: Without the love and support of my husband Kevin and my son Garrett, writing this book would not have been possible. Balancing work and writing the book, I missed out on endless regattas, other school events, and any number of social activities with them. I can't even count the number of times they had to endure frozen dinners or take-out meals, so I thank them from the bottom of my heart for being such good sports. They both really picked up the slack and encouraged me when sometimes it just seemed like too much. Between them and our amazing support system of friends and family, no one could ask for better cheerleaders.

Thanks to Phil Dyer, my colleague, friend, and mentor who introduced me to Sheryl Garrett and started us down the path of writing this book together. Thanks to Sheryl for being such a pleasure to work with and for taking a chance on me. You both had more faith in me than I sometimes had in myself.

Many thanks to Mike Baker, Jennifer Connolly and the other folks at Wiley Publishing who made this experience such a tremendous one. Thank you for allowing me the opportunity to create a product to benefit military spouses and families.

There were some sections of this book that were difficult to write and wouldn't have resonated as well without the guidance of other people. Thank you Phil for your expertise and DeDe for providing your insights.

A final thanks to my friends and fellow military spouses: Tanya Biank, Babette Maxwell, Nicole Alcorn, Krista Wells, and Robin Prior whose words of encouragement remind me daily about all that is best about the military spouse community. When we get it right, we really get it right — I cannot imagine a greater group of friends or role models.

Publisher's Acknowledgments

We're proud of this book; please send us your comments through our Dummies online registration form located at www.dummies.com/register/.

Some of the people who helped bring this book to market include the following:

Acquisitions, Editorial, and Media Development

Project Editor: Jennifer Connolly

Acquisitions Editor: Mike Baker

Copy Editor: Jennifer Connolly

Technical Editor: Phil Dyer

Senior Editorial Manager: Jennifer Ehrlich

Editorial Supervisor: Carmen Krikorian

Editorial Assistants: Erin Calligan Mooney, Joe Niesen, Jennette ElNagger, and David Lutton

Cartoons: Rich Tennant (www.the5thwave.com)

Cover Photo Credit: Kriss Russell©

Composition Services

Project Coordinator: Katie Key

Layout and Graphics: Reuben W. Davis, Christin Swinford, Christine Williams

Proofreaders: Melissa Bronnenberg, Amanda Steiner, Evelyn W. Still

Indexer: Potomac Indexing, LLC

Publishing and Editorial for Consumer Dummies

Diane Graves Steele, Vice President and Publisher, Consumer Dummies

Joyce Pepple, Acquisitions Director, Consumer Dummies

Kristin A. Cocks, Product Development Director, Consumer Dummies

Michael Spring, Vice President and Publisher, Travel

Kelly Regan, Editorial Director, Travel

Publishing for Technology Dummies

Andy Cummings, Vice President and Publisher, Dummies Technology/General User

Composition Services

Gerry Fahey, Vice President of Production Services

Debbie Stailey, Director of Composition Services

Contents at a Glance

Table of Contents

Chapter 8: Starting Out on the Right Financial Foot 97

Chapter 9: Building onto Your Financial Foundation 113

Chapter 10: Housing Options for the Military Family. 131

Foreword

I have always believed people are the heart and soul of our military and not our whiz-bang technology and state-of-the-art weapons systems. It takes a special group of people to put the nation's families before their own families and that is the sacrifice that deployed military members and their families accept on behalf of all Americans.

With more than half of all service members married, *A Family's Guide to the Military For Dummies* is a necessary, timely, and important book. Sue Hoppin and Sheryl Garrett have done a masterful job of making sense out of a gargantuan and daunting topic. Sue brings a spouse's perspective, a writer's touch, and her years of experience as a leader and advocate for improving the lives of military spouses and families, while Sheryl is the consummate consumer advocate, having worked with Congress and the courts to stop predatory lending practices, increase financial literacy, and reform Social Security.

Part reference guide, part practical advice, this gem of a book should be required reading for every new recruit and military bride. Why? Because the military is not just a job. It's one of those few professions that has a life-long impact on the entire family. Falling in love with and marrying a military member requires accepting the military lifestyle — the memorable times, as well as the hardships — as your own.

The military has come a long way in how it views families. The outdated saying, "If the military wanted you to have a wife it would have issued you one," has been replaced with, "You enlist a service member, but re-enlist a family." In the last few years, military leaders have realized that maintaining and retaining the force is linked to service members' quality of life with their families. "Quality of life" is a hot-button issue within the military community and today's military offers better resources and programs for families. But making sense of it all when you are trying to figure out rank structure and acronyms can be overwhelming for the uninitiated. *A Family's Guide to the Military For Dummies* is more than just a comprehensive guide to all things military. It's like a new friend taking you by the hand and showing you the ropes, which is reason enough to give *A Family's Guide to the Military For Dummies* a 21-gun salute.

—Tanya Biank
Author of *Army Wives,* the basis for the hit Lifetime TV show of the same name

Introduction

· ·

Do you feel like the military lifestyle should come with its own how-to handbook full of tips and insights? Well, you're not alone. Unless you were born into a military family, going behind the gates of a military installation for the first time can seem somewhat daunting. But, it's not meant to be. Everything's actually laid out to be as convenient as possible for the end user — *you*. If it seems like you need some guidance, then don't despair. Maybe you just need a little guidance from someone who's already been there and done that.

We wrote this book to help you figure out the ins and outs of military life as well as share with you financial insights that you may not always have ready access to. When you're living on a tight budget, it may not always seem possible to save that emergency fund never mind the kids' college fund, but you'd be missing out. Our goal is to let you know that military life is entirely compatible with financial stability.

We share some tips and information with you on concepts that will make you look at saving and investing not as *nice to do* things, but rather as *must do*. Remember that the sooner you get started, the more time you have to take advantage of compounding interest. Maximizing your military benefits and saving a little at a time will help you attain financial independence.

Along the way, you will meet other military spouses and family members who will help you along your journey. But, if we can give you a head start by sharing some information, then our time and effort was well spent.

About This Book

A Family's Guide to the Military For Dummies is designed to share with you an overview of the military lifestyle. You can discover everything from the traditions of the military to community resources available to support you. You're not likely going to read the book from cover to cover, but that's alright. We've written it so that each chapter is somewhat autonomous. As you're flipping around, you may see some references made to other chapters, but they're well marked. If you're approaching utilizing this book as a reference, then the index or Table of Contents will be invaluable to you. Refer to those whenever you're looking for a specific topic.

But, if you're really curious about the military lifestyle, then by all means, work through the book chapter by chapter. We've laid it out in a simplistic and intuitive manner. In the beginning chapters, we start off with a beginner's look at the military and military infrastructure then progress on to more complex matters such as deployments and financial benefits. Use the information as you need it.

If you find that this book just whets your appetite for more knowledge, take advantage of the websites we provide and the other organizations and resources we point to throughout the book. The great thing about the military is that there is no shortage of people and resources out there to assist you on your journey. Buckle in and enjoy the ride!

Conventions Used in this Book

While writing this book, we used a few conventions throughout the pages in order to make your life just a little bit easier. Here's what you can expect:

- ✔ We use italics when we define a word or phrase that's important to understanding a topic. And when we get especially excited, we might throw in some *italics* for extra emphasis.

- ✔ When you see text in **bold,** you can expect it to be either a step in a numbered list or a key word in a bulleted list.

- ✔ All Web addresses appear in monofont.

- ✔ When this book was printed, some Web addresses may have needed to break across two lines of text. If that happened, know that we haven't put in any characters (such as hyphens) to indicate a break. So, when using one of these Web addresses, just type in exactly what you see in this book or on the Cheat Sheet and ignore the line break.

Foolish Assumptions

Believe it or not, as we set out to write this book, we formed some preconceived ideas about you our dear reader. In order to provide the insights and advice you need, we have made some assumptions about you:

- ✔ You're either married to someone in the military or interested in the information presented here.

- ✔ You're curious enough to want to know the inside gouge (information) on the military lifestyle.

✔ You have access to the Internet. Although this isn't a requirement, access to the Internet will help you take advantage of the tips we share regarding web resources.

✔ You're interested in learning about your military and financial benefits so that you can get your family on the road to financial independence.

✔ You want to know and take advantage of everything out there to help you thrive within the military community while also helping you achieve your own personal goals.

✔ You're no idiot! In fact, you're so smart that you realize that in order to thrive in your military lifestyle, you need to know everything that's out there to support you and your family.

How This Book is Organized

A Family's Guide to the Military for Dummies is organized into six parts touching on different aspects of the military lifestyle. Financial tidbits are woven throughout.

Part 1: Reporting for Duty

The military lifestyle can seem quite foreign to most newcomers. In these chapters, you discover more about the basics. We take you on a quick tour of a traditional military installation and learn more about the traditions that make the military so unique.

Part II: Understanding Your Financial Issues and Benefits

One of the greatest reasons to join the military is to enjoy the many financial and military benefits available to you and your family. Unfortunately, many people are unfamiliar with their benefits and leave a lot on the table. In this section, we discuss your basic pay and benefits as well as more complex topics such as home ownership and education. After you have a better understanding, we introduce you to other benefits available to you outside of the traditional military infrastructure.

Part III: Supporting the Military Family

Separations are a challenge to maintaining strong military families. Children need to be incredibly resilient to thrive under the transient military lifestyle. Fortunately, there are a number of systems in place to support military families. In this section, you'll learn more about the resources out there available to support you and your family.

Part IV: Mastering Deployments

As a novice at deployments, you might look around at the more "veteran" families and think, "Wow, they really have it together." The chapters found in this section will help you understand all the stages of deployment as well as how you can prepare more adequately.

Part V: Transitioning Out of the Military

Whether through separation or retirement, leaving the military can be potentially quite traumatic unless you understand the pay and benefits available to you. This section will help you understand your transition benefits as well as how to roll your military benefits into future employee compensation and benefits packages.

Part VI: The Part of Tens

A hallmark of the *For Dummies* series, the Part of Tens highlights our top ten lists for best benefits for military spouses, biggest financial military benefits, and the ten worst scams against service members.

Icons Used in This Book

As you flip through this book, you'll see a lot of icons, which are there to draw your attention to specific issues or examples. Check them out:

This icon alerts you to common pitfalls and dangers that you must be on the lookout for when managing your personal finances or simply moving along in your military life.

If you don't read anything else, pay attention to this icon, which points out information we just had to stress because it *is* that important for you to consider.

If you're looking for some inside information or a time-saving tool you can use immediately, then the text marked by the Tip icon is what you want.

This icon gives you technical info that you don't *have* to know to understand the rest of the section, but we sure think it's interesting to read about!

Where to Go from Here

If you're a novice to the military lifestyle, start at the beginning. However, if you're at a different stage of life, go ahead and turn directly to that section of the book. You'll see parts dealing with everything from deployments, supporting military children to transitioning out of the military. You'll be able to find anything you're looking for quite easily by referring to the index or table of contents.

Remember: Don't worry about reading this book from cover to cover (unless you want to!). Use the bits and pieces as you need them. Every experience is different, and our dearest hope is that you can find enough information and guidance among these pages to provide some comfort and support to you.

Part I:
Reporting for Duty

The 5th Wave
By Rich Tennant

"At 1700 hours position yourselves along the perimeter of the living room. As they enter we'll hit them with the nuts and bread sticks. At 1750 hours Dolores will move to their right flank and advance with the drinks, driving them from the kitchen. As they weaken from dancing we'll cut off their supplies and force them into the driveway."

In this part . . .

Before you can embrace the military lifestyle, you need to understand the basics. In this part, you'll get a primer on military protocol and traditions. You'll also learn the basics of what you can expect on a military installation.

Chapter 1

Living Life As a Military Family

In This Chapter

▶ Becoming acquainted with military culture

▶ Maintaining flexibility

▶ Talking the talk

▶ Getting to know everyone

▶ Figuring out if living on the installation is for you

Some people believe that being in the military is no different than working for a major corporation with multiple outlets around the world. But what corporation do you know requires *all* their employees to be available 24 hours a day, 7 days a week, and 365 days a year?

Military service is a demanding way of life and there are very few people willing to sign on the dotted line and add themselves to the 1 percent of our nation's population that makes up this nation's All Volunteer Force.

If your servicemember is part of this All Volunteer Force, welcome to the club. Life in the military is wrought with its own challenges and rewards. But success is 90 percent attitude. Throughout this chapter, we draw a broad picture of what sets military families apart from their civilian counterparts, talk about some of the idiosyncrasies of the military, as well as let you know what you can expect right off the bat.

Getting a Grasp on the Military Culture

The military certainly retains its own culture. When your servicemember joins the military, you're exposed to a tight-knit community of people supporting a cause greater than themselves and dealing with issues that the average soccer mom would never encounter. In the sections that follow, we help you understand the military culture by giving you an idea of why servicemembers join and stay in the military as well as how connected you become to your community.

Believing in something bigger than yourself

Ask 100 people why they chose to *join* the military and you'll probably get about 100 different answers that might include travel, thrills, opportunities, money, and benefits. For those of us with wanderlust, the promise of travel still serves to lure some to military service. Certainly with the *temporary duties* (TDYs/TADs) and opportunities to be stationed overseas at exotic locations, wanting to see the world is as good a reason to join the military as any other. There are also some thrill seekers who are drawn to the military by the promise of adventure and tough challenges that only jumping out of airplanes or landing on an aircraft carrier can deliver.

Many choose service as a way of upholding family tradition. For some, it's all they know. If they're military brats, they may loath to imagine any other life. Others are looking for job security or opportunities to learn new skills and better themselves. The benefits of the *Montgomery GI Bill* (MGIB) still draw people looking for a way to finance a college education. Although there are definite financial benefits to military service, not too many people are going to say that they did it solely for the money. So what keeps people in through the deployments, family separations, and constant moves? Simply said, that belief in something bigger than themselves. Ask 100 people why they chose to *stay* in the military and you'll probably only get a handful of answers that include honor, pride, and a desire to serve their country. The decision your servicemember made to join the military means that you are now part of this great tradition.

Making lifelong connections

The military seems to draw together a diverse group of people from all walks of life. However, that common bond of believing in something bigger than yourself ensures that you already have a strong tie to the friends you make in the military.

You'd think that the constant moving would guarantee that you are forever saying goodbye to friends and starting over again. To a certain extent, that's true; but in the military, you never say goodbye, just "hope to see you again soon." With a finite number of installations you can be stationed to, chances are good that over the years, you'll keep running into some of the same people over and over again.

Don't burn bridges because you never know when you'll run into that annoying soccer mom again somewhere down the road.

Civilian friendships are forged over shared experiences such as attending the same schools, vacationing in the same places, and living in the same small town for your entire life. The military's not so different. Think of a culture where you all move in the same circles. Even though you'll move from base to base, you stand the likelihood of living in the same towns (although at different times), vacationing in the same military hot spots, and going to the same base schools. Your best friends become those who served with you on the PTA board, the mother of your son's best friend, or your neighbor on base who watches your kids so you can get a haircut or make a commissary run without your screaming toddler in tow.

So what's different about the military? Well, some of your best friends will also be the ones who help you weather that second, fourth, and fifth deployment. The ones you call at 3 a.m. because the news just reported some casualties in the field. They're the ones who babysit your kids who are running a 101 degree temperature when you can least afford to miss another day of work. They are the same people who cry with you because your spouse is passed over for a promotion or rejoice with you because he or she is chosen for one. They understand without words what you are going through because they have walked in your shoes. Your military friends become an extended family and these are relationships that you will come to count on throughout your time in the military.

Like everything else worth having, these lifelong connections need to be nurtured. There are certain things you can do to develop and maintain these strong connections:

- ✔ Meet the other families in your unit or squadron.
- ✔ Get involved.
- ✔ Be there for your friends and recognize when they might need some extra care and attention.
- ✔ Stay in touch.
- ✔ Share your milestones (such as promotions, graduations, and new additions to the family).
- ✔ Make the effort to send change of address cards.
- ✔ Send those annual holiday cards and letters.
- ✔ Follow the golden rule: Always write in pencil.

Being Flexible — the Key to a Happy Military Life

If you're the type of person who likes to control your surroundings, you're going to have to let that go. After your servicemember joins the military, you're no longer in charge of your life. Of course, you still have some input, but ultimately, your life is out of your hands.

With all the things you can't control, you may find it easy to start thinking that you have become an unwitting pawn in someone else's life. Don't get sucked into that mentality. True, military life demands that you look at things from a different perspective than civilian life. Moving every 2 to 4 years gives you an opportunity to recreate yourself every time. Think of the opportunities you can have that others can only dream of. While your civilian friends can only look at pictures of the great works of art, you can visit them in Paris, London, or Florence. Your friends at home learn a second language in an academic setting while you have the opportunity to immerse yourself in other cultures and languages. You get the idea — it's all in the perspective. Rather than lamenting about how the military limits your choices, start thinking about how it broadens your horizons.

In the sections that follow, we give you some advice on how to control the things you can control and let go of the other stuff . . . for now. Maintaining a good outlook ensures that you will be open to opportunities that present themselves.

Adjusting to different directions

So you may be thinking that your servicemember is given orders, you follow them, and that's that. Well, that's just the beginning. A lot can happen between being given an order and preparing for it. Be prepared to adjust to situations, such as the following examples:

- ✔ Just when you think you're headed to Hawaii on assignment and begin dreaming of Mai tais on the beach, a change in orders occurs and you're headed to Iceland — start dreaming about geysers and five-foot snow drifts!

- ✔ Your servicemember deployed in the last year and is not due to deploy again for another year, but the needs of the service prevail and you learn that he or she's scheduled to be on the next plane out for another rotation.

In the military, nothing is carved in stone.

Adapting to a changing homelife

You need to be flexible with your home as well. With bases spread out across the United States and overseas, imagine all the different floor plans you can look forward to. One assignment you might be living in a 1,500-square-foot ranch-style home and the next assignment, your same family could be expected to fit into a 900-square-foot apartment-style home. That gorgeous, comfortable overstuffed couch that seemed like such a great idea in Oklahoma might be a little less so when it won't fit into your little apartment in Japan. And the ceiling to floor drapes that were to die for in your German house with the tall ceilings, huge windows, and great light may not be as attractive in Florida when you're having to drill into cinderblock to hang them and then once you get them hung up, they block out all the natural light coming in through those teeny tiny hurricane-friendly windows.

Regardless of how well you might plan, none of your furniture will fit into the parade of houses you'll ultimately live in throughout a military career. At least, not necessarily into the rooms they were intended for. More than a few military families have had to live with a sideboard in the bedroom because that's the only place it would fit. And there's nothing stranger than seeing a huge, ornate crystal chandelier from Prague hanging in the foyer of a prefab base home in Grand Forks, North Dakota. As a fellow military spouse, you quickly learn to ignore these anomalies and sympathize with the need to adapt and make do.

Keeping education and employment flexible

The need to remain flexible is nowhere more evident than in spouse employment and education. There has been many a spouse who started a bachelor's degree at one institution only to finally graduate seven years and four different universities later. And what military spouse doesn't have numerous gaps in his or her résumé with a strange and seemingly unrelated range of jobs held over the years? The desire to create a life for yourself and the need to balance it with your servicemember's military service is a challenge that has faced military spouses throughout the years. More information on military spouse employment and education can be found in Chapter 11.

Unlike a lot of your civilian friends, you don't have the luxury of sticking around to finish your degree or work to climb the corporate ladder and build seniority. But think of it this way: How many other people get the opportunity to meet people from all different walks of life, travel around the United States, and possibly live in a foreign country?

Traveling the world . . . If you want to

Join the military, see the world. This is still true. Depending on how adventurous you are, you can see as much or as little of the world as you want to. Some people will spend their entire career in the continental United States. Others will grab any chance they can to travel. In this section, we tell you how, between overseas assignments and *space available* (Space-A) seating on military flights, opportunities to see the world abound.

Overseas assignments

If you've ever been curious about other countries and are offered an overseas assignment, seize the opportunity. You'll never get a better chance to immerse yourself in another culture. The greatest thing about being stationed overseas with the military is that you have all the benefits of living in a foreign country with a security blanket. Regardless of what foreign locale you may be stationed to, as soon as you make it back on base, the rules change, and you're back in Little America. Back to the familiar fast-food outlets, commissary, and exchange (more about these in Chapter 4). What could be better than the adventure of living overseas with all the comforts of home?

Space-available travel

If you want to see the world and aren't fortunate enough to be stationed overseas, take advantage of your Space-A (space-available) benefits. Forget reading just about riding in a gondola in the canals of Venice or gazing at the geishas in old Kyoto. With some time and research, you can soon be on your way to traveling there for next to nothing.

Space-available travel is one of the greatest privileges extended to servicemembers and their dependents. The premise is simple, if there are extra seats available on the military aircraft flying around official cargo and personnel, and if the crew is not restricted by mission constraints, extra available seats are released to space-available travelers.

There are six categories of Space-A travelers, and seats are allocated by descending order with Category 1 (CAT-1) being the highest and Category 6 (CAT-6) being the lowest. Within the categories, passengers compete based on how long they have been registered in the Space-A system for seats on the flight.

Space-A flights are unreliable and should only be attempted by people who have a lot of time and flexibility. At any given moment, a flight might be terminated without notice and you may have to purchase a commercial ticket back. In other words, if your sister's getting married Wednesday on the west coast and you have to be back on the east coast by Saturday, Space-A is not your best option. However, given enough time, Space-A travel is a great and affordable way to see the world.

To address the questions of who's eligible and how Space-A travel works, check out the most up-to-date information on the Air Mobility Command fact sheet: `http://www.amc.af.mil/questions/topic.asp?id=380`.

In addition to the official information, there are entire books and Web sites dedicated to the ins and outs of Space-A travel, but here are some basic things to remember:

- ✔ Space-A travelers can register up to 60 days before their desired date of travel.
- ✔ Military personnel need to be on leave orders to register for Space-A.
- ✔ Although there is no cost in travelling on a military aircraft, there are some costs associated with traveling on a commercially-contracted airplane.
- ✔ If your flight has multiple legs, you can get bumped off at any time.
- ✔ Show times for military flights have a way of changing based on the needs of the mission, and there is no obligation to notify Space-A travelers of these changes, so stay close to the terminal or at least check in frequently for updates.
- ✔ While large Air Force terminals are your best bets, virtually any U.S. Navy, Army, or Marine airfield will also have Space-A flights.
- ✔ Travel light because different aircraft have different baggage restrictions. With a small plane like the C-21, you may be limited to 30 pounds of luggage.
- ✔ Travel with ample cash or credit cards because you never know how long you'll be out and food and lodging at some locations can really add up. Besides, you never know when you'll have to shell out cash for a return ticket home.

Speaking in Code: Learning the Military Language

So what does it mean when you're telling your family and friends about your impending move and they're looking at you like you've grown three heads? Stop wondering — you've become the latest victim of speaking in military colloquialisms and acronyms. Don't worry: Everyone is guilty of it.

Even though you may resist the necessity of learning a second language, eventually, your hand is forced. You try to maintain English as your preferred language, but you find yourself unable to converse with your peers because you don't speak the same language. So, at first you find yourself peppering your conversations with military lingo here and there, but then one day, you find out that you sound just like everyone else:

- A move isn't just a move, it becomes a PCS (permanent change of station).

- A DITY is when you do the move yourself — so DITY literally means "do it yourself." And you thought some craft group thought that one up, huh?

- An installation becomes a base, a post, a station, or a camp, depending on the service and the size.

- TDY or TAD is another word for a temporary duty away from the home station.

- You're no longer stopping at Giant or Safeway on the way home; you're doing a commissary run.

- When your sister asks what you're doing tomorrow, you tell her that you have an OSC board meeting and can't miss it because you're in charge of Scholarships. You tell her that you can't stop by earlier in the day because your DH is going TDY and you've got to stop at the seamstress on base because you had earlier dropped off his new ABUs to have the Velcro sewn on. And after that, you've got to stop by the shoppette to pick up some hot sauce because there's never enough Tabasco in the MREs.

These acronyms and lingo all sound logical unless you're on the outside. To the uninitiated outsider, you're speaking a foreign language. But don't fret. After a few years, your sister will pick up that you have an Officers Spouses Club board meeting and can't miss it because you're in charge of the Scholarship program for the club. You can't stop by earlier in the day because your Darling Husband has Temporary Duty away from his home base and you've got to stop at the seamstress on base because you had earlier dropped off his new Airman Battle Uniform to have the Velcro sewn on. And after that, you've got to stop by the small convenience store on base to pick up some hot sauce because there's never enough hot sauce in the Meals Ready to Eat (rations they get in the field).

Your sister may now understand you, but just when you think you've got the lingo down perfectly, your DH is given a joint assignment (with a different service) and you realize that the language doesn't translate from service to service. Army does not speak Navy; Navy does not speak Air Force; Air Force does not speak Marine, and so on and so on. Just when you think you're getting ahead, you're back at square one! Don't worry about it: Everyone is in the same boat. Even though there is a movement afoot to think "purple" (terms and programs that transcend all services), each branch of service likes its own service idiosyncrasies. So just embrace your service's culture and language freely. Once you understand the natives, you'll begin to settle in.

Embracing the Place Where Everybody Knows Your Name

Forget keeping up with the Joneses. The military is a great equalizer. When everyone wears uniforms, shops at the same stores, belongs to the same clubs, sends their kids to the same schools, and shows up at the same hospital, keeping up with the Joneses tends to be a nonissue.

Better yet, not only are you all doing the same things, but at parties, you know everyone, and if you don't, everyone wears nametags! Imagine it, no more pregnant pauses or awkward silences because you can't remember the name of the guy who's walking toward you with an expectant look on his face. One quick glance at the nametag and you're back in business. What could be better?

And it still gets better: How about an additional patch that makes it easy to identify the other people in your unit? It doesn't even matter if you know them; that kinship of being in the same unit is an automatic icebreaker. No more wondering about a person's name and no more hunting for something in common with someone. The military boosts your social quotient, and you don't even need to develop any additional skills!

Choosing to Live on the Installation — Or Not

Living behind the fences of a military installation provides a fair amount of comfort to many people. In addition to living in a guarded, gated community, you're living among your peers, people who understand exactly what you're going through. In a traditional neighborhood, people come from all walks of life and work in different career fields. Neighborhoods on a military installation take the term "cookie cutter" to an all new level. While the types of homes may vary, every person in those homes has the same employer — Uncle Sam.

People choose to live on base for one or more of the following reasons:

- ✔ **You can save money.** You have no out-of-pocket expenses associated with living on base:

    - Utilities are covered.

    - The installation or privatized housing contractor takes care of maintenance issues that arise.

- ✔ **You have ready access to resources and services.** Some of the greatest benefits are attached to brick and mortar buildings on the installation. Since most base housing is either on the base proper or at least very close, the commissary, exchange, and hospital or clinic become much more accessible (more about these services in Chapter 4).

- ✔ **You find comfort being surrounded by other military families when your servicemember is deployed.** Because your neighbors understand what you're going through, they will invite you to dinner and watch your kids in a pinch. Sometimes you'll come home frazzled the day before inspection to find that your lawn's already been mowed because your neighbor knew your husband was gone and did it while he was doing his own. Everyone keeps an eye out for each other and that can be quite comforting.

Of course, you have to do your part as well as in any community, civilian or military:

- ✔ Residents are expected to maintain their quarters in an acceptable manner that includes maintaining the lawn and taking care of routine maintenance issues. Your installation housing office can give you the specific parameters of what "acceptable manner" and "routine maintenance" mean as each base differs in its regulations and requirements.

- ✔ Standards are maintained through weekly inspections.

- ✔ Warnings can be issued for violations and, with enough warnings, you can be kicked out of base housing.

On the flip side, some people choose not to live on base because of the exact same reasons other people *want* to live on base. All that closeness and support makes them feel like they're living in a fishbowl. The lines between your public and private lives fuzz a little and some people feel like they're never able to get away from work. For those reasons and more, many people choose to live off base. Find out more about your other housing options in Chapter 10.

Chapter 2

Figuring Out Customs and Courtesies

Y ou're probably coming into military life with all sorts of preconceived notions and beliefs. Some may be grounded in reality, but we bet that the majority of what you think you know about the military comes from popular television shows or novels.

In this chapter we do what we can to separate the truth from the rumors and help make you a little more comfortable with the military. In this chapter, we help you understand rank, expectations, and the military hierarchy. We also explore your servicemember's place in the military structure and how that affects you.

Separating Myths from Reality

As an outsider looking in, you may have heard some interesting stories about the military. Now that you're being welcomed into the fold, you need to take a little time to separate the myths from the realities of military life. And we do just that in this section so that you can get a more realistic view of your new life.

Below we give you some of the more common myths circulating out there regarding the military. Jumping into this new lifestyle, we suggest that you take the blinders off and figure out the lay of the land. Part of this exercise involves letting go of some of your preconceived notions and learning about some of the things that make the military lifestyle so special. Get your reality check from the following list:

Myth: Officers are better educated than enlisted troops.

Reality: It is true that all officers do have bachelor's degrees and will often have to obtain master's degrees or doctorates to progress to the higher ranks, but nearly 75 percent of enlisted troops also have some level of college education or experience. So rank is not necessarily a good indication of education or socioeconomic background.

Myth: People join the military because they get in trouble with the law and have to choose between going to jail and joining the military.

Reality: Actually, you could say the exact opposite is true. Brushes with the law could serve to disqualify people from military service.

Myth: Military spouses hold the same rank as their servicemember spouse and are accorded all due honors and respect.

Reality: Good manners require that you should be polite to everyone, but military spouses do not hold any rank — unless they are also servicemembers, of course.

Myth: The military encourages groupthink and all servicemembers are automatons.

Reality: Military members are representative of American society at large. They are as diverse a population as any other.

Understanding Rank and Military Hierarchy

Okay, we admit it: Rank can seem a bit overwhelming, but that's where we come in. In the following sections we give you the details of rank in all branches and describe who does what and where they came from. If you have a general knowledge of rank and the structure and basically understand who falls where, you can get along just fine and pick up the rest on an as-you-need-to-know basis.

Checking out the different ranks

As you start to navigate the military lifestyle, you naturally begin to wonder how the uniforms correspond to rank. At first you feel like you're trying to read signs in a whole other language: You know the symbols should mean something, but you can't understand the code. Well, don't worry. We not only unlock the code for you in this section, but we also give you the info you need to navigate your way through rank and its nuances.

Regardless of the branch of service, you'll run into two types of rank: officer rank (see Figure 2-1) and enlisted rank (see Figure 2-2). But each type of rank looks different, depending on the branch of service. Figures 2-1 and 2-2 can help you sort it all out.

Okay, so your head may spinning with all of these symbols, but before you throw your hands up in frustration, take heart. Despite all of the differences, the following list shows you some commonalities that exist across the services:

- ✔ **E** stands for **enlisted.** When people enlist, they generally come in as an E-1. However, based on other discriminating factors such as completion of certain academic requirements, troops can receive advanced pay grade status up to E-4 when they enlist.

- ✔ **W** stands for **warrant officer.** Warrant officers are highly trained specialists, are not required to have college degrees (although many of them do), and outrank all enlisted personnel. Warrant officers hold their warrants from their service secretary. After warrant officers are promoted to chief warrant officer 2, they receive a commission from the President. The Air Force has no warrant officers.

- ✔ **O** stands for **commissioned officer.** Commissioned officers are the highest rank in the military. They hold presidential commissions and their ranks are confirmed by the Senate.

  There are two types of officers:

  - **Line:** Line Officers are those in combat and support specialties.

  - **Nonline:** Nonline officers are noncombat specialists, such as chaplains, lawyers, doctors, and nurses. Most officers start off as an O-1; however, the nonline officers level of expertise in their fields may earn them a higher starting rank. Nonline officers cannot command combat troops.

Figure 2-1: Officer ranks.

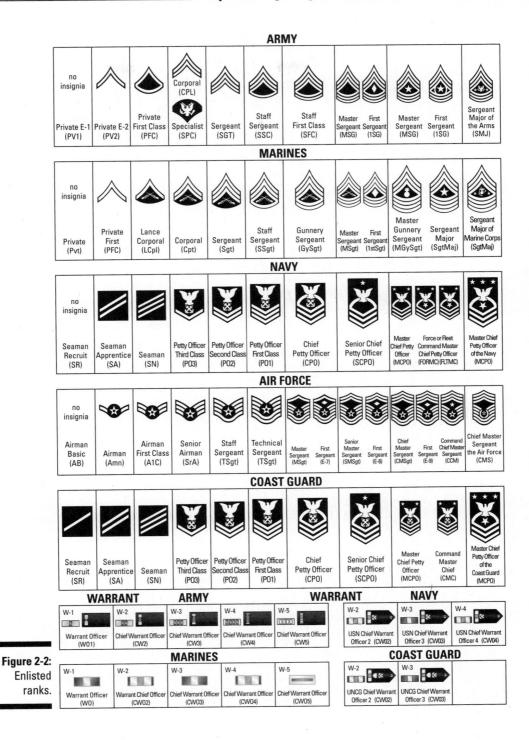

Figure 2-2:
Enlisted
ranks.

For officers, there are several different commissioning sources:

- Reserve Officers Training Corps (ROTC)
- Officers Training School (OTS)
- Officers Candidate School (OCS)
- United States Military Academy
- U.S. Air Force Academy
- U.S. Naval Academy
- U.S. Coast Guard Academy
- U.S. Merchant Marine Academy

Understanding that rank does have its place

While military spouses carry no rank, common courtesies, such as the following should prevail.

✔ Do not call an older spouse or a more senior spouse by their first name until you are given permission to. (This goes for servicemembers as well.)

✔ As your servicemember rises in rank, you're also expected to rise to the occasion and to help or mentor those who are coming up behind you. Whether you choose to accept this charge or not is up to you — as a spouse, you can't be told to do anything.

✔ After you've been around awhile, you may look around and find that you have accumulated some young friends who are looking to you as a role model. If they are struggling, they may be looking to you to provide some insights and guidance on how to navigate the military lifestyle.

Reveling in the privileges of rank

Rank does have its privileges: better compensation, bigger houses, and one of the best ones — special parking spots on base. The Air Force has recently gone away from issuing base decals, and there is widespread belief that the other services are not far behind.

Before you start gaming the system and wonder who might discover if you're parking in one of those good spots, remember that every car registered to an installation has color-coded stickers delineating between enlisted, NCOs, and officers.

Dividing officer ranks even further

You might hear other categories used to delineate between the different officer ranks. Within the officer ranks, O-1 to O-3 are called company grade officers in the Army, Air Force, and Marine Corps. In the Navy, they are called junior grade officers. O-4 to O-6 are called field grade officers in the Army, Air Force, and Marine Corps. In the Navy, they are called mid-grade officer. O-7 to O-10 are called general officers in the Army, Air Force, and Marine Corps. In the Navy, they are referred to as flag officers.

Keeping Up with Traditions and Ceremonies

The military is full of traditions and ceremonies. The traditions allow those currently serving to connect to the warriors of the past to understand the sacrifices others have made. Although the different service branches take traditions to different levels, they all have many of the basic traditions. It might help for you to understand some of these traditions and ceremonies that will now become second nature to your servicemember.

The salute

There is no tradition more integral to military life than the salute. To outsiders, it might be mindboggling the number of times a servicemember has to salute over the course of a day, so here are some inside tips to help you understand when, where, and why. To this day, rendering a salute is representative of honor, trust, and respect. Today's salute is an extension of raising your visor. The following list gives some general guidelines for saluting, geared to servicemembers:

- ✔ Salute while outdoors.
- ✔ Do not salute in no-hat/no-salute areas.
- ✔ Normally, enlisted members salute officers, both commissioned and warrant.
- ✔ Lower ranking officers also salute higher ranking officers.

Nonservicemembers *do not* salute.

Sorting through origins of the salute

While no one is really sure about the origin of the salute, legend has it that in medieval times, the right hand or "weapon hand" was raised as a greeting of friendship. It also served to show that the person was not brandishing any weapons. Tradition also held that the "inferior" person initiate the salute.

Another popular belief is that the origins of the salute stemmed back to when knights were all mounted and wore steel armor. The armor covered the body completely, so when two friendly knights met it was customary for each to raise his visor with his right hand (the left one being used to hold onto the reins) and expose his face to the view of the other.

The National Anthem

To military families, nothing inspires pride quite like the playing of "The Star Spangled Banner." If you go to a movie on base, the National Anthem is even played prior to the movie and everyone in attendance (including children) is expected to know and observe proper etiquette.

During the playing of the National Anthem:

- ✔ Those in uniform should stand at attention and salute the flag from the first note until the last note is played.

- ✔ Everyone not in uniform should face the flag and hold their right hands over their hearts.

- ✔ Those not in uniform but wearing hats should take their hats off with their right hands and hold it over their left shoulders, their hands over their hearts.

One of the things that you will notice about a military crowd is that regardless of the age of the child, every family member knows and exercises proper etiquette during the playing of the National Anthem. Children know to maintain decorum and not fidget. Don't embarrass yourself. Teach your children the correct protocol.

The Stars and Stripes

There is no greater symbol of the strength and patriotism of the United States than our flag. Twice a day on a military installation, that flag is honored with reveille and retreat.

✔ **Reveille** takes place every morning around sunrise when the flag is unfolded and ceremoniously displayed. It's hoisted up the flag pole while "To the Colors" plays.

✔ **The retreat ceremony** is at the end of the duty day. The flag is ceremoniously lowered, folded, and put away while the National Anthem plays.

When you hear the music play:

✔ You need to stop where you stand, face the direction of the flag, and stand at attention while the songs are playing.

✔ Uniformed military members should salute until the music ends.

✔ Those members not in uniform should stand at attention.

✔ If you are driving in a car on base while the music is playing, you are required to stop your car in quiet observance until the final note is played.

Reveling in inter-service Rivalry

Each of the services has its own idiosyncrasies and people choose their branch of service because certain cultures or traditions appeal to them. As an extension of this, servicemembers and families thinks that their service is better than the other. This belief manifests itself in the jokes and anecdotes that pervade military culture.

Some of the rivalries are steeped in traditions that stem back for more than a century ago, such as the Army/Navy football rivalry. These are the types of rivalries that tear families apart and make belligerent fools out of otherwise rational people.

All kidding aside, these inter-service rivalries serve to build on culture and pride in service. But, don't let the nonsense and joking fool you — once there's a mission on the table, professionalism prevails and it doesn't matter what branch of service they're in, servicemembers all work toward the common goal.

Ceremonies

Military milestones such as a Change of Command or a Retirement are observed with formal ceremonies. These types of events, recognizing the contributions and accomplishments of different members, serve an important purpose of drawing the unit together and building esprit de corps (camaraderie within the unit). You can find out more information on ceremonies in Chapter 4.

Other events that serve to build unit morale include the various military balls and celebrations that you'll be invited to attend, including Dining Outs and Birthday balls. These events are integral to military and unit tradition. They serve as ways to tie you to those who have gone before you and those who will come after you. These ceremonies and celebrations provide a great environment for members of the unit to bond and socialize outside of the stressful work environment. It's important for you to attend as many as you're able to. These moments are what set apart a military career from just any other job. More information on military events is found in Chapter 4.

Finding Your Place in the Grand Plan

Unlike your spouse, you didn't enlist in the military. This fact may leave you feeling like you're in limbo — your servicemember has plenty of things going on, but you may be unsure of how you fit in. However, spouses are an important part of the military community, and the sections that follow explain to you how to get connected and involved.

Getting involved . . . or not

You are free to pick and choose what activities to participate in. With over 60 percent of military spouses working outside the home, many spouses don't have time to take part in a lot of the activities, and they don't necessarily identify themselves as military spouses. For them, military service just happens to be their servicemember's job.

If you choose to take that viewpoint, you're missing out. While you may have your own life in the civilian world, certain aspects of military life, such as deployments and the transient lifestyle, are better addressed by experts on the installation. No one can give better support and advice to you and identify more with your situation than other military spouses or support systems.

Of course, you can't be told to do anything. So any involvement you choose to have with your military community is purely voluntary on your part. However, as your servicemember rises in the ranks, you may be expected to become more involved in unit activities. You may be asked to take charge of some events or aspects of the family support groups. Don't view this as an invasion of your privacy or as a mandate. While you're always free to decline, be flattered that you were asked and view your involvement as opportunities worth taking advantage of.

Making friends

Military spouses carry no rank. As a civilian, you're free to befriend whom-ever you wish. However, keep in mind that the fraternization rules are still in place for the servicemembers. Given the fraternization rules, doing things together as couples can be challenging (or impossible) between enlisted and officer families.

Watching Your P's and Q's: Party Protocol

Protocol sounds stuffy and may just make you think of rules, rules, rules. But protocol simply lets you know what to expect and ensures that everyone works off the same sheet of music.

Protocol covers just about everything in the military, including parties. And the military *loves* to throw parties. Chances are good that you'll be invited to any number of social events. Some will be optional, but some will be manda-tory for you to attend. Knowing what's expected of you will help you master any situation with ease and confidence.

Of course, you need to know what's expected of you, so we give you some good guidelines to follow in this list:

- ✔ Always RSVP to the phone number provided well before the deadline even if you are unable to attend.
- ✔ Do not RSVP to people when you see them out and about because they may not be focused on the event and may forget to annotate your response.
- ✔ Do not bring extra guests.
- ✔ Do not bring children unless the invitation specifically states that chil-dren are allowed.
- ✔ For events held at someone's home, never arrive early. People need the time to get ready.
- ✔ If you know you're going to be more than a few minutes late, call your host or hostess a few days in advance and let them know.
- ✔ Follow the dress code.

✔ Bring a hostess gift to express your appreciation. The gift does not have to be very extravagant. It can be anything from fresh flowers to a bottle of wine or a box of chocolates.

✔ Always write a thank-you note. Although you should write a thank-you note immediately following the event, it's never too late to acknowledge a kindness.

If issuing invitations yourself, make sure you let people know what the dress code is. No one likes to be over- or underdressed.

Don't be intimidated by the guidelines above. These guidelines should serve you well. However, if you forgot them or get confused, just fall back on all those lessons your mom taught you. Good manners will always prevail.

Chapter 3

Getting Around Military Bases

• •

In This Chapter

▶ Stepping onto the installation

▶ Getting familiar with your new surroundings

▶ Finding a place to sleep

▶ Getting your shopping on

▶ Eating and finding entertainment and activities for all ages and interests

▶ Taking care of personal needs like banking and medical care

• •

Your military life centers around military installations, also commonly known as bases. You need to know what it takes to get onto the installation, what to expect once you get there, and how to find your way around. If you're already in the military and have access to your current military installation, you may not really know what goes on in all those buildings you see. This chapter introduces you to the facilities that make up a military installation.

Defense Enrollment Eligibility Reporting System (DEERS)

Do wish you could live a meaningful existence? We're not talking about the philosophical, existential notion of "I think, therefore I am" type of existence. In the military, unless you're registered in DEERS (Defense Enrollment Eligibility Reporting System) you simply don't exist. Servicemembers get automatically enrolled, but before you can begin using your military benefits, you, too, need to enroll in DEERS. But never fear! In the sections that follow, we give you all the information you need to register, as well as update your info, in DEERS. Plus, we let you in on what DEERS is and what it can do for you.

Making sense of DEERS

You probably know by now that the military *loves* acronyms, but we'll bet you'd like to know exactly what DEERS is and what good it does for you to register in it. DEERS is simply a database of those people who are eligible for TRICARE.

After you register in DEERS, you can take advantage of the same benefits your servicemember enjoys, such as:

- ✔ Getting a military ID
- ✔ Shopping at the base exchange
- ✔ Using military healthcare
- ✔ Gaining complete understanding of all military-related acronyms (okay, so to really get this you need to check out the Appendix, but it's okay to dream!).

Registering in DEERS

To enroll, fill out a DD Form 1172 (an Application for Department of Defense Common Access Card and DEERS Enrollment) for each eligible family member and be prepared to provide two forms of identification, which need to include one picture ID and one additional piece of supporting documentation such as a marriage or birth certificate and/or Social Security numbers. DD Form 1172 can be found online at `http://www.tricare.mil/mybenefit/Download/Forms/dd1172-2.pdf`.

Verifying and updating information

Only your servicemember can update your record in DEERS. Be sure you get your record updated whenever you or your servicemember experiences a significant life event including:

- ✔ Change in your servicemember's status
  - • Retiring or separating from active duty
  - • National Guard or Reserve member activation or deactivation
- ✔ Change in your servicemember's service status (i.e. enlisted to officer, branch change)
- ✔ Change in marital status (married or divorced)
- ✔ Having a baby or adopting a child
- ✔ Change of address (moving for any reason)

Of course, we didn't include every life event in this list, but you get the idea. Anytime you or your servicemember experience a significant life event, update DEERS within 30 days. If you don't, you may experience a break in your benefits.

Your servicemember can verify and update DEERS in one of the following ways:

- ✔ **In person:** To add or delete family members, servicemembers can visit a local ID card office. They can locate an ID office nearby by visiting the Rapids Site Locator at http://www.dmdc.osd.mil/rsl/owa/home. They can search for the nearest office by ZIP code, city, or state. After they have that information, they should call the office to verify its location and business hours first before they venture out.

- ✔ **By phone:** Servicemembers can call the Defense Manpower Data Center Support Office at 1-800-538-9552 (TTY/TDD for the deaf: 1-866-363-2883) to update addresses, e-mail addresses, and phone numbers.

- ✔ **By fax:** Servicemembers can fax address, e-mail address, or phone number changes to the Defense Manpower Data Center Support Office at 1-831-655-8317.

- ✔ **By mail:** Servicemembers can mail changes to the Defense Manpower Data Center Support Office (ATTN: COA, 400 Gigling Road, Seaside, CA 93955-6771). They must also mail supporting documentation if they're adding or deleting a family member.

- ✔ **Online:** Servicemembers have two options for updating personal information online:

  - • Visit the DEERS Web site (https://www.dmdc.osd.mil/appj/address/indexAction.do): Follow the steps to update address, e-mail address, and phone numbers.

  - • Via the Beneficiary Web Enrollment Web site: The site is linked directly to the DEERS database, so when they update information via this portal, it not only updates DEERS, but also with your *regional contractor.*

If your servicemember (commonly referred to as a *sponsor*) isn't available, authorized family members can update information in DEERS with a notarized DD Form 1172 or a Power of Attorney (for more on the importance of filling out this form or a Power of Attorney, see Chapter 9).

Making It Official — Getting a Military ID Card

After you register in DEERS (if you haven't registered, see the section earlier in this chapter, "Registering in DEERS"), you should immediately visit the Pass and ID office to get a military ID card. Military ID cards have to be renewed every four years.

Because you can't physically enter a military installation on your own without a valid military ID card, you need to get an ID card if you fit one of the following categories:

- ✔ The spouse of a servicemember
- ✔ A dependent child over the age of 10 and under the age of 21
- ✔ A dependent full-time student under the age of 23

After you know where you're going, be sure to call ahead and verify the hours of operation before venturing out. Some installations even have a phone number you can call to get an anticipated wait time. Be prepared to bring the necessary supporting documentation.

Every person requiring a military ID card has to be present at the ID office, along with the servicemember (also called a sponsor). If the sponsor is unavailable due to deployment or other reason, eligible family members can still acquire military ID cards with a power of attorney. Refer to Chapter 9 for more information on power of attorney forms.

Taking In the Town

If you have an ID card (if not, you need to check out the section earlier in this chapter, "Making It Official — Getting a Military ID Card"), you can get through the installation's gate on your own and take a look around. To different degrees, military installations are similar to self-sufficient little towns. Like Any Small Town, USA, you can find housing areas, dining options, shopping, clubs, office buildings, and any number of other businesses.

The people you see running around your "town" are the military personnel and civilians who work there, family members, and other vendors doing business on the installation. Other than being a gated community, you probably won't find too many differences between your installation and the town that you grew up in. But to guide you through it all, we've provided an overview of the things you need to check out first.

Getting Your Rest

People need places to lay their heads, and military installations provide different types of housing to accommodate different people (refer to Chapter 10 for an in-depth review on housing options). The following list gives you an idea of what to expect:

- ✔ **Dorms and barracks:** Some single servicemembers live in dorms and barracks on base.

- ✔ **Housing areas:** For families, options range from high rises to single-family homes, depending on the installation. The housing areas are laid out very much like any other street and community you might see in your hometown and can include playgrounds, skate parks, and other amenities for the residents.

- ✔ **Billeting/Lodging facilities:** Lodging facilities range from single rooms to larger accommodations designed for families.

  The larger accommodations are generally called *temporary lodging facilities* (TLFs). To get an idea of what these are like, imagine an extended stay hotel. TLFs are meant to accommodate families and vary in size, but typically have separate bedrooms, a complete kitchen, eating and living area.

Military installations make lodging available to:

- • **Servicemembers visiting the installation on business**

- • **Families *pcs'ing* (moving) in or out of the area:** After families move out of housing (whether on base or off), families in transit move into TLFs on the installation while wrapping up their business and waiting for their impending moves. When pcs'ing, families could be in residence at these TLFs for weeks on end, so the facilities tend to be quite spacious, much like a moderately-sized apartment.

- • **Eligible leisure travelers:** While installations give priority to those on official business (like servicemembers on business or families pcs'ing), eligible leisure travelers visiting the area can also make reservations at TLFs on a space-available basis. For more information, you should consult the installation Lodging Office.

 In many cosmopolitan areas, accommodations on the installations are at a premium. Make sure your servicemember makes reservations as soon as he has orders in hand. If the installation has no room available and gives you a nonavailability slip, you need to reserve lodging somewhere that's convenient to where you're doing business or plan on focusing your house hunting.

Shopping

What's a town without some shopping options? Forget Giant, Safeway, and Shopper's Warehouse; you've got the commissary. And although you may not have Penney's, Sears, or Macy's, you've got the exchange. If you're feeling confused just read the sections that follow — we straighten you out with descriptions of both as well as other places you may find on base to shop at.

Commissary

The Defense Commissary Agency or DeCA, as servicemembers commonly call it, operates a chain of nearly 300 commissaries worldwide in support of military personnel and their families. As an authorized user, you will be able to purchase your groceries at cost plus 5 percent. The DeCA Web site boasts that the average overall savings for patrons is 30 percent on your purchases compared to other commercial grocery stores.

Commissaries come with their own idiosyncrasies, but just follow a few simple rules of the road, and you can look like a seasoned pro in no time:

✓ **Keep right.** To maintain order, keep to the right while shopping in the aisles. It is a military base, after all.

✓ **Yield to uniformed personnel.** During peak work hours, military in uniform have priority at a number of the checkout stands.

✓ **Be prepared to tip.** The baggers helping you with your groceries work strictly for tips. They bag your groceries, provide carry-out service, and load your vehicle. You're expected to tip for this service. Standard tipping guidelines suggest that you tip 25¢ to 50¢ per bag.

✓ **Tip even in the quick checkout lanes.** Even if you go through the quick checkout lanes, if a bagger handles your groceries, you're still expected to tip before you grab your bags and leave the store. At these lanes, the baggers "help you out" by providing a tip jar as a reminder to tip before you exit. Throw in some pocket change and be on your way.

Several times a year, the commissaries run case-lot sales, which are very popular with young families and retirees alike. Commissaries advertise the sale well in advance, so be on the lookout and mark your calendar. If you have the storage space in your home, they're a great time to stock up on nonperishable items and other things you use in bulk. Be prepared to invest a couple of hours though, because as we mentioned before, these events are very popular and well attended.

In case you're one of those people who becomes easily overstimulated by the plethora of sundry items available at grocery stores, take heart — outside of a decent array of groceries, you won't find too many extras at your commissary. While you can find candy and a limited selection of magazines at the checkout stand, for cards, gifts, and other small items you might otherwise find at a commercial grocery store, you have to go to the exchange.

Exchanges

All of the exchanges fall under one of four major systems: Army and Air Force Exchange Service (AAFES), Navy Exchange Service Command (NEX), Marine Corps Exchange (MCX), and the Coast Guard Exchange (CGX). Eligible shoppers can shop at any of the exchanges, regardless of service affiliation.

Just as with the commissary, eligible shoppers are roughly defined as those holding a valid military ID card and include active-duty, retired, National Guard and reserve members and their families, some disabled veterans and their families, surviving spouses, and former spouses. Restrictions and limitations do apply so to be on the safe side, check with your local exchange for their policy.

On average, two thirds of exchange earnings go to supporting Morale, Welfare and Recreation (MWR) programs. More about MWR activities later in this chapter. While the savings at the exchange are not quite as robust as the average savings you'll experience at the commissary, the greatest benefit of shopping at the exchange is that purchases are tax-free. If you find an item advertised for a lesser amount at another store, bring in the flyer and they will match the price.

If you live far away from an installation and want to take advantage of the savings, the exchanges also have online and mail-order components.

Checking out the inside of an exchange

Exchanges differ in size, but general layouts resemble those of retail stores such as Wal-Mart and Target in that you'll be able to find a range of items such as household goods and apparel. Where they differ is that you will also find high-end, luxury goods such as quality handbags, china, crystal, and jewelry. When you think of the exchange, it is the main store that will immediately come to mind. However, at some installations, the exchange can be quite large and include additional specialty stores located outside of the main store building. Generally speaking, stores will sell goods such as uniforms, furniture, toys, appliances, electronics, and outdoor items including seasonal plants, grills, and outdoor furniture.

When we first suggested that a military installation is like a small town, we weren't exaggerating. In addition to the main store and the satellite specialty stores, you will often be able to find additional concessionaires and vendors. Most common are the barber and beauty shops, which are commonly part of the exchange mall.

Installation barber shops may be the last great deal with haircuts still costing under $10 including tip.

Other concessionaires might include phone, flower, or optical shops, and food vendors such as: Anthony's Pizza, Cinnabon, Charlie's Steakery, Taco Bell, Robin Hood, and Burger King. You get the idea. We're not talking about fly-by-night mom-and-pop vendors here. We're talking about names that you know and love.

Gassing up

Although the majority of people do live off the installation, they still make an outing out of coming on base to do their grocery shopping and combining it with other errands such as a haircut, a quick run to the exchange, lunch, and filling up the gas tank on the way out.

The exchange systems also run gas stations on base. Within the continental United States (CONUS) the price of fuel on base may or may not be less expensive than the surrounding area. However, outside the continental United States (OCONUS) the price of gas on the installation is considerably less expensive than what you will find on the economy (locally). If you find yourself running low on fuel while tooling around Europe and can't make it on the installation, the exchange services run a very competitive gas coupon program that allows eligible users stationed to the overseas installation to purchase Petroleum, Oil & Lube (POL) coupons. The coupons can be used at participating gas stations and ensure reasonably priced fuel on the local economy with participating vendors.

Shoppettes

Many times, the gas stations on the installation will be attached to a shoppette. If you find yourself needing just a couple of items and the idea of running to the exchange and fighting the crowds exhausts you, take heart — you can run into the shoppette, grab your few items, and be on your way.

As with the main exchange, shoppettes come in different sizes. On the basic end, they will resemble a larger gas station store or 7-Eleven style facility. On the larger end, you might be able to find seasonal items, a good assortment of books and magazines, as well as alcohol. Some facilities might also include a video rental section, photo shop, and laundry and dry cleaning facilities.

Overseas, these shoppettes are a great connection to the pop culture back home. When you're surrounded by foreign-language films and magazines, it's comforting to be able to find English-language movie rentals. More than one family has made a ritual out of picking up American new release rentals and a pizza on base for a Friday family movie night before heading back home to their small villages.

Class 6

Known by different names, the package store or Class 6 as it is commonly referred to, is in layman's terms, a liquor store. Generally you can find it housed within a shoppette, but sometimes you may come across a stand-alone facility. You can choose from a pretty decent selection of beer, wine, and spirits at reasonable prices. The Class 6 offers many of the same services you would find at a regular liquor store, so if you're having a huge event and need a tap and a keg, you know where to look.

Eating on the Installations

If the choices at the exchange mall aren't doing it for you in terms of dining options, take heart, you've got some other avenues open to you.

The dining hall

Dining halls (also known as chow or mess halls) exist primarily for unaccompanied servicemembers who live on the installation. Imagine a college dorm and chow hall — it's the same principle. For the privilege of three or four square meals a day, the servicemembers' Basic Allowance for Subsistence (BAS) is deducted from their pay. Because the dining halls generally provide decent food for reasonable prices, other servicemembers routinely pay to eat at the dining hall. Depending on the installation, other people who want to eat at the dining halls such as active duty family members or retirees may also be able to do so for a fee.

The Air Force in recent years has been downsizing many of its services and facilities to save money. As a result, they have closed a number of their dining halls, giving airmen back their BAS and requiring them to fend for themselves. This has been received with mixed results. Some people lament the loss of the dining facility, but others relish the options available to them.

The clubs

Food and entertainment have always drawn servicemembers and their families to the clubs. When a servicemember's social life used to revolve around the installation, the clubs did brisk business. Ceremonies celebrating promotions, changes of command, and retirement guaranteed that social life centered on the clubs. One of the greatest appeals of the clubs remains their convenience. It's easy just to walk across the base for lunch with your coworkers instead of jumping into a car and driving off base. Happy hours and live entertainment would entice some people back after work. Themed dinners such as: Mongolian barbecue, prime rib, or seafood feasts as well as nice Sunday brunches drew people back to the clubs with their families in tow.

In more recent times with people moving off the installations and families busier than ever, the clubs are not as well attended as they used to be outside of official events. However, catering and banquet facilities still make the clubs popular locations for holiday parties, weddings, farewell parties, and luncheons.

The three different types of clubs you may encounter are the

- Officers' Club
- Non-commissioned Officers' Club
- Enlisted Club

Single membership and family membership are open to all active duty and retired U.S. and foreign military, Reservists, National Guard, DoD, and Federal personnel. Where the separate clubs exist, your eligibility for the club is determined by the servicemember's rank. Many installations have gone to consolidated clubs combining the clubs into one entity and making it open to all, regardless of rank. There is a charge for membership that entitles you to discounts in the club restaurants and facilities. You will also receive a monthly member's newsletter that will come with additional coupons.

Membership at the club covers the entire family, so you do not need to be accompanied by your service member to use the facilities. This is quite handy in a culture where at any given time, a significant number of the military population will be deployed. It isn't out of the ordinary to see large tables of moms and kids dining together at the club during the holidays. Faced with another holiday without dad, it's sometimes just easier to meet your friends at the club where they make an effort to provide a kid-friendly environment and some entertainment to distract the children so that the moms can eat.

At many clubs, a dress code is still in effect that generally prohibits you from wearing certain items of clothing during different times of the day and encourages certain standards at other times. It is always wise to check out the requirements at the club or on the website before visiting.

Having Fun with MWR

Shopping and eating alone cannot sustain you. At some point, you'll long for the companionship of others and start looking around for other diversions. Luckily for you, you won't have to look far.

MWR stands for Morale, Welfare, and Recreation and represents a network of programs, services, and activities that exist to enhance the lives of servicemembers, their families, military retirees, civilian employees, and other eligible participants. MWR activities run the gamut from family, child, and youth programs to recreation, sports, entertainment, and travel and leisure activities.

Fitness and sports center

The fitness and sports center is open to military ID card holders past a certain age. The age restrictions vary from installation to installation and those younger than 18 who have access usually have other restrictions attached to their use of the facility. For all users, there is a dress code in place regulating what can and can't be worn at different areas of the fitness centers for decorum purposes as well as to prevent damage to equipment and the facility.

The fitness centers resemble any other good-sized gym you might find out in town. In addition to the standard fitness equipment, you'll find a gamut of other extras such as massage therapy, fitness assessments, and classes. If you're lucky, your installation will also have an indoor pool attached to the gym. In addition to the personal classes and training sessions, staff will also coordinate intramural sports and tournaments that foster friendly competition.

Access to the fitness center is free of charge, but there will be costs incurred with extras such as locker rentals, classes, massages, and other services.

Skills development center

Working out is a great way to stay in shape and to blow off steam, but sometimes you just want other options when it comes to relaxing. If you find yourself in this position, head over to the skills development center. It has facilities and classes on almost anything you have ever wanted to learn how to do.

The wood hobby shop is equipped with machinery and tools for experienced and novice woodworkers alike. Every first-time user is required to attend a mandatory safety briefing before using the shop. There is a nominal hourly fee for use. If you're a little unsure of yourself, have no fear, there is staff on hand to help you out.

Frame shops are also a popular fixture at the skills development center. You will no doubt soon have your own "I love me" wall consisting of framed certificates, farewell plaques, and various other collectibles. The skills development center and frame shop are the birthplace of many of these mementos. In addition to being a full-service custom frame shop, they often have a self-help area where you can frame your own work. If you don't know how but have always wanted to learn, they also hold classes from time to time.

Classes don't just end with learning how to frame. The arts and crafts centers offer numerous classes in a myriad of different fine arts and crafts. You'll be able to take advantage of everything from cake decorating and holiday and seasonal crafts to painting, drawing, and kids' crafts.

Everything else

Most of the buildings you see on your installation that involve any sort of activity for you or your family will fall under the umbrella of MWR. A short list includes: bowling center, skills development center, movie theater, outdoor recreation, automotive center, recreation centers, library, child development center, youth and teen centers, and swimming pool (some of the more family-oriented buildings are discussed in the following section, "Focusing on the Family). If you need it, are interested in it, or are looking to take classes in it, chances are MWR's already thought of it. A number of installations are even fortunate enough to house some the nation's best golf courses.

Attending a movie on base is like going to a movie at any other movie theater with one big difference. Before the beginning of each movie, the national anthem will play and everyone in the audience is expected to stand and extend all due courtesies. The anthem will generally be accompanied with video on the movie screen, depicting military scenes.

Focusing on the Family

The old saying used to go, "If the military had wanted you to have a wife, they would have issued you one." Today, with over 50 percent of servicemembers married, that attitude doesn't fly. Leadership understands that important issues of staying in or getting out are made around the kitchen table, so every effort is made to provide support to military spouses and families. After all, servicemembers are only able to be effective at their jobs if they know their families are well taken care of.

Family support center

Regardless of whether or not you want to be involved, it's important to know what's going on, so stay informed. Go to all the briefings you are able to attend. The deployment, smooth move, and other briefings provide you with the official information you'll need to learn about the resources available to you. Don't wait until you need the information to go looking for it.

Known by different names depending on the service branch, the Marine Corps Community Services, Navy Fleet and Family Support Centers, Airmen and Family Support Centers, and Army Community Services — family support centers are the backbone of military family life.

Looking for assistance with your résumé? Have you always wanted to take classes in basic investing and finances? How about some items from the loan closet to tide you over until household goods arrive at the installation? You'll find all these and more at your family support center.

If you are new to a base or facing an impending move, the family support centers are a great place to start your search for information as well as everything from deployment support to ongoing classes and education on all aspects of the military lifestyle.

Child development center

Understanding that long hours and deployments are an integral part of military life, every effort is made to ensure that high-quality, affordable childcare is available to military families. As you drive around your installation, chances are good that you will see the child development center (CDC). Some installations are even large enough to warrant more than one facility.

The majority of military childcare facilities are accredited by the National Association of Education of Young Children (NAEYC), recognized as a leading accreditation system to set high professional standards for early childhood education programs. Once upon a time, childcare centers were viewed more as child-minding facilities. This is no longer the case. In order to work at the CDC's, providers must go through a training program and will continue their training throughout their employment. The goal is to provide children with a stimulating environment where they can grow and develop.

The centers generally provide care for children between the ages of 6 weeks and 12 years old. Although the majority of CDC users are under the age of 5, the centers also run a school-age program known as school-age care (SAC). CDC costs are determined on a sliding scale and based on a family's total income. For the school-age program, the costs are further determined by hours of use.

Some centers also offer a limited number of drop-in hourly care slots. Reservations can be made up to one month in advance and are given out on a first-come, first-serve basis. With hourly care, there are a maximum number of hours per child per week.

Because the child development centers are so affordable and convenient, there is usually a long waiting list. For those who cannot get into the CDC, there are other options available to you discussed in Chapter 12.

Youth and teen centers

During certain times of the year, you'll see a building with a line of parents, some in uniform, some in civilian clothes, clutching a fistful of forms, waiting patiently for their turn. What are they waiting for? The privilege of registering their kids for activities on base through youth and teen services.

Understanding that military youth and teens face the same societal pressures as their peers with the added stressors of frequent moves, deployments, and other issues unique to the military lifestyle, military youth programs seek to provide enriching activities for children in a safe environment. By partnering with highly regarded institutions such as the 4H Club and the Boys & Girls Clubs of America, they are able to offer a wide range of activities such as after-school programs, academic assistance, youth sports, pre-teen/teen programs, classes, adventure programs, arts and crafts, field trips, music, dances, and summer camps.

Picking Up on Personal Services

The installation has plenty of fun for the family, entertainment, and shopping available, but the installation goes beyond that to provide some more basic personal services that anyone would like to have close to home, such as auto repair, banking, and medical services. These sections give you the rundown of each.

Auto hobby shop

In addition to the gas station on the installation, some will also have an auto hobby shop or service station. Like any retail facility, the auto hobby shop provides services such as oil changes, tire rotations, inspections and detailing. For those who have the time and inclination, the hobby shops also offer self-repair facilities with automotive tools and lifts. There is a nominal lift fee as well as an hourly stall fee. Rentals occur on a first-come first-serve basis and hobby shop staff is generally on hand to help with do-it-yourself projects.

Depending on the facility, additional services might be offered. If you've been meaning to educate yourself on basic automobile care, some shops offer preventive maintenance classes. Many shops also offer programs for the spouses of deployed servicemembers that might include a free oil change or towing within a certain range. As with everything else, check with your specific installation auto hobby shop to see what's available.

Banking

Banking on the installation even comes with some choice. For quick cash, you'll find ATM machines throughout the installation, but usually near or at the exchange or shoppette. If you need just a couple of dollars and find yourself making a purchase at the commissary, exchange, or shoppette, when you pay, you'll be able to write your check for a small amount over the total (usually around $20). At the exchange, you can cash a check for larger amounts at customer service. Check-cashing facilities are also available at the clubs for members.

Many military families maintain more than one bank account. In addition to the main account where the pay is deposited, some families will have an additional local account so that they can deposit money and cash checks with greater ease. There is usually a local branch of a national banking institution located on the installation. This has greater implications for families stationed overseas where many people utilize the on-base bank for currency exchange.

Overseas, the exchange rate is usually more favorable on base, and when you're paying for rent and utilities in cash, every cent, yen, or won makes a difference. Currency exchange is also available at the clubs, although the exchange rate may not be as favorable and there is a lower limit on the amount you can exchange.

Military treatment facility (MTF)

The military treatment facility (MTF) is what you know of as a clinic, hospital, or medical center. Some MTFs are larger than others. On the small side, they'll be similar to civilian clinics with general practitioners and outpatient services. On the larger side, they are similar to regional medical facilities housing both general practitioners and specialists and accommodate both outpatient and inpatient services. Regardless of their size, MTFs generally have an in-house pharmacy. That's where the similarities stop. Depending on the size of the installation and the MTF, the range of services can either be very basic or expansive to include specialties such as audiology, dermatology, dietetics, emergency services, family medicine, internal medicine, OB/GYN, occupational therapy, ophthalmology, optometry, orthopedics, ENT, pediatrics, physical therapy, psychiatry, surgery, podiatry, psychology, and substance abuse.

All active duty servicemembers stationed to the installation are empanelled to the MTF and go there for their primary care. Even if they have to be referred out to specialists, they will start at the MTF. More about military healthcare in Chapter 6.

Getting the Support You Need

Aside from connecting with your unit, the installation offers several different ways that you can not only get involved but also find support if you need it. The following sections tell you how.

Chapel

The base chapel is not so different from its civilian counterpart. You'll recognize the building because, for the most part, it'll be configured much like any other chapel you'll see out in town. Because of the diversity of members serving in the military, base chapels are respectful of all religions and try to have services for most denominations. This is successful to varying degrees on different installations. At minimum, most installations will try to offer Protestant, Catholic, Jewish, and some Muslim services.

There is nothing to say that if you live or are stationed on a specific installation, you have to attend services at the base chapel. It's just another option for you. Many people choose it because it's convenient and a natural extension of their small town. Many retirees also choose to come on base for Sunday services because it provides them that continued connection with the military community.

Base chapel services are similar to those you will find out in town. You'll find religious education such as CCD (Confraternity of Christian Doctrine) and Vacation Bible School for children. Like their civilian counterparts, military chaplains perform ceremonies such as marriages, baptisms, funerals, counseling, and other religious rites.

Some slight differences you might notice are that the exterior of a base chapel generally conforms to the architectural style of the base (i.e. not always attractive looking). Religious icons will either be generic or interchangeable and outside of Sunday service, the chaplain wears a uniform. Military chaplains also serve in the military and are primarily responsible for meeting the spiritual needs of servicemembers and their families. Like regular troops, they are eligible for the same benefits and promotion opportunities. They also PCS and are deployable, so they're very knowledgeable on issues facing servicemembers who serve downrange. Unlike many of their civilian counterparts, military chaplains are particularly sensitive to the issues of reintegration facing servicemembers coming back from a deployment and their families because they have faced the issues themselves.

Clubs and groups

If you want to expand your contacts outside of the unit and want to meet other spouses around base, there are any number of clubs and groups you can join that will open up your social life.

Most bases will have both an Enlisted Spouses' Club and an Officers Spouses' Club. Over the years a small number of clubs have consolidated to preserve numbers. Regardless of the demographics of the different Spouses' Clubs, they are generally arranged in the same manner.

Some thumb their noses at these clubs because they think they're dinosaurs and have no place in today's modern military lifestyle where most spouses work outside the home and others are so busy they don't have time for the many activities. A lot of people view the socials and functions as frivolous, but they underestimate the importance of these clubs in building lasting friendships. It's also easy to make snap judgments about the frivolity of a club when you don't understand the philanthropic side of these organizations.

In addition to the monthly activities, many Spouses' Clubs run thrift shops that serve the military community in three ways:

- ✔ Allowing young families access to affordable, gently used items.
- ✔ Providing a place for families to consign items they no longer need and to make a little money.
- ✔ Finally, the funds generated by thrift shop activities go right back into the base community in the form of charitable donations and scholarships for military children.

While you may be envisioning chicken scratch, the stores make everything from tens of thousands stateside to overseas where gift shops generate hundreds of thousands of dollars for charity.

So maybe we've piqued your interest enough for you to go check out your local Spouses' Club. Fortunately, they're getting easier to find because many of them now have web sites. Even better, some of the clubs are linked to one another through their web sites. If you can't find a web site for the clubs at the base you're moving to, you can usually get a membership application at the officers' or enlisted club on base once you get there.

In larger areas with high concentrations of military installations and personnel, area spouse groups (across the services) will join together for a Joint Spouses' Luncheon. The speaker is usually a national celebrity. Past speakers include: General Peter Pace, President Bush, Lee Woodruff, and Art Buchwald. These joint luncheons are always fun to attend and provide you with a way to meet spouses from other service branches.

The Base Chapel also provides you with other opportunities to meet other spouses through groups such as Protestant Women of the Chapel (PWOC). If you have a DODDS school on base, the Parent Teacher Student Association (PTSA) will provide you with additional opportunities to get involved. You get the general idea. Regardless of where your interests may lie, there are any number of groups and associations around base for you to affiliate with. It's just a matter of getting out there and finding them.

Family Advocacy Programs

Although there are any number of ways to stay busy and get involved, some-times it's not enough to offset the stressors of the military lifestyle. As with any-thing else, there is an uglier side to military life, and if you or anyone you know is a victim of abuse, the counselors and experts at Family Advocacy can help.

In addition to the assistance they provide to families experiencing the trauma of abuse, they are also the go-to resource for child and spouse abuse prevention. In the interest of preventive education, *Family Advocacy Programs* (FAP) offers classes in topics such as crisis management, parenting, and anger management. For new parents, they also support groups available.

Clubbing with the new "Wives Club"

Historically, clubs consisting of spouses of ser-vicemembers were called Wives Clubs, but as the ranks of male spouses began to grow, some of the clubs changed their name to Spouses' Clubs.

Each club is led by an elected Executive Board. In addition to the Executive Board, there are additional committee chairs for everything from Special Activities and Programs to Newsletter and Scholarships. These committee chairs are members of the club who volunteer to be in charge of their committees for the board year. The chairs of these committees in addi-tion to the Executive Board make up the Board of Governors. Advisors to the board are the spouses of the senior leadership on base.

Check out the basic specs of a Spouses' Club:

- The Board of Governors meets every month.

- The frequency of Executive Board meetings varies from club to club.

- The board year generally runs from June to May.

- You pay dues to belong to the clubs.

- Clubs normally have a general meeting every month.

There are some traditional functions that repeat themselves every year because they are so popular. These include some sort of special activities sign-up or community fair, bingo, and a recognition ceremony for scholarship recipients.

Chapter 4

Connecting with the Military Community

*1*t's somewhat scary to think about moving every two or three years into a brand-new situation and having to start over. Fortunately, the military has a structure in place that ensures that you have people, resources, and programs out there to support you from day one.

Connecting to the Unit

The unit patch servicemembers wear on their uniforms represents tradition, history, and belonging. For the servicemember, much of their identity is tied to the unit. In these instances, the common adage is very true — you don't get to pick your family. For better or worse, through the shared experiences and deployments, your unit will become your extended family for the duration of your time at the installation.

Depending on how active your unit is, your life could very well revolve around the command. Servicemembers will arrange official functions such as Hails and Farewells, deployment briefings, fundraisers, parties, and picnics. All of these events are important to unit morale and serve to build esprit de corps (morale/unit cohesion).

Utilizing your sponsor

When your servicemember receives an assignment, your family will be offered a sponsor from the *gaining unit* (unit that you will be assigned to when you move). You can always choose to decline a sponsor, but why limit the resources available to you? Your sponsor will act as liaison to your new installation and unit.

In addition to making sure you receive a newcomer's packet consisting of information about the base and possibly the local area, your sponsors should make themselves available to answer any questions you have. Sponsors will be particularly important when you are moving overseas. Because working with different cultures and time zones can be somewhat overwhelming, sponsors try to help by doing things such as making hotel reservations and arranging for transportation to and from the airport.

When moving overseas, you won't even have a driver's license yet and chances are, neither will your servicemember spouse. Therefore, sponsors become much more important to your survival and the success of your PCS (move) and transition.

As with everything else, the quality of sponsors varies. You will have some that will do the bare minimum that is required of them, or you will have others who really do view it as their job to make your transition to your new base as smooth as possible by providing you with as much information as they can get their hands on. Remember to take notes because your service-member will have the chance to be a sponsor as well and knowing what information was important to you as you were moving will come in handy.

Keeping contact info current

The first few days to weeks at any new job are spent attending meetings and filling out mountains of paperwork. Why would you think the military would be any different? Really, the only difference is that the servicemember will be filling the forms out *in uniform!* In the course of filling out all the paperwork, your DH or DW (darling husband or darling wife) will be asked to fill out an informational sheet for the unit roster.

There are generally two rosters that are maintained. One is the roster used for official correspondence and information. The other is a social roster that you will opt into if you're interested in receiving information on other activities. Even if you don't think you want to be terribly active, you should opt into the social roster so that you receive all the information and stay in the loop.

The unit can't support you if they don't know you exist. The relationship works both ways. You should also get contact information and phone numbers for the rear detachment (those servicemembers left behind) before your servicemember deploys in case a situation arises and you need help.

For a multitude of reasons, it is also imperative that you keep your contact information up to date throughout your time at the base. Information on the rosters is used to generate newsletter mailings. The information is also used for other initiatives such as the phone trees. Because they are a quick way to disseminate information, volunteers making the calls need to be able to rely on good, up-to-date data.

Chances are good that you'll be asked to provide detailed driving directions to your house from the installation. If you move, be sure you keep this up to date. Programs such as Mapquest are not always a reliable means of finding directions to newer housing developments.

Staying in the loop

Good communication is essential to the success of any squadron or unit. At any given time, there are a multitude of support systems and programs available to you. It's up to you to find them. No one's going to come knocking on your door offering up a menu of everything that's available to you.

The best way to stay in the loop is to maintain an open line of communication. As mentioned earlier, keep your information up to date so that you continue to stay up to date with all the news and developments. Newsletters are an important connection. In addition to reading the unit newsletter, you should make a habit of reading the base paper. It's the equivalent of reading your hometown paper and easy enough to pick up during your next trip out to the BX or commissary. Installation commands and commanders use the base paper as the official means of disseminating information to the general base population, so it's a good way to find out what's going on or what new and interesting might be coming soon.

Marking military family milestones

Just as with any family, your military family will experience milestones that will need to be acknowledged. This acknowledgement generally comes from individuals (if you feel like you know those involved well enough), but an official acknowledgement also comes from the unit in the form of some type of gift or recognition.

In determining what to do and when, unit spouses will decide a *standard operating procedure* (SOP) for acknowledging milestones such as births and weddings. As mentioned earlier, this usually involves a gift of some kind. In addition to gifts, units might also choose to deliver meals to new moms as well as people who are under the weather, or for other occasions. Regardless of what is decided, every effort will be made not to leave anyone out. The general rule of thumb being: Only do for one what you can do for all.

The unit Commander and his/her spouse might also choose to acknowledge milestones on their own with an additional gift or memento aside from the official unit gift. They will generally also try to pay a visit to people who are in the hospital or laid up at home.

Attending Hails and Farewells

When you join a new unit, one of the first events you'll attend is a Hail and Farewell. This is when you and your family are officially welcomed into the fold of the unit. Hails and Farewells are official functions organized by the unit but well attended by the families. The purpose of these events is to welcome incoming members of the unit and farewell to outgoing members and their families. The events can take the shape of anything from potlucks to restaurant events. Regardless of where the events are held, they're an important time to mingle and get to know other members of the unit and their families.

When the servicemembers are deploying together, getting to know each other better, and sharing very close quarters for long stretches of time, you'll be happy to be able to put the faces to the names. Knowing a little more about the people your spouse is deployed with is an easy way to feel more involved when you're separated by thousands of miles.

When you leave the unit and the base, one of the last events you attend will be the Hail and Farewell. This is always bittersweet as you'll see the new families becoming welcomed into the unit just as you're being farewelled and saying good-bye to your friends.

Discovering other social activities

Hails and Farewells are only the beginning of unit activities. This means that you will have the opportunity to attend various parties and picnics, such as the following:

  ✔ **Fundraisers:** From time to time, the unit will also have a fundraiser, and you might be asked to volunteer. Be prepared to sell donuts or breakfast burritos, man a gift-wrap table, or wash cars. It's all for a good cause. Money raised during these fundraisers goes toward defraying the costs of unit activities.

✔ **Spouse events:** In addition to the occasional parties and official events, unit spouses will also meet approximately once a month. These spouse gatherings/coffees are generally held in the evening at someone's house. People who are interested in hosting the event will sign up and be responsible for refreshments and sometimes arrange for a speaker or program of some sort.

The first time you attend a spouse coffee, you'll probably be asked to pay your dues. These dues usually go to pay for the cost of Hail and Farewell gifts. In many units, only those spouses who pay dues will receive a farewell gift upon departure.

Unit spouse events are not segregated by rank and everyone is invited and encouraged to attend.

Making merry with holiday parties

The holidays are particularly fun for families with young children. The spouses work very hard to pull together children's parties and rally the families for activities centered around kids' activities, usually around Easter, Halloween, and Christmas. You'll be invited to the various egg hunts, costume parties, and visits with Santa. Kids have a lot of fun at these parties; you have even more fun because you get a chance to visit with your friends while your kids are happily engaged in supervised activities. But to make sure that these activities make a splash and make everyone feel included, follow these reminders:

✔ **Volunteer.** If you really enjoy these parties and can help, volunteer to do so. It's always challenging to find enough hands to help make the events memorable.

✔ **Include everyone.** Although the kids' events are fun, not everyone in the unit is married and even those who are don't always have kids. Successful units will ensure that their activities are inclusive and equally welcoming to single members of the unit, married couples without children, as well as families.

✔ **Make babysitting arrangements well ahead of time.** Call your babysitter before December because sometime around December the unit will also have a holiday party just for the adults that you won't want to miss. This usually involves dinner, dancing, and possibly some type of entertainment from members of the unit (generally very humiliating and not meant to be taken seriously).

✔ **Make the annual holiday party a priority.** If you can't attend anything else throughout the year, you should really make an effort to at least go to the annual holiday party. Most everyone will be there with their spouses and it's a great time to touch base with your friends and meet the other people in your unit.

Understanding the ins and outs of Dining In and Out

A unit might decide to hold a Dining In to honor a visiting dignitary or to farewell departing members. Dining Ins are strictly for members *in* the unit, and spouses are not invited. Dining Outs are essentially the same event, only they also include members from outside the military. They are similar to the Dining Ins with an important difference. Spouses are included. Both events are very formal, and if you're invited to attend a Dining Out, plan on wearing a ball gown or the male equivalent.

Chances are good that you will go your entire *tour* (assignment at a base) without being invited to a Dining Out, but it's worth mentioning because it represents a grand tradition of building *esprit de corps* and boosting unit morale. The sections that follow help you get in and out of the Dining Out with ease.

Following the rules

Every Dining In and Out is regulated by the Rules of the Mess that govern the evening's events. Here are some examples of common rules:

- The President is the final decision maker and is never wrong.
- Thou shalt arrive within 10 minutes of the appointed hour.
- Thou shalt not bring hats or caps into the mess.
- Thou shalt make every effort to meet all guests.
- Thou shalt move to the mess when thou hearest the chimes and remain standing until seated by the President.
- Thou shalt not bring cocktails or lighted smoking material into the mess.
- Thou shalt not leave the mess whilst convened. Military protocol overrides all calls of nature.
- Thou shalt participate in all toasts unless thyself or thy group is honored with a toast.

Speaking of toasts, there will be *many* toasts — don't drain your glass with any one toast because it is a violation of the mess to toast with an empty glass. Speaking of violations, you're probably wondering who would ever know and who would care? Believe it or not, each Dining In or Out has an appointed Mr. Vice who extracts penance from offenders. Traditional penance is to send the offender to the Grog bowl where he or she needs to partake of the grog. Sounds straightforward, doesn't it? Well, every trip to the Grog bowl involves a little ceremony. If you get any part of the ceremony wrong, you have to start all over again!

Keeping up with the pomp

What's a military event without many ceremonies? Part of the evening's festivities will involve concocting the grog, usually of an alcoholic slant. Nowadays, there is generally nonalcoholic grog available.

In addition to appreciating all the pomp and circumstance and trying to keep all the toasts and traditions straight that take place during a Dining Out, you might be a little worried about how well you'll do. Well, stop worrying. As with everything else in life, good manners will serve you well. More about basic protocol in Chapter 2.

Combat Dining Out

You may be lucky enough to be invited to a Combat Dining Out. Unlike Dining Ins or Outs which are quite formal, this type of event is much mellower and definitely does not involve any formalwear. While a Combat Dining Out might retain some elements of the more formal Dining Out, the rules are generally more relaxed; there might even be some type of obstacle course or activity involved, and it tends to be much more appealing to the younger people in attendance.

Marking Military Milestones

A military career is full of milestones: graduations, promotions, changes of command, and retirements. Every event is worthy of recognition and a ceremony. Just as you would attend festivities surrounding momentous events in your family, the military's no different. Your unit and your military friends become an extended family of sorts. You should attend as many ceremonies as you are invited to.

Promotions

Promotion parties are given by officers or NCOs shortly after being being notified that they have been promoted. Sometimes held in the squadron, sometimes held at the club or at a different location, promotion parties may be done in conjunction with a group of people being promoted around the same time. In addition to the party, there's also the promotion ceremony where the orders are read and the new insignia is pinned on. The promotion ceremony occurs when servicemembers are able to pin on their new rank.

Change of command

Change of command ceremonies are set up to pass on the authority, accountability, and responsibility from the old commander to the new. This formal ceremony ensures that the troops know who is in command and also serves to demonstrate the new commander's commitment to the unit.

The outgoing commander, the new commander, and the next highest level of command are present at the ceremony. The outgoing commander relinquishes command back to the higher level command who then entrusts the command to the new commander. This is literally done by passing the unit colors, also known as the guideon from the old commander to the higher command and then to the new commander. The symbolic action is meant to signify passing the baton.

Once the unit colors have been passed from one commander to the other, the new commander then addresses the troops while the old commander slips out to his or her next assignment, riding off into the sunset. A change of command ceremony is wrought with a mix of emotions for everyone involved. If the outgoing commander was a popular one, people will feel somewhat conflicted. While you might be happy that the commander is moving on to bigger and better, you may be somewhat apprehensive about the new commander, not knowing what to expect.

Personal feelings aside, it is important that everyone pay their respects to the old commander and his or her family and support the new leadership team by showing up to the ceremony and staying for the following reception.

Retirement ceremonies

After 20-plus-some years of service to their country, servicemembers are entitled to a retirement ceremony to acknowledge their accomplishments throughout their career in service to their country. If you are invited to attend these ceremonies in support of other members of the unit or other friends, try to attend. Retirement ceremonies are important to provide retiring servicemembers and their families a tangible acknowledgement of their faithful service and contributions. Though it may be hard to imagine, one day that'll be you and your servicemember on that stage, and you'll be happy to look out over a sea of faces who have meant so much to you throughout your military life.

Just because your servicemember spouse has a formal retirement ceremony doesn't mean you're no longer part of the military family. On the contrary, you've earned a lifetime of benefits through your dedicated service. A military retirement is a milestone you can be proud of. Don't think of this as an ending. Think of it as a beginning for the next chapter of your lives (more about military retirement in Chapter 21).

Finding Support within the Installation

At times, you may feel that you need more support than your unit can or is qualified to offer. If you are fortunate enough to live on or near an installation, there are any number of support systems for you to tap into:

- ✔ **Chapel:** Not only can you attend services and ceremonies at the chapel on base, but also military chaplains can offer support to servicemembers coming back from a deployment and their families. Remember that military chaplains have faced the issues themselves and can thus be quite helpful.

- ✔ **Family support centers:** Family support centers can be a backbone of support by providing you with loads of information about deployment, as well as providing you with classes and education on military life.

- ✔ **Clubs and groups:** Participating in groups and clubs can give you an even greater sense of belonging. Even outside of the unit, you can find clubs and groups to belong to, such as groups associated with your religion, the school, as well as the Spouses' Club.

- ✔ **Family Advocacy Programs (FAP):** Face it — you're going to get stressed out. If that happens, or if you or anyone you know is a victim of abuse, the counselors and experts at Family Advocacy can help. FAP is your resource for child and spouse abuse prevention as well as preventive education classes, such as crisis management, parenting, and anger management. They even have support groups for new parents.

For more on any of these facilities or programs, check them out in detail in Chapter 3.

Part II:
Understanding Your Financial Issues and Benefits

The 5th Wave
By Rich Tennant

"I just think we need to make provisions in our Will for disposition of our property. Who'll get Park Place? Who'll get Boardwalk? Who'll get the thimble and all the tiny green houses?"

In this part . . .

Understanding all your military and financial benefits can be somewhat overwhelming. In this part, you'll get an overview of what you can expect as well as suggestions on how to maximize your benefits and begin building your financial foundation. You'll also learn about other educational and employment programs out there to support you.

Chapter 5

Deciphering Military Compensation

In This Chapter
▶ Figuring out your sources of income
▶ Understanding your pay statement
▶ Clarifying what's taxable

Servicemembers get paid in a number of different ways, which is a great thing, but it's not simple. Your family member will receive base pay, allowances to help pay for different types of things, and possibly additional income, known as special pays. And once you get it figured out, it'll change. Luckily it only changes for the better; with annual pay raises, longevity raises, promotions, increases in special pays, and allowances.

This chapter explains your servicemember's primary income sources, the leave and earnings statement (LES), and what part of this income is taxable. We know, you may have just snoozed, especially when you saw "taxable." But we promise that if you keep thinking, "Money!" as you read the chapter, you'll become a pro at wading through the LES and all things related to military income — score!

Sifting through Sources of Pay

Basic pay, allowances, and special pays are affected by your service-member's military occupation, pay grade, where he's stationed, and if he's deployed. But, don't worry. In the sections that follow, we give you the information you need to sort through the many pieces and parts of military compensation. And, the more pieces and parts that apply to your family, the more income you have to work with to meet your needs and goals.

Basic pay

Think of this as your servicemember's base paycheck. Basic pay rates are the same across all branches of the service. The only differences in basic pay are pay grade and, to a much lesser extent, the number of years your servicemember has been in the service.

Additional pays

All military who've been in the service for the same length of time and have the same pay grade receive the same basic pay. Your servicemember may qualify for additional pays because of his unique training or specialty, where his duty station is located, and whether he's in a combat zone. Your family may also receive allowances for some food, clothing, and shelter. And the following sections break down all of the additional pays you may encounter.

Hazardous duty pay

Heck, if your loved ones are in harm's way to serve our country, it's nice to know that they're getting paid more. And considering there is an endless number of activities and situations that are dangerous, the military has a number of ways to compensate your servicemember exposed to these dangers:

- ✓ **$225 per month for Hostile Fire and Imminent Danger Pay:** Additional pay for those occasions when your servicemember is subject to hostile fire or explosion.

- ✓ **$50 to $150 per month for Hardship Duty Pay:** For servicemembers living and working in extremely difficult living conditions or enduring excessive physical hardship.

- ✓ **$150 per month for Hazardous Duty Incentive Pay:** In addition to living and working in a danger zone, under extremely difficult living conditions, your servicemember may also perform particularly hazardous duties, such as jumping out of airplanes or handling explosives.

- ✓ **$150 to $350 per month for Hazardous Duty Incentive Pay for Flying:** Servicemembers, known as aircrew (everybody on the plane except the pilots), receive this additional pay. Pilots are paid additionally for their job specialty (more on specialty pay in the section, "Unique training and specialty pay," below).

Your servicemember is entitled to any two of these hazardous duty pays that apply to them at any one time.

Unique training or specialty pay

Each branch of the armed services pays extra if your servicemember acquires the unique skills or specialized training for certain military occupations and may also be eligible for certain special bonuses. Here's how it works:

✓ **Monthly specialty pay**

- $125 to $840 for aviation officers

- $50 to $730 for sea duty

- Up to $340 for diving duty

- Up to $1,000 for proficiency in a foreign language, presuming the military has deemed that foreign language critical.

✓ **Special bonuses**

- **Reenlistment:** Bonuses vary depending on servicemembers' unique training or specialty, their Military Occupational Specialty, and how long they initially served. They may also be eligible for additional reenlistment bonuses if they possess a skill designated as critical by the Secretary of Defense or Homeland Security or are willing to accept undesirable assignments.

- **Pilot:** Up to $25,000 per year for aviators remaining on active duty after the end of their initial enlistment.

- **Nuclear:** Up to $20,000 one-time bonus is available to Naval officers upon their selection for nuclear power training duty. An additional annual pay of up to $22,000 is provided for their technical qualifications for duty in nuclear propulsion plants. And if they sign a long-term contract, they may be entitled to an additional $25,000 bonus each year.

- **JAG:** Up to $60,000 is available to officers who complete ten years of service as a judge advocate. This bonus goes a long way toward paying off big law school loans.

- **Medical:** Special pay is awarded to medical officers if they agree to remain on active duty for at least one year. Remaining on active duty after their initial service obligation period provides up to $14,000 per year of additional pay.

- **Dental:** Up to $30,000 is available to officers who contract to serve on active duty for four years. An additional $7,000 to $27,000 per year is paid for their unique skills, and even more, if they are board certified.

- **Veterinary:** Veterinary officers are eligible to receive awards of $2,000 to $5,000 per year depending on their years of service. In addition they receive an extra $100 per month in special pay.

- **Special Warfare:** Officers who remain on active duty in special warfare service for at least one year may be entitled to receive a continuation bonus of up to $15,000 per year, for each year they serve on special warfare duty.

Allowances

In addition to your servicemember's basic paycheck and any additional special pay they may earn, your family also receives allowances.

These allowances aren't all that different from the ones your parents may have given you as a kid. The military pays servicemembers and their family allowances to help cover increases in the cost of living, as well as additional expenses related to food, clothing, and shelter — and a few other related items.

Cost of living allowances

Maybe you're one of the lucky families who live in a warm, beautiful place like Southern California or Miami or other wonderfully expensive areas like Boston, New York, or Seattle. Housing, gasoline, auto insurance, and sometimes even food may cost significantly more where you live than many other areas of the country. Since your servicemember's basic pay is the same as his or her counterparts stationed in far less expensive parts of the country, the military provides a monthly Cost of Living Allowance (COLA) to help make up this imbalance in compensation.

Cost of living allowances depend on your servicemember's assigned duty station, pay grade, length of time in the service, and whether there are dependents. If you live in a location that the military regards as a high-cost area, you will receive a COLA increase regardless of whether you live on or off base. Visit www.military.com/COLA to calculate the current COLA adjustment for various locations and your personal situation.

Basic allowance for subsistence

This allowance (BAS) is intended to offset the cost of food for the service-member — not the family — and the amount is adjusted annually. The monthly BAS paid to your officer is about $200 and the amount provided to your enlisted servicemember is almost $300. This allowance is paid to all servicemembers regardless of whether they dine in the mess hall or offbase.

But don't get too excited thinking that you've got $300 in extra cash because your servicemember dines at the mess hall. Government provided meals are only partially subsidized.

Clothing allowances

Your officer receives a one-time payment clothing allowance after commissioning to buy clothing. Enlisted servicemembers receive uniforms and an annual clothing maintenance allowance. If your servicemember is required to wear civilian duds as part of his duty assignment, the service will provide an allowance for this additional expense.

Per diem

Should servicemembers travel on official military business they are entitled to a daily cash allotment to reimburse them for the cost of food and lodging. This is known as per diem.

Per diem is set to reimburse servicemembers, to cause them not to go into debt on a business trip. Find out the per diem rate for a given location, at `http://perdiem.hqda.pentagon.mil/perdiem`, prior to the trip and budget accordingly.

Housing allowances

Basic Allowance for Housing, also known as BAH, is provided to servicemembers to adjust for the additional costs of living offbase. The actual amount of BAH is based on the local rental housing market, your servicemember's pay grade, and number of dependents. When it comes to considering your servicemember's housing allowance, keep the following things in mind:

- ✔ BAH is a set amount per month. Remember your actual housing expense can be substantially higher than your BAH. Visit `http://www.military.com/benefits/military-pay/basic-allowance-for-housing-rates` for current rates by geography, pay grade, and dependent status.

- ✔ The Basic Allowance for Housing is paid out automatically when you apply for off-base housing. You may use this money to help cover your housing expenses whether you rent or purchase your home. Refer to Chapter 10 for more on housing options and what may be the best choices for your family.

- ✔ If you and your spouse are both employed by the military, each of you is entitled to the Basic Allowance for Housing. If you live together, one of you can claim BAH with dependents and the other must register at the single rate.

✔ Your family receives the highest total BAH pay if the servicemember with the highest pay grade claims the dependents.

✔ If servicemembers are stationed overseas and live offbase, they don't receive BAH. Instead they receive a special Overseas Housing Allowance, or OHA. This allowance is intended to offset the actual cost of rent, utilities, and recurring maintenance expenses. Unlike BAH for your state-side counterparts, OHA is not a set monthly amount.

✔ If you are eligible for Overseas Housing Allowance, you also qualify for a move-in housing allowance to cover the purchase of necessities; one-time fees, such as real estate agent fees or lease taxes; and reimbursements for required security expenses.

✔ If you are unable to stay in government housing when you first report to a permanent duty station outside the continental United States (OCONUS) for some other reason beyond your control, you may be eligible for an overseas temporary lodging allowance, generally up to 60 days.

Dislocation allowance

If you and your servicemember must relocate due to a change in duty stations or as required by the government, a dislocation allowance or DLA, ranging from about $1,800 to nearly $4,000, is granted to help offset your relocation expenses. The DLA rate is dependent on pay grade.

This allowance does not apply toward the costs your family incurs locating to the first duty station after your servicemember's initial training.

Family separation allowance

If your servicemember must be away for more than 30 days, you may be entitled to the Family Separation Allowance of $250 per month. If your servicemember is assigned to a permanent duty station where dependents are not allowed or if your spouse is on duty on board a ship at sea for more than 30 days you'll be entitled to the Family Separation Allowance.

Taking time off — Leave

Your servicemember earns two and a half days leave per month, or 30 days each year. The civilian world calls it vacation pay and usually limits employees to two weeks per year. And they don't qualify for any vacation until they've completed at least 12 months of employment. But, then again, civilians are almost never on call 24/7.

Leave can accumulate for up to 75 days — over two full years.

If servicemembers don't use their leave — they lose it.

Announced July 01, 2008, members can now carry over 75 days leave rather than the previous 60 days into the next fiscal year. Servicemembers who are unable to take leave because of operational duties may carry forward as many as 120 days leave for up to three or four years depending on circumstances. And this carry-over happens automatically. No authorizations or paperwork are required to get this carry-over. If servicemembers retire or transition out of the armed forces with unused leave, they may receive a cash buyout of their unused leave. Enlisted servicemembers may now sell back up to 30 days of special accrued leave earned in a combat zone or designated contingency operation. This is an especially valuable benefit in that leave earned under these circumstances is not taxed. And you can't cash out more than sixty 60 days worth of leave.

Demystifying the pay statement

In the military your payroll information statement, is known as the leave and earnings statement (LES). All active duty, retired military, and civilians employed by the armed services receive an LES at the end of each month. You might be paid twice a month, but you'll still only receive a monthly LES. And, really, who wants one more frequently than that?

If you're like most people you probably won't spend much or any time reviewing your LES. However, we strongly advise that you thoroughly review your LES any time you may have a change in pay, deductions, or allotments. If the government accidentally overpays your servicemember and the money gets spent — when the error is discovered — you are responsible for making up the overpayment. Review the LES to make certain errors, for or against you, don't go undiscovered.

The easiest and most efficient way to view, or print, the LES is online at www. myPay.com. The following section highlights the key points to review on your spouse's leave and earnings statement. See an example and detailed explanation for each entry on your LES at www.dfas.mil and check out an example of what an LES looks like in Figure 5-1.

Explaining the LES

The Leave and Earnings Statement is only one page long, but it does pack in a lot of information. We'll touch on the highlights here (see Figure 5-1 for a picture of an LES):

↗ **Section A:** On the top line, you see your servicemember's personal information, pay grade, years of service, expiration date of current contract, and the period date covered by the statement.

↗ **Section E:** You'll find all the information you need about the leave part of the LES in this section. It starts out with the beginning balance, adds 2.5 days per month, shows adjustments for leave taken during the current fiscal year (the government runs on a October 1 through September 30 fiscal year), and shows you the remaining leave available.

↗ **Section G:** In this section you find out about taxes — the number of exemptions claimed, state, federal, Social Security, and Medicare taxes paid this period and year to date.

↗ **Section I:** Your Basic Allowance for Housing is illustrated in this section.

↗ **Bottom half:** A listing of all the types and amounts of pays (entitlements), deductions, and payments are displayed on the bottom half of the LES.

↗ **Net pay:** Now we're talking, right? The total (net pay) number toward the bottom of the LES is probably what you're most interested in. This is the amount of cash that will be deposited directly into your bank account.

If you have any questions about your servicemember's LES, consult with your disbursing/finance office.

Allotments

An allotment is money that your servicemember elects to have withheld from his pay and directed toward loan payments, retirement savings, and charitable contributions.

You should take advantage of this convenience as much as possible. It costs nothing to have bills paid or to make investments or contributions directly out of your paycheck. It is very convenient! No checks to write, desired expenditures get made, and you didn't have to think about it or to lift a finger. You've got much more important or at least fun things to do with your time than paying bills. The only downside to allotments is that your servicemember is limited to the number of total allotments they can have at any a time.

The sections that follow show you what you need to know about allotments.

U.S. NAVY
LEAVE AND EARNINGS STATEMENT

	PERIOD COVERED
	01–30APR92 43081

I O	NAME, LAST, FIRST, MI	SSN	PAY GRADE	YRS	LEAVE ACCOUNT

					BEG LV BAL	LV EARND	LV EARND	END LV BAL	BAL TO	PAIDLV
	CHRISTMAS, MARY (N)	123-45-6789	01	00	000 0	12 0	05 0	007 0	000 0	000 0

EARNINGS

BASIC PAY	1565.00	ADV PAY	83.33
BAQ WITH DEPENDENTS	426.20	SCLI FOR 100,000	8.00
BAS	130.30	FEDERAL TAX	110.80
VHA WITH DEPENDENTS	11.15	FICA TAX	100.56
		STATE TAX	32.19
		ALLOTMENT	60.00
TOTAL EARNINGS	2132.65	TOTAL DEDUCTIONS	394.88

NET PAY (1565 + 426.20)   1991.20

PAYMENTS POSTED SINCE LAST LES:
  14APR92   721.20, DDS, DSSN 8522, NPR   0500
  01MAY92   721.25, DDS, DSSN 8522, NPR   0603

BASED ON CURRENT INFORMATION AT DFAS YOUR PAY IS
EXPECTED TO BE:
  MAY92   MID-MONTH PAYMENT AMOUNT   721.00
  MAY92   END-OF-MONTH PAYMENT AMOUNT   721.00

REMARKS:
TOTAL ADVANCE OF PAY 1000.00 – BALANCE OUTSTANDING   666.68
TAX STATUS CHANGE TO MO2 EFFECTIVE APR89
DAILY NORM EFFECTIVE 01MAY92IS 56.08
NAVY AND MARINE CORPS RELIEF SOCIETY NEEDS YOUR SUPPORT;
FUND DRIVE 4 MAY–6JUN

PERSONNEL AND PAY LV COMPENSATION

BAL	AND DUE AND OF LAST NO DON'T LV	TOTAL EXPENSES	TOTAL			M I S C	DDS			
	00	1833 33	390 33	1442 45	00		DDS	00	30,500	22APR89
TAX	MO2	1338 90	5355 60	521 95	1338 90	5355 60	402 21	5355 60	154 98 AL	
SVC	09DEC88	000000		09DEC88 AC				00 00	00 2705	
FIELD										
USE ONLY										

Figure 5-1:
A sample
LES.

Discretionary allotments

You can add up to six discretionary allotments (by completing DD Form 2558) at any time. You can also discontinue or change the amount of your discretionary allotments at any time — it's at your discretion, hence the name.

Use the maximum of six discretionary allotments to have your required monthly expenses such as loans, insurance premiums, and savings contributions paid automatically for you each and every month. Discretionary allotments should be utilized to their fullest extent. Set them up and use them! Make all of your required expenditures, including saving and investing – yes, this is a requirement – before you have a chance to spend the money. You'll be glad you did!

Key items to consider for your discretionary allotments:

- **Rent or mortgage payments**
- **Insurance premiums:** auto, renter's or homeowner's, commercial life insurance
- **Loans:** auto, home, school, or personal
- **Investments:** Thrift Savings Plan, IRAs, mutual funds, or money market accounts

We talk more about the benefits and strategies of paying your bills and saving and investing automatically in Chapter 8.

Nondiscretionary allotments

These types of allotments work exactly the same way as discretionary allotments, with the exception that the type of expenditures allowed are very limited; you can have more of them, but you can't start and stop these allotments at will. If you have any questions about allotments, contact your assigned pay office. If you have additional questions contact the Defense Finance and Accounting Service (DFAS) at 800-390-2348 or visit online at www.dod.mil/dfas.

If you owe back taxes or pay court-ordered child support, you must make these payments through your nondiscretionary allotments.

Making Sense Out of Taxes

We know you're patriotic, red-blooded Americans just dying to abide by the laws of our great country. While it's your duty to pay all the taxes you owe, you have the right not to pay a penny more than you must. In the following sections we highlight what of your income is taxable and what isn't, and what you may be able to do to minimize your total tax bite.

Understanding what compensation is taxable

Everything is included — unless it's excluded! All the time — almost! Oh, that's right. We said we'd make *sense* of your taxes. Here we go . . .

Unless your family member's pay is received for service in a combat zone, the following income sources are taxable for federal income tax purposes:

- Basic pay:
  - Active duty
  - Special schooling and training
  - Cost-of-living allowance (CONUS)
- Special pay (see details in the section "Additional pays")
- Bonuses (see details in the section "Additional pays")
- Pay taken in lieu of leave
- Personal allowances paid to high-ranking officers
- Student loan repayments by the government
- Incentive pay (see details in the section "Additional pays")

The following list outlines the tax-free benefits you receive:

- Living Allowances
  - Basic Allowance for Housing (BAH)
  - Basic Allowance for Subsistence (BAS)
  - Overseas Housing Allowance (OHA)
  - Cost-of-living allowance (OCONUS)
- Moving allowances
- Travel allowances
- Miscellaneous
  - Uniforms for enlisted members, uniform allowance for officers
  - Professional education, required for service

- Childcare assistance

- Qualified educational expenses for dependents

- Discounts at the exchange

- Space-available (Space-A) travel

- Legal assistance

- Medical and dental care

- Burial services, death gratuity payments

- Veteran's disability payments

- Group life insurance

- Survivor Benefit Protection premiums

You may not feel like you're rolling in the dough, but if you had to earn a civilian paycheck equivalent to your after-tax military compensation, it would take a whopping big number!

Commissioned officers' combat zone pay is only excluded from income taxation up to the highest rate of enlisted pay available with the maximum time in service, plus imminent danger or hostile fire pay.

Exploring ways to reduce your tax bite

Everyone wants to reduce their taxes, and we have some ideas just for you listed below:

- **Housing:** Owning a home is one of the most significant ways you can reduce your tax bite. But don't buy a house just to save on taxes. There are many more important issues that should be considered, other than tax savings, and we elaborate on these issues in Chapter 10.

   You can deduct mortgage interest and real estate taxes on your home even though you pay a portion of these expenses with tax-free BAH pay!

- **Thrift Saving Plan (TSP):** Another very useful and beneficial strategy to reduce your taxes is to contribute to your TSP. More on retirement savings options and strategies are found in Chapter 9.

- **Education:** You can invest money for your children's education and save taxes by utilizing 529 plans or Coverdell Education Savings Account. We elaborate on these strategies in Chapter 9 as well.

Make sure that you have your tax return prepared by a professional who has substantial experience serving military clientele. Many offer discounts to military personnel — just ask!

Chapter 6

Taking Care of Yourself: Health and Dental Insurance

*O*ne of the most significant financial benefits servicemembers and their families receive from the military is healthcare. To emphasize just how important healthcare benefits are, consider that nearly one-third of the average retiree's expenses are eaten up by healthcare costs. The amount younger civilian families pay for healthcare is typically much less, but it's still hundreds, if not thousands, of dollars every year.

Less than 60 percent of the civilian workforce has medical insurance, and far fewer have dental, vision or prescription drug coverage. When a civilian retires she almost never has employer-provided health insurance, and even if she does it's not guaranteed to be around throughout her retirement years. However, those employed in, or retired from, the armed forces and their families have access to very affordable, quality healthcare and insurance guaranteed for life by the U.S. government.

This chapter explains your family's military healthcare plan choices, how to determine which option is best for your family, and how to access benefits.

When we say family, we're talking spouse, widow or widower (if not remarried), unmarried children under age 21 (under age 23 if a full-time student), and dependent parents and in-laws. Also, former spouses qualify if they are not remarried and they are not eligible for private medical insurance.

Exploring TRICARE

Your family has three primary military healthcare programs to consider under TRICARE. TRICARE gets its name from the three primary care plans that make up the military health system. Participants in these plans are called beneficiaries. Servicemembers with family covered by TRICARE are referred to as sponsors. In the following section we hit the highlights of each plan and talk about which plan might be best for your family's needs and circumstances.

Breaking down the basic of TRICARE

When you explore your options with TRICARE, you need a basic understanding of how it works and even some basic terminology. First, we give you an overview of each of the three primary plans.

TRICARE consists of three primary care plans. Before we delve into the details of each, here is a quick snapshot of each plan:

- *TRICARE Standard* provides you with the greatest flexibility to choose healthcare providers, without a referral or pre-authorization, but it also costs the most. It is available worldwide.

- *TRICARE Extra* is more restrictive and less expensive. You pay the same annual deductibles as those with Standard; however your share of medical costs is 5 percent less. This plan is only available in the continental United States (CONUS).

- *TRICARE Prime* is like an HMO and is geared toward preventive care. It is the least expensive option, but your choice of healthcare providers is limited. You pay nothing — or very little — under most circumstances.

  All active-duty servicemembers and activated Guard and Reserve are *required* to enroll in TRICARE Prime or one of the Prime options depending on where they live and work. All other eligible beneficiaries *may* choose to enroll in TRICARE Prime. If eligible beneficiaries don't enroll in TRICARE Prime, they are automatically covered by TRICARE Standard and Extra.

Here's some terminology you might run into:

- *Authorized* healthcare providers may be part of a *network* of contracted providers who accept TRICARE negotiated payments and file claims for you.

- Other *authorized* healthcare providers are *non-network* providers, meaning they have no contract with TRICARE, and they limit their services to a case-by-case basis. You may or may not be able to access TRICARE paid services from authorized non-network providers. Be sure to ask before receiving treatment.

✔ *Participating* providers accept TRICARE benefits as payment in full, file claims for you, and you won't incur additional costs for their services.

✔ However, if they are *non-participating* providers they may charge you up to 15% more than the TRICARE allowable charge. You'll likely be responsible for paying for treatment at the time of service and filing your own claims with TRICARE for reimbursement.

TRICARE will only pay for care provided by *authorized* providers. Medicare certified hospitals must participate in TRICARE for inpatient care. However, for outpatient care, providers have the choice whether or not to become authorized providers.

To find out if *your* provider is TRICARE-authorized, check with your regional TRICARE Service Center at `http://tricare.mil/contactus`.

TRICARE Standard

If you select TRICARE Standard you have the flexibility of using any TRICARE-authorized civilian doctor or hospital, or your local Military Treatment Facility (MTF).

You may have to wait for treatment at your MTF, because TRICARE Prime beneficiaries get priority. TRICARE Standard folks will be served on a space-available basis.

With TRICARE Standard:

✔ You don't have to pay for your coverage.

✔ You are responsible for annual deductibles of $50 or $100 per individual and $150 or $300 per family per fiscal year depending on your sponsor's status and rank. However, when you receive treatment at your MTF, no deductible applies.

✔ If your sponsor is active-duty or an activated member of the Guard or Reserve your share of outpatient, clinical preventive and emergency services are 20 percent, up to $1,000 per family per year. All other eligible beneficiaries pay 25 percent of allowable charges incurred after the annual deductible is met.

✔ Your cost for hospitalization is $15.15 per day, subject to a $25 minimum, if your sponsor is active-duty or an activated member of the Guard or Reserve. All other eligible beneficiaries pay the lesser of $535 per day, or 25 percent of the cost of hospitalization, plus 25 percent for any additional professional services, that aren't included in your bill from the hospital.

✔ TRICARE Standard is available to everyone who is eligible for TRICARE benefits, *except* active-duty servicemembers, activated Guard, and Reserve and dependent parents and in-laws.

- ✔ Referrals are not required; however, you may be required to obtain authorization for certain medical treatments and services. Check with your regional Service Center for verification.

- ✔ Be aware that many non-network providers will not file a TRICARE Standard claim on your behalf. It is your responsibility to pay the health-care provider and then apply for reimbursement from TRICARE.

- ✔ You should file your TRICARE Standard claim immediately after services are rendered. Use DD Form 2642 when filing claims. For assistance completing the claim form, consult your regional TRICARE Service Center. Once the claim form is completed, mail one form per envelope to your regional TRICARE Service Center.

For the complete list of contact information and the mailing address for your regional TRICARE Service Center visit http://tricare.mil/contactus.

TRICARE Extra

TRICARE Extra is the military's PPO, or preferred provider option. It is available to all people eligible for TRICARE coverage in the continental United States, except active-duty servicemembers and activated Guard and Reserve. If you opt for TRICARE Extra, you may select civilian physicians and health-care providers from a network of authorized managed care support contractors. Your provider choices are more limited than with TRICARE Standard; however, you're responsible for fewer costs.

With TRICARE Extra:

- ✔ You don't have to pay for your coverage.

- ✔ You are responsible for annual deductibles of $50 or $100 per individual and $150 or $300 per family per fiscal year depending on your sponsor's status and rank. However, when you receive treatment at your MTF there is no deductible.

- ✔ If your sponsor is active-duty or an activated member of the Guard or Reserve, your share of outpatient, clinical preventive and emergency services are 20 percent, up to $1,000 per family per year. All other eligible beneficiaries pay 20 percent of the allowable charges incurred after the annual deductible is met.

- ✔ Your cost for hospitalization is $15.15 per day, subject to a $25 minimum if your sponsor is active-duty or an activated member of the Guard or Reserve. All other eligible beneficiaries pay the lesser of $250 per day, or 25 percent of the cost of hospitalization, plus 20 percent for any additional professional care services that aren't included in your bill from the hospital.

✔ TRICARE Extra is available within the continental United States to everyone who is eligible for TRICARE benefits, *except* active-duty servicemembers, activated Guard and Reserve, and dependent parents and in-laws.

✔ Under TRICARE Extra your healthcare provider files your claim forms for you when you receive treatment, and you may still receive care from your military treatment facility; however, it's on a space-available basis only.

✔ Referrals are not required; however, you may be required to obtain authorization for certain medical treatments and services. Check with your regional Service Center for verification.

The major difference between Standard and Extra is that your share of the cost after you've paid your annual deductible is 5 percent less with Extra. And your healthcare provider must be part of the network.

TRICARE Prime

If you're like most military families TRICARE Prime is your best choice of healthcare plans. It's the lowest cost option, but there are a few limitations. It's kind of like a civilian's HMO. You can save a lot of money, you never have to file insurance claim forms, but you do have restrictions on your choices of doctors and hospitals. And TRICARE Prime may not be available where you live.

Active-duty servicemembers are automatically enrolled in TRICARE Prime when registered with DEERS.

For a listing of Military Treatment Facilities, hours, contact information, and summary of services visit http://www.tricare.mil/mtf. For a directory of TRICARE providers, visit www.tricare.osd.mil/providerdirectory. And you can update information directly at the TRICARE website at http://www.tricare.osd.mil/deers.

As a TRICARE Prime beneficiary:

✔ You see doctors and medical personnel at your local military treatment facility MTF.

✔ You are assigned a *primary care manager* (PCM) who is your personal medical care provider and advisor. They provide routine healthcare, coordinate referrals to specialists, assist with prior authorizations, and maintain your healthcare records.

When your primary care manager provides you with a referral to a specialist, they also file the referral with TRICARE. The specialist to whom you are referred will contact TRICARE to obtain authorization. TRICARE must authorize certain medical treatments and procedures before you receive care.

As a TRICARE Prime beneficiary you should always consult with your primary care manager at your military treatment facility before receiving medical treatment from any specialist or other healthcare provider — unless of course — you or a family member are experiencing a healthcare emergency.

✔ You have first priority for appointments at military treatment facilities. And, if for some reason, MTF care is not available, your primary care manager will refer you to a TRICARE network provider.

✔ Active-duty servicemembers, as well as Guard and Reserve members and their eligible family members, are not subject to any charges if they are directed to a network provider or referred to a non-network provider by their primary care manager.

✔ If you happen to need hospitalization, there is a nominal charge at military treatment facilities. Check with your local MTF for specific details. If your primary care manager directs your active-duty servicemember or activated Guard or Reserve member to a TRICARE provider for hospitalization, you should incur no cost. However, you and all other eligible TRICARE Prime beneficiaries will be charged $11 per day, subject to a $25 minimum.

✔ Services of a non-network provider without a referral from your primary care manager may be accessed through your Point of Service option of TRICARE Prime. The Point of Service option is not available to active-duty servicemembers. You are subject to a deductible of $300 per individual and $600 for the family each fiscal year, and 50 percent of all allowable charges beyond that point. There is no annual maximum out-of-pocket cost for Point of Service charges.

✔ If you don't get authorization before (non-emergency) treatment — you'll get smacked with some very hefty medical expenses!

✔ Eligible family member must each be enrolled individually. Refer to Chapter 3 for details on initial enrollments and updating your information as necessary.

If you have health insurance provided through civilian employment you should review all plan options. TRICARE Prime may not be your best option when you have other health insurance.

If you work through your primary care manager to supervise and coordinate your family's healthcare, if you avoid using services from a healthcare provider without a referral and authorization, and if care is available in your area, you can receive great healthcare all paid for by the government.

TRICARE Prime Remote

If you live more than 50 miles away from the military treatment facility your family can still participate in a program very similar to TRICARE Prime — it's called TRICARE Prime Remote. The only difference is the medical professionals providing your care. Instead of obtaining treatment at your local military treatment facility, you see a local civilian healthcare provider who is part of the TRICARE authorized network.

Activated Guard and Reserve members and their families meeting the same distance requirements are also eligible for TRICARE Prime Remote.

For more information about TRICARE Prime Remote call 888-363-2273 or visit `http://mybenefit/home/overview/Plans/PrimeRemote`.

TRICARE Prime Overseas

This program works the same as TRICARE Prime in areas where there are military medical facilities and a network of civilian providers.

If a provider is not available in your location, you may have your share of Point of Service costs waived by getting your primary care manager to refer you to a Regional Medical Service Center, which is a TRICARE authorized healthcare provider. But the Point of Service option is not available to active-duty servicemembers or activated Guard or Reserve members.

For assistance with TRICARE Prime Overseas, call 888-777-8343 or visit `http://mybenefit/home/overview/Plans/PrimeOverseas`.

Vision benefits

TRICARE Prime participants (age three and older — although special rules apply for newborns and infants or if you or a family member has diabetes) are also entitled to vision benefits, including comprehensive eye exams once every two years. You don't even have to work through your primary care manager for a referral or authorization unless you can't or don't want to see a network provider. TRICARE covers some surgeries and treatments for diseases and conditions of the eyes. You can even get free eyeglasses from your local military treatment facility.

Vision exams are only provided to servicemembers and their families who have TRICARE Prime coverage. Those families covered by TRICARE Standard or Extra are not eligible unless the exam is necessary due to a covered medical condition.

For additional information about all military health programs, visit the TRICARE website at `http://www.tricare.osd.mil` or call 877-363-6337.

Prescription drug coverage

If you, your servicemember, or any of your family members have TRICARE health benefits, you are eligible for TRICARE's Prescription Drug plan. The prescription drug coverage is the same for all military healthcare plans, and it is available worldwide.

You can use one of the following ways to have your prescriptions filled:

- ✔ **Military pharmacy:** The military treatment facility pharmacy is your best option if your prescription is available at the MTF. You can get a 90-day supply at no cost. It's a good idea to call ahead to verify that your prescription is available.

- ✔ **Mail-order pharmacies:** Mail order is a great alternative if your prescription drug isn't available through the MTF. You can save a lot of money, but you do have to plan in advance — note the key words "mail order." Depending on the pharmacy, the mail service, and your location it could take several days to receive your prescription. For more information visit the TRICARE Mail Order Pharmacy Program online at http://www.express-scripts.com/TRICARE.

- ✔ **Network pharmacies:** If you need your prescription filled *immediately* and it's not carried by your local MTF, your best option is to obtain it through a network pharmacy. There are over 54,000 network pharmacies in the United States and in U.S. territories. To find a network pharmacies check out http://member.express-scripts.com/web/pharmacyLocator/openPharmacyLocator.do?portal=dodCustom&net=1991.

- ✔ **Non-network pharmacies:** Lastly, your more expensive option is non-network pharmacies. Fortunately, it is highly unlikely that you would have to utilize a non-network pharmacy given appropriate notice.

Prescription drugs can take a substantial bite out of your budget. Make certain that you fully utilize all of your military benefits by taking advantage of the TRICARE Prescription Drug program.

Summarizing healthcare options

Selecting the TRICARE plan best for your family essentially boils down to:

    Whether TRICARE Prime is available in your area, and

    Whether access to your personal physician is worth the additional expense

We've included some common situations that might help steer you into the right direction of which plan to choose:

✔ The more flexibility you need or desire, the more expensive your health-care. Also, if you want priority access to your military treatment facility, then TRICARE Prime is the plan for you!

✔ If you're really attached to your doctor and you're not subject to relo-cating, TRICARE Standard might be the best fit for you, but only if your doctor isn't a participating network provider in TRICARE. If they are, you could save a little money with TRICARE Extra. Ask your doctor or refer to the network provider list.

✔ If you live on or near a military installation and don't currently have a doctor or a strong attachment to your primary physician, TRICARE Prime is the way to go! You'll save a lot of money, receive prompt and quality care at your local MTF — and well — what else do you really need?

Enrolling in TRICARE

Active-duty servicemembers and activated Guard and Reserve *must* enroll in one of the TRICARE Prime options. All other eligible family members *may* choose to enroll in TRICARE Prime — if available in your area — or you may use one of TRICARE's other health plan options. For everything you need to know about enrolling in TRICARE visit https://www.hnfs.net/bene/enrollment/enrollment_activities_current_beneficiaries.htm.

Enrollment is *not* necessary for TRICARE Standard or Extra! Coverage is automatic if you remain eligible through DEERS. Refer to Chapter 3 for more information on DEERS.

If you have access to the Internet, the easiest way to enroll is online at http://www.tricare.mil/mybenefit/home/Medical. Because you'll need certain information to complete your enrollment application whether you're enrolling online, mailing your enrollment application to your Regional Contractor, or submitting your enrollment application to the TRICARE Service Center representative in your area, go to the Web site and follow these steps:

1. **Establish your profile.** Click on the link entitled My Profile in the top left-hand corner and answer some brief questions about your servicemember's status and your geographical location.

2. **Click on Enrollment at the top of the next screen.** From the Enrollment page you can download enrollment applications and look up TRICARE Service Centers and Regional Contractors.

To enroll online you will need to have your "myPay PIN" or a valid, Common Access Card (CAC) and have your active-duty servicemember establish a Family Member Account (for active-duty personnel only). Your servicemem-ber must log in to the Family Account Manager with his or her CAC and select which family members are to receive a family account. This creates a separate account for each eligible family member. Family members can then log onto the site with their unique Family Account number.

Once you're logged into the site you can complete your TRICARE enrollment, update your address, and change your primary care manager.

If you prefer to mail in your enrollment application, you'll need to obtain a copy of the application from the above-mentioned website or have your regional contractor mail you an application kit. Complete the application, sign it, and mail it back to your regional contractor.

You may find it most convenient just to drop by your local TRICARE Service Center, pick up a copy of your enrollment application and primary care manager change form, complete the form on the spot, and return the completed form to a service center representative.

After your application has been processed you will receive a package by mail, including a welcome letter identifying your primary care manager, if one has been assigned to you, and enrollment card for each family member that you enrolled. You'll also receive a copy of the TRICARE handbook.

You should keep a copy of your enrollment application until you receive your military ID cards, which state your TRICARE eligibility on the back. If you need nonemergency medical treatment before you receive your ID cards, be sure to contact your Regional Contractor to verify that you have coverage and determine who has been assigned as your primary care manager. Remember to contact your primary care manager before seeking treatment.

Sizing up TRICARE Health Benefits for the Guard and Reserve

Your family has three primary military healthcare programs to consider if your Guard or Reserve servicemember is activated for more than 30 consecutive days. Those options include TRICARE Standard, Extra, and Prime.

Checking the basics of your options

- ✔ *TRICARE Standard* provides you with the greatest flexibility to choose healthcare providers, without a referral or pre-authorization, but it also costs the most. This program is available worldwide.

✔ *TRICARE Extra* is more restrictive and less expensive. You pay the same annual deductibles as those with Standard; however, your share of the medical cost is 5 percent less. It is only available in the continental United States (CONUS).

✔ *TRICARE Prime* is like an HMO and is geared toward preventive care. It is the least expensive option, but your choice of healthcare providers is limited. You pay nothing — or very little — under most circumstances.

Here are some facts that cover all plans:

✔ Your activated servicemember is eligible for TRICARE Prime, Prime Remote, or Prime Overseas, depending on their location.

✔ Your maximum annual out-of-pocket cost is $1,000 for your family.

✔ You can get dental benefits.

✔ If your servicemember is not currently activated for more than 30 consecutive days or is not a member of the Selected Reserve, you and your family are *not* eligible for TRICARE benefits.

TRICARE Reserve Select

TRICARE Reserve Select is available worldwide to most Selected Reserve members and their families while not on active duty. You have the freedom to manage your own healthcare and utilize any TRICARE authorized provider. You may also access care at a military treatment facility.

With TRICARE Reserve Select:

✔ The current premium for servicemember and family coverage is $253 per month.

✔ There is also an annual deductible of $50 or $150 per individual and $100 or $300 for the family each fiscal year, except when you receive treatment at an MTF and then no deductible applies. The ranges are dependent on your servicemember's rank. E-4 and below pay the lesser deductible, while E-5 and above pay the higher deductible.

✔ Your share of most medical services, devices, and supplies including outpatient, clinical preventive, laboratory and X-Ray, maternity, ambulance, and emergency services are 15 percent of allowable charges if approved and provided by a network provider. If services are rendered by a non-network provider, your share of allowable charges is 20 percent.

✔ Your cost for hospitalization, newborn care, or inpatient skilled nursing treatment is $15.15 per day, subject to a $25 minimum.

✔ In most cases, there is minimal or no cost to access treatment at a military treatment facility. However you may have to wait awhile since treatment is provided on a space-available basis only.

✔ You generally have to pay for services when they are rendered and seek reimbursement by submitting a claim form to TRICARE Reserve Select.

TRICARE Reserve Select may be an excellent option if you are eligible. This military healthcare program provides comprehensive healthcare at a reasonable cost and includes the TRICARE Prescription Drug coverage. Refer to the section "Prescription drug coverage," earlier in this chapter for more information on the drug plan.

For more information visit http://www.defenselink.mil/ra/html/tricare.html.

Understanding Dental Benefits

The TRICARE Dental Plan (TDP) is dental insurance and is available to you and your family if your servicemember is active-duty or activated Guard or Reserve.

Active-duty servicemembers and activated Guard and Reserve members are not eligible for the TRICARE Dental Plan, but don't you worry; they receive free dental care from the military dental treatment facilities.

Before you check out the coverage in Table 6-1, keep the following facts about TDP in mind:

✔ For you and your eligible family members, the monthly premiums for TDP are $11.58 for one person and $28.95 for two or more family members. The first monthly premium is due upon enrollment, but going forward you'll likely want to have the ongoing monthly premiums deducted from your servicemember's pay as a discretionary allotment.

✔ The maximum annual benefit any one beneficiary can receive is $1,200. The lifetime maximum orthodontic benefit is $1,500 per beneficiary.

✔ Once enrolled in TDP you must continue the coverage — and pay premiums – for at least 12 months. After that, your enrollment commitment is only month to month.

✔ If your spouse is in the National Guard or Reserves you, your servicemember, and your kids can enroll in the TRICARE Dental Plan. Contact United Concordia Companies at 888-622-2256 for specific details or enroll online at www.UCCI.com.

✔ The TRICARE dental plan covers all of the costs for diagnostic, emergency, and preventive services. Table 6-1 illustrates your cost — based on your servicemember's status and rank — should you or your children need any of these services.

Table 6-1	Breakdown of the TRICARE dental plan		
Services	*E1-E4 CONUS*	*E5 + CONUS*	*All pay grades OCONUS*
Office visit, Basic restorative, Post surgical services, and Sealants	20%	20%	0%
Endodontic, Periodontal, and Oral Surgery	30%	40%	0%
General anesthesia	40%	40%	0%
Orthodontic (limitations apply), Non-basic restorative, Implants, and Miscellaneous services (not available OCONUS)	50%	50%	50%

For more information visit www.TRICAREdentalprogram.com, or call 800-866-8499 if you're in the continental United States or 888-418-0466 OCONUS.

Explaining Your Benefits

As a TRICARE beneficiary you receive statements – also known as an EOB or Explanation of Benefits – which look a lot like a bill. These EOBs are sent to you shortly after TRICARE receives a claim request. Your EOB lists details about the claim that was submitted, the allowable amount, how much TRICARE paid, if there was other insurance, and how much you are responsible for paying.

You're also provided with information about how much your individual and family deductibles are each year and how much of that deductible you have met as of the EOB statement date.

It is very important that you review each Explanation of Benefit statement immediately upon receipt to make sure the information is correct. If you have any questions about information reported on your EOB, contact your healthcare administrator immediately.

Chapter 7

Maximizing Military Benefits

*Y*our family's military compensation goes beyond just your servicemember's base pay. The military provides a number of significant monetary benefits, including free relocation assistance, financial counseling, and legal services. These benefits alone can be worth thousands of dollars to you and your family. In this chapter we highlight the major financial benefits, beyond your paycheck and your health and dental benefits, and discuss how to access and maximize those benefits.

Tapping into the Family Support Center

The average military family moves about once every three years. The Family Support Center is available to help you assimilate into your new community — whether it is your first station or your fourth — the Family Support Center is a great resource when you're new to "town."

Centers are available on all installations to assist in your transition and help you with any questions that you may have. The centers are staffed with people who've been through transitions, deployments, and reunions. They have spouses in the service and kids in the local schools. They are information central when it comes to what's going on in "town." The center staff can help you locate day care, get you the scoop on schools, provide you with the rundown on recreation programs to help the kids meet new friends, and fill you in on all the activities and events that you need to know about as a new member of the community.

The Family Support Center is command central for family support information, benefits, and programs. Take advantage of this resource on your military installation.

To find your local Family Support Center visit www.militaryinstallations. dod.mil.

Accessing Military OneSource

If you need assistance or support beyond what may be available through your local Family Support Center, or at a time when the center isn't open, you can also tap into the Military OneSource service. They have trained specialists who can assist you in virtually all areas of military family life. The subject matter covered ranges from transitioning and relocation, pre- and post-deployment issues, military benefits, financial matters, and much more.

Military OneSource hotline is available 24/7 to all active-duty servicemembers, Guard, and Reserve and their immediate family members.

If you've got questions about local schools or how to arrange a vacation with military lodging and transportation or your five year old is having nightmares because his daddy is away, stop by your local Family Support Center or call the Military OneSource at 800-342-9647. This is what they're there for — and so much more — at no cost to you!

Traveling Space-A

Join the service and see the world! There's a lot of truth to that statement if you want to make it happen. Your family can travel for free with the military's special travel benefits — but there's a little art and luck involved.

Space-available flights, also known as, space-A flights enable you, your servicemember, and family to take advantage of the unused seats on Department of Defense aircraft.

Space-A flights can be of great value, but you need to have some flexibility, know the rules, and do some research ahead of time. Unfortunately, there's no publicly available online central booking system for space-A, like Travelocity. But if you have access to a military computer you can login to the Joint Operational Support Airlift Center (OSA) at https://josac. tanscom.mil/newfltschedules.htm and check the daily OSA space-available flight schedule.

There are several ways to sign up for a space-A flight:

- ✔ You can sign up online at `www.spacea.info/signup`.
- ✔ Fax your request on an Air Mobility Command Form 140 (available at `http://www.spacea.info/signup/amc140.pdf` to the installation near you that provides space-A travel).

When considering space-A travel, keep the following in mind:

- ✔ **Be prepared to wait.** Space-A travelers are never guaranteed a seat, and you may spend a lot of time in the terminals waiting to see if you can get on a flight at all. Bring some snacks and reading material!

- ✔ **Forget luxury.** If you do get a flight it might be on a cargo plane not really designed for passengers. Needless to say, it can be difficult to travel on a space-available basis with your family. However, we wouldn't be wasting your time telling you about space-A travel if it wasn't worth it!

- ✔ **Remember the requirements.** To take advantage of space-A travel, your servicemember must be on leave at the time they submit a travel request and remain on leave status throughout the travel time requested.

- ✔ **Do your homework.** To successfully travel on a space-available basis, spend some time doing a little homework and try to be as flexible as possible on your dates and destinations. That way you can make the most of this wonderful military benefit!

Traveling on a space-available basis is dictated by your eligibility and priority level. First, there has to be empty seats. Then priority is given in the following order:

Category I – Dependent on Emergency leave

Category II — Environmental Morale Leave (EML)

Category III — Active Duty on Ordinary Leave/House Hunting

Category IV — (EML) Unaccompanied Dependents

Category V — Permissive TDY/Students/Overseas Command — Sponsored Dependents

Category VI — Retired Military, Guard, and Reserves

Looking into Lodging Bargains

As a military family you can access lodging on bases, at temporary housing facilities, and hotels, resorts, and guesthouses all around the world. There are more than 400 military installations offering temporary lodging facilities and thousands of other temporary military lodging around the world.

Each branch of the service has its own special lodging programs and discounts. However, servicemembers and their families aren't restricted to just their branch of the Armed Forces. For more information contact your Family Support Center or visit http://www.temporarymilitarylodging.net.

Protecting Your Rights — Legal Issues

As a military family you have many legal rights and protections. Unfortunately, laws had to be passed to help ensure that your rights are upheld and protected. Fortunately, the Armed Services extend a helping hand with legal issues, and we break down those issues as well as how to find legal help in the following sections.

Getting the lowdown on the law

The Servicemember's Civil Relief Act (SCRA) is the body of law that helps insure your family's legal rights. The law covers all active-duty servicemembers, activated Guard and Reserve, and their dependent family members. These laws were put in place to allow your servicemember to focus on their job and minimize undue financial hardship on your family. To further minimize hardship on your family, the Armed Services provides legal assistance to all active-duty, Guard and Reserve members, and their dependent family members.

Below we list the highlights of SCRA that you need know:

- **Limit on interest rates:** Interest rates that you must pay on any loan or debt that you had prior to going on active duty are limited to no more than 6 percent a year. However, this cap on your interest rates is not automatic. You must notify your lender in writing requesting this benefit.

- **Stay of proceedings:** If you're involved in a lawsuit you can request a delay, if the delay is necessary due to your servicemember's service.

- **Statute of limitations:** Your active-duty servicemember's service to our country will not be taken into account when determining the statute of limitations on legal proceedings brought by or against you.

✔ **Health insurance reinstatement:** If you have health insurance prior to reporting to active duty, SCRA requires your civilian health insurance company to reinstate your coverage when your servicemember completes their service.

✔ **Home foreclosure protection:** Your mortgage company can't foreclose on you if you have a mortgage prior to active duty and you can illustrate that military service is the reason you can't afford to make your mortgage payment.

✔ **Eviction protection:** Your landlord also has to be more flexible if you are renting your home and can't keep up with your rent payments because of your servicemember's duty.

✔ **Business lease termination:** You can terminate a business lease contract that you or your spouse had prior to active duty if reporting to duty would make continuing that lease unreasonable.

That doesn't mean you can walk away from back payments or that you're off the hook the day active-duty orders are issued. You're still responsible for all past and, in most cases, through the end of the next month.

And be sure the lease holder gives written notice to the landlord! If your servicemember is the leaseholder and they're deployed overseas or for some other reason unavailable, you want to have power of attorney in place so you can handle this! Your Legal Assistance Center attorney can draft a power of attorney for your servicemember.

✔ **Eliminates double taxation:** If you work in one state, but your legal residence is in a different state, SCRA prevents the state in which you're employed from taxing your income. Only your state of residence may tax your income. Hopefully your legal residence is one of the few states without state income tax.

In addition to the protections provided under SCRA, Guard and Reserve families and servicemembers receive additional protections under the Uniformed Services Employment and Reemployment Rights Act (USERRA). One of the major provisions under USERRA is a law that requires employers to reemploy Guard and Reserve members when they return from deployment, under most cases. Not only is the employer required to reemploy servicemembers returning to the civilian work force, but employers must also reemploy servicemembers in a position comparable to the one they had prior to going on active duty.

Finding legal assistance

Consult with your Legal Assistance Center if you're having trouble meeting your financial obligations or if you have any questions or concerns about any of your rights under the laws. There are a lot of nuances to these laws, but fortunately the Legal Assistance Centers are here to assist you — at no cost — it's all part of your military benefits.

In addition to answering questions about your legal rights and protections, your Legal Assistance Center can assist you by drafting a will, healthcare directives, and powers of attorney. Legal assistance attorneys can also answer questions and give advice about your income taxes or any other personal legal issue.

To find a Legal Assistance Center near you visit `http://legalassistance.law.af.mil/content/locator.php`.

Reviewing Your Military-Provided Life Insurance

The military provides servicemembers and their family members with access to high-quality, affordable group life insurance programs. In the following sections we highlight the major features and benefits of each of these programs.

Servicemembers' group life insurance

Servicemembers Group Life Insurance (SGLI) is available to all active-duty servicemembers and members of the Guard and Reserve. Servicemembers are automatically covered for $400,000 of death benefits. The monthly cost for coverage is $29 and is automatically deducted from their pay. The premium cost to insure your Reservist who is not on active duty is $25 per year for $250,000 of insurance.

If servicemembers determine that they need less coverage or decide to decline coverage entirely because they have no need for life insurance, which is highly unlikely, or they have alternative coverage, servicemembers must complete the SGLI Election and Certificate Form 3286 to reduce or cancel coverage.

SGLI has a couple of major benefits:

- The premiums stay level for the duration of servicemembers' military careers.

- Servicemembers can convert to Veteran's Group Life Insurance (VGLI) — with no medical underwriting — upon transitioning from the military. So, if servicemembers have health concerns upon transitioning from the military this VGLI conversion benefit is a major deal! However, if servicemembers are healthy, they very likely can obtain more cost-effective life insurance through other insurance companies.

Conversion from SGLI to VGLI must take place within 120 days of service to avoid medical underwriting.

Perhaps $400,000 sounds like more than enough life insurance to support you and your family should something happen to your spouse. But if you have one or more young children, it's highly likely that you'll need additional life insurance coverage on your servicemember. In Chapter 8 we explore how to compute exactly how much life insurance your family needs. It is not uncommon that your family will need more than $400,000 worth of life insurance, but that's the maximum your spouse can qualify for through SGLI. Fortunately there are some military friendly (that is, they don't have a war clause) life insurance companies through which you can obtain additional life insurance coverage. Check out the following web sites for additional information:

- www.AFBA.com
- www.AAFMAA.com (Army and Air Force)
- www.navymutual.org (Navy and Marines)
- www.MOAA.org (officers)
- www.USAA.com
- www.USBA.com

Traumatic SGLI

In addition to the $29 per month for $400,000 of Servicemember's Group Life Insurance (for more on SGLI, check out the section above, "Servicemembers' group life insurance"), a $1 per month premium is automatically included for Traumatic Injury Protection coverage. Traumatic Injury Protection is mandatory coverage.

Traumatic Injury Protection provides a benefit between $25,000 and $100,000 if your servicemember sustains one of the following traumatic injuries:

✔ Loss of sight, speech, or hearing

✔ Loss of one hand or foot, or a major injury to the hand

✔ Severe paralysis, burns, or brain injury

Family service group life insurance

Families Servicemembers Group Life Insurance (FSGLI) is just like it sounds. It is a life insurance program for you and your dependent children if your spouse is insured under the SGLI program.

You can purchase up to $100,000 of coverage for yourself and up to $10,000 for each of your dependent children. The cost of your coverage if you're under age 35 is only $5.50 a month. The premium increases every five years; however the cost is still very competitive through at least age 50. There is no cost for coverage for eligible dependent children.

For more information on Family Servicemembers Group Life Insurance visit www.insurance.va.gov/sgliSite/fsgli/sglifam.htm.

Exploring Your Retirement Benefits

Unlike any other employer, the U.S. government provides full retirement benefits if you've served in the Armed Forces for 20 years or more. Imagine: You and your servicemember could be in your late 30s or early 40s and receive one half of your servicemember's base pay for the rest of your lives. That additional income provides you with opportunities that other people can only dream of at that stage in life.

The financial value of these retirement benefits alone could easily be worth more than $500,000. It would take savings of about $13,000 per year to accumulate that sum of money in 20 years.

Finding out how retirement benefits are calculated

Servicemembers are eligible to receive a monthly retirement paycheck equal to 50 percent of their highest 36 months average base pay if they retire after 20 years of service. At 30 years of service the retirement benefit increases to 75 percent of the highest 36 months average base pay.

Basic pay used to calculate retirement benefits for members who entered service prior to September 8, 1980 is final basic pay, rather than the average of the highest 36 months of basic pay.

This retirement benefit is calculated by multiplying the number of years of service times 2.5%per year.

- ✔ 20 years × 2.5 = 50%
- ✔ 25 years × 2.5 = 62.5%
- ✔ 30 years × 2.5 = 75%

An extraordinary feature of your retirement benefit is the cost-of-living adjustment equal to the national consumer price index (CPI). So, every year you might receive a cost-of-living raise in your retirement paycheck. The only reason we say "might" is because it is possible for the CPI to stay level or go down in a given year. However, it almost always goes up, usually between one and 3 percent per year.

There is another way to calculate your retirement benefits. This program is called the Career Status Bonus, also known as, CSB/REDUX. This retirement program is more complicated than the standard retirement system mentioned above, and for the majority of servicemembers this program does not make sense.

In the CSB/REDUX system, your benefits are based on a multiplier of 2 percent per year times the number of years of service beginning at 20 years. So your military benefit at 20 years would only be 40 percent of your final base pay.

Why would anyone be inclined to accept 40% when they could have 50%? Well, a bonus check of $30,000 can induce many people into taking this reduced monthly benefit. And by the way, not only do you receive a reduced monthly benefit, but your cost-of-living adjustment is also reduced by 1 percent per year.

When servicemembers reach their 15th year of service they must choose between taking the CSB/REDUX and the traditional military retirement program.

Choosing a retirement program is a huge decision and can be extremely costly if you make the wrong choice for your family. Although CSB/REDUX can be hazardous to your financial well-being, there are times when the CSB/REDUX program may be appropriate as long as you tread carefully. Refer to Chapter 20 for additional considerations to think about with regard the Career Status Bonus decision. For great information and helpful calculators on the military retirement plan visit `http://www.defenselink.mil/militarypay/ retirement`.

Chapter 8

Starting Out on the Right Financial Foot

. . . .

In This Chapter

▶ Exploring the fundamentals of personal finance

▶ Evaluating what you must have

▶ Protecting your family against common risks

▶ Beginning your investment portfolio

. . . .

*Y*our family is either in the midst of or embarking on a new military career and just getting by financially, but now you're ready to dedicate your energy to get your financial house in order. Order and discipline — it's the military way! And those characteristics are extremely helpful in building and maintaining a successful personal financial life. In this chapter, we cover all the essential issues you face financially and provide you with the guidance that — along with your discipline — enables you to achieve a rock solid financial foundation.

Determining Your Required Monthly Expenses

What amount of money do you *really* need to live on? The appropriate answers don't sound like — I need the latest cellphone. We're really talking about food, clothing, shelter, medical care, and insurance that we must have. Most of these required expenses are provided by, or supplemented by, the military.

The following is a list of the types of *required* expenses incurred by a typical military family.

- ✔ **Shelter:**
  - Home mortgage or rent
  - Utilities: electric, gas, water, sewer, trash pickup, and basic telephone service
- ✔ **Protection:** Life, disability, homeowners, renters, health, and auto insurance
- ✔ **Healthcare/medical and dental care**
- ✔ **Prescription drugs**
- ✔ **Childcare**
- ✔ **Savings:** minimum of 10 percent of gross income
- ✔ **Food:**
  - Groceries: basic essentials only
- ✔ **Clothing and clothing maintenance**
- ✔ **Basic hygiene:**
  - Personal: toothpaste, deodorant, haircuts
  - Household: laundry detergent, toilet paper
- ✔ **Transportation:**
  - Automobile loan or lease payment
  - Auto maintenance
  - Gasoline
  - Other: tolls, parking, public transportation
- ✔ **Legal requirements:**
  - Real estate and property taxes
  - Child support
  - Alimony
  - Other debts: school loans, personal loans, credit cards, and so on

You may notice that some of your family's monthly expenses don't appear on the above list. That could be due to an oversight on our part, or more likely, it's because these expenses are not *required* expenses.

You won't find an expense category for dining-out, entertainment, subscriptions, health club memberships, summer camp, birthdays, charitable contributions, cable television, or mobile phones. These types of expenses, although very common and convenient, are discretionary expenses.

The above list contains items that are required to sustain life, or keep you from going to jail, if you don't pay those bills. All other expenses are discretionary — in other words — you choose how to spend, or if to spend, any money on these items.

Making it automatic

We strongly recommend that you utilize the allotment feature of your military paycheck to automatically have required monthly expenses deducted from your pay before the balance is deposited into your checking account. Use allotments to pay for as many of your required monthly living expenses as possible. Utilizing allotments provides you with two great benefits:

- ✔ Your savings and investments happen automatically before you have the opportunity to spend the money.
- ✔ Your bills get paid automatically, so you never have to worry about being late on a payment because you're PCSing, or just busy doing more enjoyable things than paying bills.

Discretionary allotments can include the following:

- ✔ Commercial insurance premiums
- ✔ Thrift Savings Plan and other investment contributions
- ✔ Mortgage or rent payments
- ✔ Auto and student loans

Nondiscretionary allotments include the following:

- ✔ Purchase of U.S. savings bonds
- ✔ Child support payments
- ✔ Delinquent taxes

To sign up for or change your allotments, complete and submit DD Form 2558 to your Assigned Pay Office.

You may find that you have more regularly occurring required monthly expenses than you are allowed to pay through your discretionary allotments. If that is the case, you can do the next best thing by setting up automatic monthly withdrawals from your checking account to cover the balance of these expenses automatically.

Establishing Emergency Reserves

If you get into a car accident, your dear sister needs a helping hand, or your tree falls on your neighbor's fence, where are you going to get the money to resolve these problems? The best answer is — your emergency reserves.

Recognizing the reality of not having reserves

Unfortunately, without having easy access to cash in your checking or savings accounts, or a money market mutual fund to take care of legitimate emergencies; you might have to tap alternatives that aren't nearly as appropriate or financially attractive. Maybe parents or other family members can bail you out. Maybe you can get a home equity line of credit or borrow against your 401(k) or Thrift Savings Plan. Possibly the only option is credit cards or payday loans.

Payday loans are the (legal) lender of last resort. You should exhaust all options before even thinking about a payday loan!

Reserving funds for financial emergencies

The best strategy to protect your family from unforeseen financial emergencies is to establish adequate emergency reserves. The most common types of accounts to consider are savings accounts, money market accounts, and money market mutual funds.

We list some ways to get started that you should consider when establishing your emergency reserves:

- ✔ A great place to get started with an emergency reserve account is the bank that you use for checking.

✔ As a military family you may find it most convenient to work with a national bank that has branches in most cities. However with today's online banking options, you may get better pricing and more personal attention working with the community bank or credit union, such as the Pentagon Federal Credit Union `http://www.penfed.org`.

✔ You can open a savings or money market account at a bank or credit union with as little as $100 to $500.

✔ You can start an emergency reserve account online through an online bank such as ING Direct (`http://www.INGdirect.com`). They have very competitive rates on their Orange Savings account — and it's very easy to open and make additions and withdrawals to the account online. You can open this account with as little as one dollar, add contributions to the account anytime you want, and when you need tap into this reserve account you can do so online very simply by transferring money directly into your checking account.

The age-old question is: How much money should you keep in your emergency reserve accounts? Well, that depends entirely on your comfort level and the security of your income. We are extremely confident that the U.S. government is going to be able to make payroll. However, if you have a job that provides income required to help meet your family's living expenses, if your spouse is reassigned to a new duty station, and you have to terminate your employment, that move could put a significant crimp on your lifestyle.

Given that it could take a number of months to adjust to your new duty station and possibly acquire new employment, we feel that it is only prudent to have at least six months' worth of required living expenses, which are not covered by your servicemember's paycheck, in cash reserves accounts.

If you determine that your required monthly living expenses for your family total $4,000 per month and your servicemember's total compensation covers $2,800 of that expense, you should have no less than $7,200 in your cash reserve accounts ($1,200 per month times six months equals $7,200).

Building and Maintaining a Solid Credit History

Establishing a solid credit history takes time and persistence, but the effort pays off in many ways. The stronger your credit report and the higher your credit score, the less you have to pay when you borrow money. Your credit history also impacts the cost of your auto and homeowner's insurance, and possibly your ability to obtain employment or advance in your current career.

The key factors in building and maintaining a solid credit history include the following:

- **Establish credit in your own name.**
  - Secured credit cards are a great way to establish credit if you cannot obtain credit through traditional methods such as an auto loan or a Visa or MasterCard account.
  - Avoid borrowing from finance companies and signing up for credit cards issued by retail stores.
- **Pay your bills on time.**
- **Limit your outstanding balances to 30 percent or less of your total credit line.**
- **Avoid opening new accounts.**
- **Don't delete old, good credit history off of your credit reports, even if those accounts are no longer being used.**
- **Obtain copies of your credit report from all three credit bureaus at least every 12 months** from `http://www.annualcreditreport.com` and verify that all of the information on the report is accurate.
- **File a dispute with the credit bureaus if you find any inaccuracies.**

For more information about building and maintaining good credit check out *Understanding Credit For Dummies* (Wiley).

Obtaining Appropriate Insurance Coverage

Military families just cannot afford to be without certain types of insurance. Fortunately, your health insurance is provided through TRICARE. In the following section we hit on the other major areas that a military family needs to consider to make certain that they're fully and appropriately insured.

Servicemember's life insurance

All active-duty servicemembers and activated Guard and Reserve are eligible for up to $400,000 of Servicemembers Group Life Insurance (SGLI; see Chapter 7 for more details). For nearly every military family, the maximum amount of insurance through SGLI is warranted, appropriate, and very cost effective. However, there are instances when your family needs more coverage on your servicemember than what is available through SGLI. So you have to check out commercial life insurance companies and shop their policies.

Most commercial life insurance companies are not necessarily "military friendly." Those insurance companies who aren't military friendly include clauses in their life insurance policies that state they will not pay claims if death occurs during the act of war.

The following is a list of Web sites that provide additional coverage for your servicemember above and beyond what is provided through SGLI:

- ✔ http://www.afba.com
- ✔ http://www.aafmaa.com (for Army and Air Force)
- ✔ http://www.navynutual.org (for Navy and Marines)
- ✔ http://www.moaa.org (member officers only)
- ✔ http://www.usaa.com
- ✔ http://www.usba.com

We suggest that, at a minimum, servicemembers should have at *least* 10 times their annual income (basic pay, allowances, and incentives) in life insurance coverage. And most likely you'll be best served buying a term life insurance policy, which has a level premium equal to or greater than the number of years until your youngest child graduates from college. A 15- or 20-year level term policy might be in order.

Refer to *Personal Finance Workbook For Dummies* (Wiley) for specific instructions on the type of life insurance policy that works for you and how to calculate more precisely how much insurance you may need.

Family member's life insurance

If you work outside the home, and your family is dependent on the income that you generate, you should also have life insurance.

You can purchase up to $100,000 of coverage for yourself and up to $10,000 for each of your dependent children through the Family Servicemembers Group Life Insurance (FSGLI) program (see Chapter 7 for more info). The cost of your coverage if you're under age 35 is only $5.50 a month. The premium increases every five years, however the cost is still very competitive through at least age 50. There is no cost for coverage for eligible dependent children.

For more information on Family Servicemembers Group Life Insurance visit www.insurance.va.gov/sgliSite/fsgli/sglifam.htm.

The $10,000 per child coverage (which is free with the purchase of spousal coverage) provided by FSGLI life insurance should be sufficient.

Spousal disability insurance

Did you know that there's actually a much greater chance that you will become disabled for more than 90 days, than it is that you will die before age 65? And, if your family is dependent upon your income, you really should have disability insurance to provide income replacement in the event you're unable to work for an extended period of time due to injury or illness.

Many employers provide 60 to 70 percent of your salary as a long-term disability insurance benefit. This benefit will be taxed to you just like earned income. So, if you need 100 percent of your income to maintain your family's lifestyle, in the event of your disability your family will have some painful financial adjustments to make. So even if your employer provides 60 or 70 percent of your salary as a long-term disability benefit, you should investigate purchasing as much additional disability insurance protection as you are able to buy.

You may not have any long-term disability insurance provided by your employer. In this case, you should purchase an individual, commercial long-term disability insurance policy. This type of insurance generally kicks in after you've just been disabled for six months and the benefits continue until age 65.

Don't worry about the insurance company trying to sell you more disability insurance than you may need. If your family is dependent on your income, you need all the disability insurance protection the insurance company can sell you.

Obtaining an individual, commercial long-term disability insurance policy is very appropriate for a military spouse who works outside of the home. The benefit of obtaining your own individual policy is that it is portable and you can take it with you to the next duty station. If you rely on employer-provided long-term disability insurance alone, when you leave that employer, you lose your long-term disability insurance coverage.

It costs more to have your own individual policy; however, this assures that you will always have coverage should you need it. If your family needs your income — you need disability insurance!

Homeowner's or renter's insurance

You buy insurance to protect you from the risks that you can't afford to bear. Losing your home in a fire or flood, or sustaining significant damage due to hail or windstorms, can undermine even the best laid financial plans. The sections that follow describe both homeowner's and renter's insurance as well as how to estimate the value of your belongings.

For more information refer to *Personal Finance Workbook For Dummies* (Wiley).

Homeowner's insurance

If you own a home and you have a mortgage, you're required to have adequate homeowner's insurance protection. In the unlikely event that you own a home outright (your mortgage is paid off), you still need homeowner's insurance to protect from catastrophic losses.

Not only do you need to take inventory of the contents within your home, but you also need to provide documentation of the physical structure itself.

Contact your homeowner's insurance agent to have them review the adequacy of your homeowner's insurance protection periodically.

Renter's insurance

If you rent your home you should obtain a renter's insurance policy to protect your family from the financial hardship of losing your home and its contents.

Many renters do not carry renter's insurance. If you are one of these people, please recognize that this is a severe shortcoming in your financial foundation. The contents of your home can very easily be damaged or destroyed by a flood, fire, theft, or many other forms of destruction. People who rent homes are at no less risk than people who own the physical structure in which they reside. All families should have insurance to protect the contents of their home and homeowners should also have coverage on the structure itself.

Renter's insurance is very reasonably priced depending on what part of the country you live and how much your property is worth. For many renters their insurance policy costs $200-$300 per year. Yes, that's a lot of money. However, think about what you're buying for that cost. You are purchasing insurance that will provide you a place to stay and the money to replace all of the items and property that is damaged or destroyed. This could easily total tens of thousands of dollars.

If your family rents your residence, you should obtain sufficient coverage to replace all of the property in your homes. Look for a policy that provides full replacement value coverage.

Estimating the value of your belongings

It's challenging to estimate the value of your belongings. Take one drawer or closet for example. Go through that drawer or closet and estimate how much it would cost to repurchase all of the items that you see. Now carry on with that exercise throughout your entire home. Add up the value of all of the items in your kitchen, your families' clothing, the kids' toys, books, electronics, and collections and so on.

Videotape the contents of your home in intricate detail. Record the serial number, make, and model of all items where this is possible. Walk through each room of your home and videotape every item, including the contents of drawers and closets. While videotaping describe to the viewer what you are showing them. Store a copy of this videotape in a very safe place, such as your safety deposit box. This videotape may be the best evidence of the value of your property, if you ever have to make an insurance claim.

If you're fortunate enough never to have to make an insurance claim, you can have a lot of fun with this video years from now, looking back at your old stuff, your digs, and what you used to think was attractive.

Automobile insurance

If you own a vehicle and you or anyone else ever drives it, or you have a loan on it, you need automobile insurance. Depending on the value of your vehicle and your state's requirements, the type of automobile insurance you must have will vary.

For state-by-state regulations on required automobile coverage visit `http://info.insure.com/auto/minimum.html`.

The following are the key types of coverage:

- **Collision:** If you're in an accident, collision insurance provides coverage to replace or repair your vehicle — regardless of who is at fault.

- **Comprehensive:** In the event of hail damage or a tree smashing your car (risks not included in automobile collision coverage), you are covered under this type of insurance.

- **Personal injury protection:** This coverage provides for medical and other expenses resulting from an accident for the people specified in the policy.

- **Medical payments:** This feature provides a limited amount of insurance to help cover medical expenses for you and your passengers resulting from an accident.

- **Bodily injury and property damage liability coverage:** Your insurance company pays damages if you injure someone or their property in an auto accident.

- **Uninsured and underinsured motorists liability coverage:** If you're in an accident with another driver who doesn't have enough, or any, liability coverage this protection allows you to collect for damages that you personally experience from the accident.

There are some key mistakes people make when buying automobile insurance. They often pay too much for their insurance because their deductibles are too low. At the same time, they are inadequately covered for liability exposure. So choose a deductible (your portion of the damages) for both collision and comprehensive coverage that is at least $500 to $1,000 each (the higher the risk you bear, the lower your insurance cost). Make sure that your liability coverage for bodily injury, property damage, uninsured motorist, and under insured motorists is at least $100,000 per person and $300,000 per accident.

You should only buy insurance to protect you from losses that you cannot afford to bear on your own. A little scratch or a minor dent in your fender are not the type of catastrophes for which you should be filing an insurance claim.

Beginning Investing

Everyone has to start some time, and the sooner the better. Make the commitment to get started investing. For the balance of this chapter we give you the guidance to confidently begin investing for your most cherished life goals.

Investing according to your purpose

Before you make your first or next investment give some thought as to the reason you're accumulating money:

- ✔ Are you building up cash reserves that need to be available at a moment's notice in the event of an emergency?
- ✔ Are you accumulating funds to be available for the down payment of a home or another short-term need or objective?
- ✔ Or are you saving money to help pay for a child's college education or for your own retirement?

The purpose of your savings and investments dictates what type of accounts and options are appropriate for each objective. Consider these examples and see where you fit in:

- ✔ **Need money in one to five years:** Savings accounts, money market accounts, and money market mutual funds are savings vehicles that work when you're accumulating funds that you need to tap into in the short term.

✔ **Need money in more than five years:** If your time horizon is longer than five years and you're somewhat flexible about what time period you need to pull your money out, you can consider many more investment options. Growth mutual funds, individual stocks, and real estate may all have a place in your long-term investment portfolio.

The longer you can commit to an investment (that is, the longer your time horizon) the more opportunity you have for long-term growth.

✔ **Need money for retirement:** You can take advantage of some wonderful retirement planning vehicles that enable you to take advantage of long-term growth opportunities while deferring taxation on your investment gains in these accounts until retirement or possibly avoid taxation altogether.

Your servicemember's Thrift Savings Plan (TSP) and traditional IRAs are examples of retirement vehicles that enable you to defer taxation on the gains within your retirement accounts until you begin withdrawing funds in retirement.

Any earnings that you have in Roth IRAs accumulate tax-deferred until retirement and then you can pull out distributions tax-free. You never have to pay taxes on the earnings within your Roth IRA account!

Leveraging time

When asked what he considered to be the most powerful force in the universe, Albert Einstein responded — compound interest! And the true magic of compound interest occurs over time.

The power of compound interest through time is illustrated in Table 8-1. Presuming you haven't begun to save for your retirement in any meaningful way and you plan ultimately to retire at age 65, Table 8-1 reflects what percentage of your total income that you should be saving.

Table 8-1	Checking out the Power of Compound Interest
Current Age	*Savings Required to Replace Current Income*
18	5%
25	9%
30	13%
35	20%
40	32%
45	51%
50	87%
55	can't compute!!!

Notice how significantly the savings requirement escalates as your time horizon shrinks. If you start saving for retirement when your servicemember joins the armed forces and if you save just 5 to 10 percent of your gross income, by the time you are age 65, you'll have enough money to support your standard of living, no matter how long you might live. Unfortunately, if you're 35 years old you have to save at least twice that much just to end up at the same place. And, if you're 45 years old, I sure hope you'll have a military retirement benefit, because if you haven't started saving for retirement by now, being able to retire at 65 and maintain your standard of living is nearly impossible.

Compound interest needs *time* to do its magic!

Getting started

Of course, you need to get started on your investing right away, and nothing reflects better how early investing can be a huge benefit to you than Rob and Bob in Figure 8-1.

Check out the following great places to start, depending on your goals:

- ✔ **For your short-term and intermediate-term goals,** such as cash reserves or accumulating funds for the down payment on a home, consider using the ING Orange Savings Account available through http://www. INGdirect.com. There is no minimum account balance to get started, the savings account pays a very competitive interest rate, its completely liquid, and its FDIC insured. You should have money directed as a discretionary allotment from your servicemember's paycheck directly to this type of account each month.

- ✔ **For your retirement goals,** you should utilize your servicemember's Thrift Savings Plan (TSP) and Roth IRAs. Once again, these contributions can be set up as discretionary allotments directly from your servicemember's paycheck.

   To enroll in the Thrift Savings Plan servicemembers need only complete the TSP enrollment form available on the Web at http://www.tsp. gov, or they can obtain an enrollment form and additional TSP materials at your local Family Support Center. Servicemembers may contribute as little as 1 percent to a maximum of $15,500 in 2008 or $20,500 if age 50 or older.

Age	Bob Contribution	Ending Value	Contribution	Bob Ending Value
19	1,200	1,296	0	
20	1,200	2,696	0	
21	1,200	4,207	0	
22	1,200	5,840	0	
23	1,200	7,603	0	
24	1,200	9,507	0	
25	1,200	11,564	0	
26	1,200	13,785	0	
27	1,200	16,184	0	
28	1,200	18,775	0	
29		20,277	1,200	1,296
30		21,899	1,200	2,696
31		23,651	1,200	4,207
32		25,543	1,200	5,840
33		27,586	1,200	7,603
34		29,793	1,200	9,507
35		32,176	1,200	11,564
36		34,750	1,200	13,785
37		37,530	1,200	16,184
38		40,533	1,200	18,775
39		43,776	1,200	21,573
40		47,278	1,200	24,594
41		51,060	1,200	27,858
42		55,145	1,200	31,383
43		59,556	1,200	35,189
44		64,321	1,200	39,300
45		69,466	1,200	43,740
46		75,024	1,200	48,536
47		81,025	1,200	53,714
48		87,508	1,200	59,308
49		94,508	1,200	65,348
50		102,069	1,200	71,872
51		110,234	1,200	78,918
52		119,053	1,200	86,527
53		128,577	1,200	94,745
54		138,863	1,200	103,621
55		149,973	1,200	113,207
56		161,970	1,200	123,559
57		174,928	1,200	134,740
58		188,922	1,200	146,815
59		204,036	1,200	159,856
60		220,359	1,200	173,941
61		237,988	1,200	189,152
62		257,027	1,200	205,580
63		277,589	1,200	223,323
64		299,796	1,200	242,484
65		**$323,779**	1,200	**$263,179**
Total Invested	**$12,000**		**$44,400**	

Figure 8-1: Rob and Bob's return on investment

Moral of the story . . . Bob invested $100 per month for the first ten years in the service. Rob waited to begin investing until he was 29 years old. Rob had to invest almost four times as much money, but never caught up with Bob . . . because Bob started saving earlier.

Assumption: 8% annual return

Thrift savings plan contributions can be invested in the following accounts:

- Government Securities — G Fund

- Fixed Income Index — F Fund

- Common Stock Index — C fund

- Small Cap Stock Index — S Fund

- International Stock Index — I Fund

- Lifecycle Funds — L Fund (target date maturity funds)

Roth IRAs can be purchased from banks, stockbrokers, financial advisors, or directly with mutual fund companies. The least expensive way to invest in a Roth IRA account is by doing a little research on your own and investing your Roth IRA into a no-load, low-cost mutual fund. For more information on mutual fund investing, check out *Mutual Funds For Dummies* (Wiley).

A great company to consider is T. Rowe Price. You might want to take advantage of one of their target retirement portfolios `http://ira.troweprice.com/retirement_funds/?phone=6066`. You simply select the year of your ultimate retirement and a target date portfolio will be selected for you. Each portfolio has a variety of stocks and bonds. The younger you are the more exposure you have to stocks and the more opportunity you have for growth. As you age the portfolio automatically begins to shift toward a more conservative allocation. Each portfolio is designed to give you a broad range of large-cap, small-cap, and international stock exposure as well as some bond exposure.

You can begin a Roth IRA with T. Rowe Price with as little as $50 per month, as long as you continue to add at least $50 per month to the account. Of course we're recommending that you make these contributions automatically, preferably as one of your discretionary allotments.

For the calendar year 2008 you can contribute $5,000 dollars per person if you're under age 50 and $6,000 per person if you're 50 or older.

Chapter 9

Building onto Your Financial Foundation

In This Chapter

▶ Planning for big-ticket purchases

▶ Calculating how much you'll need to fund specific goals

▶ Organizing your financial affairs

After you have a solid financial foundation built on strength and discipline — adequate cash reserves and insurance and disciplined savings and spending — you're ready to add to that financial foundation. (If you have a shaky financial foundation, check out Chapters 7 and 8.) In this chapter we get into the financial planning aspects for specific goals in your life, such as funding a kid's college, buying a house, or preparing for your ultimate retirement. We also cover how to address subjects that everyone faces, but no one wants to think about: end-of-life issues.

Accumulating What You'll Need for Specific Goals

To get the money you'll need to pay for a big expense, such as a college education, a house, starting your own business, or eventually retiring, requires

✔ Thoughtful planning

✔ Time

✔ Discipline

✔ A lot of compromise (generally)

You'll always find competing objectives for your resources — whether those resources are time, energy, or money. So when it comes to major financial objectives, you'll frequently have to make tough decisions about what matters most to you and your family. To gain confidence in making those difficult choices, consider the following tips:

- ✔ **Write down your financial objectives.** We're sure that your objectives have been so solidified in your mind that you won't forget them. But writing out your financial objectives enables you to best compare all of your options.

- ✔ **Consider your priorities.** Especially if you have objectives competing for your money, weighing your priorities can provide you with a clearer decision.

- ✔ **Be flexible and creative.** Flexibility and creative thinking go a long way in helping you achieve your most cherished life goals. For instance, if you can't go to a traditional college because you never know how long you'll be in that location, try some online college courses or programs (see Chapter 11 for more info).

- ✔ **Make a compromise.** Reach some compromises between competing objectives. For instance, if objectives — such as, paying for your children's college education, having a vacation home, and taking early retirement — compete with each other, consider compromising as an option. You could limit your children's college options to those only in-state so that you're paying resident tuition, find a less expensive vacation home, or consider working a few more years before retiring.

- ✔ **Discuss objectives with your spouse.** Your spouse may have different objectives altogether, and even if they are the same objectives as yours, your spouse may have different priorities. Get on the same page as your spouse with regard to the goals most important in your financial lives and direct your resources accordingly.

Refer to *Personal Finance Workbook For Dummies* for some great goal-setting and communication exercises to help you and your spouse articulate your goals and establish priorities.

After you've determined the financial goals you'd like to work toward, search for that goal in this chapter to discover how to figure out how much money you'll need, how much you'll need to save, and how best to save this money.

Purchasing a Home

In Chapter 10, we explore all of your housing options and considerations as a military family. The process requires just a few steps: First, figure out how much house you can afford, then what type of mortgage is most appropriate for you, and then you can determine how much down payment you need. But those are big steps to take, ones that must be taken carefully. So, in the sections that follow, we cover how much home you can afford (presuming you want to buy one), while still having a life. We also discuss accumulating money for a down payment and the investment vehicles appropriate for this objective.

Determining how much you can spend on a house

Two important principles have to guide you through this important first step of the process of buying a home. When figuring out how much you can spend on a house never deviate from the following:

- **Total mortgage payment vs. gross income:** Your total mortgage payment (*including* taxes and insurance should *not* exceed 28 percent of your gross monthly income. So, add up all of your total compensation (before tax), multiply that dollar amount times 0.28 to arrive at the maximum amount of money you should spend on your home mortgage, real estate taxes, and homeowners insurance.

- **Debt vs. gross income:** The total monthly amount of all of your other debt payments — car loans, student loans, credit cards, and so on — *plus your housing expenses* should not exceed 36 percent of your total gross monthly income. So, add all of your monthly debt to your proposed total mortgage payment (including taxes and insurance) and divide that total by your total gross income. If the result is more than 36 percent, you should reduce debt aggressively prior to purchasing a home, or reduce the size of your target mortgage balance.

Knowing these two facts, you can work the process backwards to figure out how much you can spend on a house. So, we take you through the steps of the following example to show you just how to figure out how much your monthly payment should be, but also how to use that amount to figure out how much you can spend on a house:

1. **Figure out a total monthly mortgage payment based on your total gross compensation.** If your family's total gross monthly compensation (before tax) is $3,500, multiplying that amount times 0.28 results in $980. This is the maximum amount you should spend on your mortgage payment, real estate taxes, and homeowner's insurance per month.

2. **Check your total monthly debt — including your total monthly mortgage payment (including taxes and interest) against your total monthly income.** If your total monthly debt is $135, add to it $980 to include your total mortgage payment. Then divide that total ($1,115) by your total monthly income ($3,500). In this case, the percentage is 32 percent, and because the percentage doesn't exceed 36 percent, then you can definitely afford a total monthly mortgage payment of $980.

3. **Subtract insurance and taxes from the proposed total monthly mortgage payment.** Homeowner's insurance premiums vary greatly depending on what part of the country you live. Homeowner's insurance commonly costs between $50 and $100 per month. Real estate taxes also vary greatly. Real estate taxes frequently run about 1 percent of the home value each year. For our example, assume $100 each month is going toward real estate taxes and insurance. If you subtract $100 per month for real estate taxes and another $100 per month for insurance, the resulting balance of $780 is available to pay the principal and interest on the mortgage.

4. **Discover the maximum mortgage amount of a house you can afford, using the monthly principal and interest payment (result of step 3).** To determine how much mortgage you can afford with a payment of $780 per month, you can use an online calculator, such as the mortgage calculator at BankRate.com (`http://www.bankrate.com/brm/mortgage-calculator.asp`). With this calculator and your target monthly maximum payment in mind, just adjust the mortgage amount until you arrive at your monthly mortgage payment target. With a monthly mortgage payment (principal and interest only) of $780, and an interest rate of 7 percent, the approximate total mortgage amount on a 30-year fixed rate mortgage is $117,000.

5. **Add the down payment to determine how much home you should be able to afford.** If you had $8,000 to apply toward the down payment on a home with a total mortgage of $117,000, the purchase price of your new home could be $125,000. If you want to buy a more expensive home, you would need to come up with a larger down payment.

Of course, the Internet has a ton of great tools for home buying, but two you may consider checking out are

✔ `http://www.bankrate.com/brm/calculators/mortgages/maximum_mortgage.asp`: Use this great calculator for determining your total mortgage affordable based on your income and your other debts.

✔ `http://www.hud.gov/offices/hsg/sfh/hcc/hcs.cfm`: HUD provides a list of approved housing counseling agencies. These agents can assist you in determining your best course of action if you have too much debt.

Reviewing mortgages

There are many mortgage options available in the marketplace. The key factors in selecting a mortgage that is right for your family are:

✔ **How long do you plan to live in the home?**

How long you plan to live in the house is one of the most essential questions to consider when determining what type of mortgage may be appropriate for you. If you plan to stay in the home for more than five years, you're likely much better off to lock in a fixed rate mortgage.

If you know with great certainty that you will not own the home for more than five years, I encourage you to evaluate whether an adjustable rate mortgage may actually be more cost-effective for you. Bankrate.com has a great calculator that will enable you to calculate whether you're better off with a fixed-rate mortgage or an adjustable rate mortgage. Visit http://www.bankrate.com/brm/calsystem2/calculators/fixedvsarm/default.aspx.

✔ **Would you prefer a stable monthly payment, or can you handle the uncertainty of an adjustable mortgage?**

Depending on current interest rates, you may discover that the difference between an adjustable rate mortgage and fixed rate mortgages do not provide enough incentive for you to accept the uncertainty of an adjustable rate mortgage, just in case you end up owning that home longer than you had planned. Refer to Chapter 10 for more information about these dangers.

✔ **How much money do you have for the down payment?**

The amount of your down payment will influence the number and types of loans available to you. If you have 20 percent to put down on the purchase of your new home a conventional mortgage will likely be the most attractive option for your family. You'll receive a lower interest rate by going with a conventional mortgage. A conventional loan may also be available if you take out a first mortgage for 80 percent of the value of the home, and then a home-equity line of credit for another 10 percent. This would leave you a down payment as low as 10 percent. And, you would still qualify for a conventional mortgage, avoid PMI and get the most competitive interest rates available.

However, most young couples and families don't have the money available to put down 20 percent on a home purchase. You can check out first-time home buyer programs, which may be available in your area. Consult with a local mortgage lender about these types of programs or visit http://www.hud.gov/buying/localbuying.cfm for more information.

An FHA loan will likely be one of your most competitive options. They typically require a 3 percent down payment, maybe less. Closing costs are also minimized.

Possibly your best option, if you have little or no down payment, is a VA loan. If your servicemember has served on active duty for at least six months, or six years if your servicemember is in the Selected Reserves or National Guard, your family is eligible for a VA loan. You can purchase a home with no down payment, the interest rates are competitive, and you should incur lower costs at closing. You also avoid Private Mortgage Insurance (PMI) that is required on most every mortgage, unless you are able to make a 20 percent down payment. These premiums can add $50 to $100 or more per month to your mortgage payment for the first several years that you own your home.

✔ **Are you eligible for VA benefits?**

✔ **What are the current fixed interest rates?**

- Conventional

- FHA

- VA

  The VA actually doesn't issue the loans, they insure them. You would obtain a VA loan through a traditional mortgage lender such as a bank, savings and loan, or mortgage company.

✔ **What are the current adjustable rates?**

- 3-year fixed, then annually adjustable (3/1 ARM)

- 5-year fixed, then annually adjustable (5/1 ARM)

Coming up with your down payment

Saving for the down-payment on a home, just like any financial objective, involves determining:

✔ How much money will you need?

✔ What resources are available?

✔ How should this money be invested?

✔ When will you need it?

Assume for the sake of illustration that you would like to purchase a home for $150,000 in two years. And you want to make a down payment of 5%; so you'll need $7,500 in two years. Your servicemember is currently the only wage earner in the family. If you simply divide $7,500 by the number of pay periods that your servicemember will have over the next two years you will arrive at a specific dollar amount that should be saved per month. Using this simple formula will actually result in accumulating a bit more than the required $7,500, because you haven't taken into account the interest that will be earned on each deposit.

Given that two years is a very short time horizon, the most appropriate investment vehicle for this type of savings is a bank money market account or money market mutual fund account. Currently these types of accounts are yielding about 3 percent per year. So your excess savings only totals about $220 dollars. That's nothing to sneeze at. In fact, you'll likely find a great use for this extra money in your new home.

However, if your objective was to accumulate exactly $7,500 by the end of two years, you have two reasonable options to calculate the precise savings requirement. The first is to use a financial calculator. Another option is to use one of the many online financial calculators. One of the best is at `http://www.bankrate.com/gookeyword/news/sav/2006savmg/calc/savegoal.asp?caret=25.`

Using a financial calculator, either a handheld or an online calculator, the required savings to come up with $7,500 by the end of two years is $303.61 a month, presuming a 3 percent return is earned on your money market mutual fund account.

Set up an automatic deduction from your servicemember's discretionary allotment and have the targeted savings amount automatically deducted and forwarded to your money market account.

A great account to consider for this type of savings is available from `http://www.INGdirect.com`. You can open an Orange Savings account with as little as one dollar and add to that account as frequently as you would like. The Orange Savings account pays a very competitive interest rate, it's completely liquid, and its FDIC insured. Shortly before you need the down-payment on your new home, simply go online to INGdirect.com and authorize a direct transfer to your checking account for the amount of your down payment.

Planning for Children's College Costs

Most American families want to own their own home, have enough money to retire in comfort, and they would like to see their children obtain a college education. Sometimes saving money for all three of these objectives can really put a damper on your lifestyle. However, if you do have the desire to pay for, or help pay for, your children's college education, the sooner you get started the better.

Trying to figure out how much you need to save is all based on how much you plan to provide for your child(ren) and how much the school they attend will cost. To solve the first half of this dilemma, let's just assume that you and your spouse want to have the money available to pay for 100 percent of the cost for your child(ren) to attend college. It's much safer to save more than you'll actually need or want to spend on their college, so we'll default to saving 100 percent.

Now comes the more challenging part. Which college, or type of college, are you or your young scholar considering? The cost of a community college or junior college runs about $2,200 a year, in today's dollars. Tuition and books at a public state university could cost you about $6,000 a year. And a private college or university could easily cost you over $20,000 a year just for tuition and books.

For most young families with competing objectives; buying a home, raising children, saving money for their college and your retirement, and taking care of everyday living expenses, just getting started saving something for college is a great beginning.

However, if you feel strongly about your children attending a specific university such as — your alma mater — check out `http://www.CollegeBoard.com`. On this Web site you can find out the actual current expenses for tuition, books, and room and board at thousands of colleges and universities across the country.

You may be aware that college costs have far exceeded the rate of inflation over the last 30 years. This is another good reason for starting your savings early. Beginning an education fund for a newborn or toddler is definitely not too early! The sooner you start saving the lower your monthly savings contribution requirement.

If the after-tax rate of return you receive on your investments for your children's college education keep pace with the escalating cost of college, you should be alright saving as illustrated in Table 9-1.

Table 9-1	Saving for Different Colleges		
Age of Child	*Junior College (2 years; $4,400)*	*State University (4 years; $24,000)*	*Private College (4 years; $80,000)*
Newborn	$20/month	$111/month	$370/month
5 years	$28/month	$154/month	$513/month
10 years	$46/month	$250/month	$833/month

These savings amounts are for each child!

It's never too early to start planning for college. This includes setting the proper expectations of just how much you and your servicemember plan or are prepared to pay for your child's college education.

Securing Your Retirement

Your child can find many ways to obtain a college education. However, when it comes to retirement, there is no financial aid!

Do not forsake your own retirement to provide a college education for your child(ren), unless your children are your retirement plan. In this section we go into saving for retirement. Just because the section is positioned after college planning doesn't mean that it should ever take a back seat.

There are only four variables when it comes to retirement planning:

- ✔ You can spend less and save more now.
- ✔ You can get better returns on your investments.
- ✔ You can work longer.
- ✔ You could die earlier.

The last option really isn't a recommended planning strategy. Working longer may also not be the first thing that comes to mind. Getting better returns on your investments may have very little to do with influencing how much money you'll have at retirement — if you don't have any retirement savings yet. So, for this section let's focus on what you do have significant influence over — regardless of whether you choose to exercise that influence — saving for retirement.

The earlier you begin to save for retirement the less you have to save. Let the power of positive compound interest work for you.

Table 9-2 illustrates the percentage of your income that you need to save each and every month until retirement to ensure that you'll never run out of money no matter how long you live. This savings requirement assumes that you have little or no retirement savings now.

Table 9-2	Saving for Retirement
Your Current Age	*Savings as Percentage of Income*
18	5%
25	9%
30	13%
35	20%
40	32%
45	51%
50	87%

You could use one of many sophisticated Web-based retirement calculators or financial planning software programs to compute how much you need to save to maintain your lifestyle in retirement. However, it need not be that complicated. If you have not yet begun to save for retirement, or you have just barely begun, Table 9-2 is all you need to focus on.

If you have accumulated some savings for retirement, your actual required savings may be a percent or two less than the percentage illustrated on the table above.

For most young people, and if you're under 30, knowing how much you're going to need to live on in retirement is just a shot in the dark. So many things are going to change throughout your lifetime. Making a projection about retirement occurring decades from now, with dozens of variables, comes out with a goofy conclusion. One thing you can be certain of, your projection is guaranteed to be wrong. So, keep it simple. Focus on the following keys to financial independence and don't complicate your financial lives any more than necessary:

✔ **Focus on what you can control!** Concentrate your energies on what you have the most influence and control over — your ability to make money. You and your spouse's potential to make money is your single biggest asset. Don't let your penchant for spending it all be your biggest liability.

✔ **Live beneath your means!** Living within your means is a good start. But all that says is you're making it from paycheck to paycheck. That's not getting ahead. Living beneath your means, means that you are saving a bit of every dollar you earn.

✔ **Start now!** Don't stop until you retire — you, too, can achieve financial independence! Refer back to Table 9-2 to determine your required savings percentage.

✔ **Make it automatic!** Fund your retirement savings contributions in the following order.

- Have money withdrawn directly from your servicemember's paycheck as a discretionary allotment directly into Roth IRA accounts (presuming you don't make too much money).

- Next, if you have access to an employer provided retirement plan that has a matching contribution, such as a 401(k) plan, contribute up to the maximum amount of the matching or the amount to fully fund your retirement savings requirement, whichever comes first.

- If you don't have a retirement plan with a matching contribution, then add your additional target savings percentage to your servicemember's Thrift Savings Plan account.

Making your retirement funding automatic means that you're essentially paying yourself first using automatic deductions from your servicemember's paycheck to fund your retirement savings requirement.

The most important thing is to get started, be consistent, and save on a regular, automatic basis. Don't worry about what's going on with the economy or the stock market — just keep accumulating — when retirement comes you'll be glad you did!

Preparing for the Inevitable

You know the old phrase — nothing in life is certain except death and taxes? Well, we know when our tax return is due, but most of us never know when we're going to die. The question is not "if," but rather "when"? Given that certainty, it is only appropriate that you think about what would be best for the survivor(s) in the event of your or your servicemember's death. We call this estate planning. It sounds pretty hoity-toity doesn't it? Well, estate planning is nothing more than documenting what you want to happen to you, your dependents, and your stuff when you're gone. It also covers what happens if you're alive, but can't make decisions for yourself.

We're not estate planning attorneys. The information and suggestions provided here are for your education and empowerment. You should work with qualified legal counsel to make certain that your wishes will be carried out in the manner that would be most efficient and effective.

Fortunately, you may be eligible for free legal services through Armed Forces Legal Assistance. Refer to Chapter 7 for additional information about military legal benefits.

In this section, we show you why estate planning is so important and outline strategies you can implement to make sure that your desires are carried out if you are not around, or if you're unable to communicate your wishes.

Answering key questions to get started

As you get started, you need to answer the following key questions:

- ✔ Financial
  - What do you own?
  - What do you owe?
  - How much life insurance do you have?
- ✔ Family
  - Are you legally married?
  - Are you both U.S. citizens?
  - Do you have minor children or other dependents?
  - If you have minor children or dependents, who would you like to care for your dependent family members if you are unable?
  - If you have minor children or dependents, who would be the best custodians of the assets left to your dependent family members?
- ✔ What legacy do you want to leave for your surviving family?
  - Are there any people or causes to which you would like to leave money?
  - If you are unable to make healthcare decisions for yourself, who should make those decisions on your behalf? What if that person is not available?
  - Under what circumstances, if any, would you like your life prolonged by artificial means?
  - If you are unable to manage your financial affairs for yourself, who should manage your affairs on your behalf? What if that person is unavailable?

Communicating your wishes through legal documents

Thinking through how you'd like your family to be cared for, and where you would like your "stuff" to go, is a critical first step. However, without getting your wishes down in writing, all the thinking in the world won't make a bit of difference.

How you own property, and the beneficiaries you have designated for your life insurance and retirement plan assets, are also very critical to implementing an effective estate plan. We discuss forms of ownership and beneficiary designations in the next section. In this section, we walk you through the types of legal documents, which may be most appropriate for your family, and what you'd like to accomplish.

You very likely can receive assistance in creating these estate planning documents, at no charge, through military legal assistance! Take full advantage of your military benefits!

Wills

The most well-known estate planning document is the *will*. A will is a legal document that allows you to dictate in writing what you want to happen to your assets and appoint guardians to care for your dependents upon your death. One of the most important reasons, if not *the* most important reason to have a will, is to name the guardians for your minor children (presuming you have minor children). A will enables you to name the individual or couple who you would like to be the caretakers of your children in the event that you and your spouse are both deceased. And you shouldn't just name one person or one couple. You'll also want to name a backup or alternate guardian, in case the first individual or couple is not available or able to care for your children.

Your will also enables you to name the custodian you appoint to take care of the money you leave your minor children. Many times the guardian(s) are the most appropriate people to also serve as custodians. But, that is not necessarily always the case.

Sometimes the best caregiver, is definitely not the best money manager, and vice versa. Fortunately, by executing a will you have the opportunity to name the caregivers for your children, as well as, the custodians of their money. Without a will your state law will determine your children's guardian and custodian. Don't leave these critical decisions up to state law!

Living trusts

Another document commonly used in estate planning is a *living trust.* For most young couples and families a living trust is not necessary. However, before you immediately rule out the benefits of a living trust, let's explore a couple of the major reasons people choose trusts.

First of all, trusts avoid the probate court process. In fact, you'll often hear from many estate planning attorneys that probate is this horrible legal process that can take years and cost you a fortune. Generally that statement is grossly exaggerated. Probate does take time and it will cost more to transfer the assets through the probate court process than through title, beneficiary designation, or living trust.

Another very useful reason for having a living trust is in the event that you own a home or other real property outside of your state of residence. This is not an uncommon occurrence with a military family. With a living trust you can avoid probate in your state of residence, as well as, the state in which you own other real property.

There are a few major drawbacks to having a living trust. The first one is cost. Living trusts can cost you and your spouse $2,000 to $3,000 to have drafted by a qualified legal professional. After you get over the price tag of living trusts, the next stage is making certain that all of your property is appropriately and completely retitled into the trust, and that it maintains proper title or beneficiary designation to the trust through time. Failure to do so will make your investment worthless.

Don't misunderstand; living trusts do have a very legitimate role in many people's estate planning. However, they are not the only option, or some sort of silver bullet, that so many estate planning attorneys purport. There are other legal documents and strategies that you can use to make certain that your survivors are cared for and your stuff is transferred as you would like, that cost you substantially less than living trusts. However, if your attorney suggests a living trust, follow your attorney's advice.

Durable power of attorney for healthcare

This is an essential estate planning document! A durable power of attorney for healthcare enables you to name a person or possibly a couple of people to make healthcare decisions for you if you are unable to make them for yourself.

Both you and your servicemember should immediately obtain durable power of attorney forms, if you do not already have them in place. If you do have these documents, review them periodically to make certain they are current.

Visit your military legal assistance services office. They can get you set up with durable power of attorney for healthcare documents.

Living will

A *living will* spells out under what circumstances, if any, you want your life prolonged if you have no reasonable chance for recovery. This is another essential estate planning document that both you and your servicemember should have in place. You can also obtain these documents from your military legal assistance services office.

Financial power of attorney

The financial power of attorney form is another essential legal document required for effective estate planning. This document enables you to appoint someone to make financial decisions and manage your financial affairs in the event that you can't do this for yourself. Most couples appoint each other as their financial power-of-attorney. But, you should also select a successor, so that in the event your spouse is unable or unavailable to perform these services, you've got a backup. Your military legal assistance office can also assist you in obtaining these documents.

Given the nature of your servicemember's employment, and the fact that you may be frequently separated due to their service, obtaining the above-mentioned documents is essential to making certain your wishes will be carried out under all circumstances. Don't leave these issues to chance. Visit your military legal assistance office immediately!

Accounting for ownership and beneficiary designations

All assets that transfer by title or beneficiary designation upon death avoid probate. You can reduce probate expenses and hassles by maximizing your use of appropriate ownership classifications.

Table 9-3 lists the common forms of asset transfer strategies and indicates whether these strategies avoid probate.

Table 9-3	Asset Transfer Strategies
Strategy	*Avoids Probate*
Joint tenancy with right of survivorship	Yes
Tenants in common	No
Individual ownership	No
Beneficiary designations	Yes
Transfer on death designations	Yes
Payable on death designations	Yes
Will	No
Living trust	Yes

Titling assets

Most couples who own a home with their spouse register the house in joint tenancy with the right of survivorship. You may also have bank accounts or investment accounts registered in both of your names, as joint tenants with right of survivorship. In this form of ownership both of you have access to the account or asset and can transact certain business on behalf of the other. In the event of the death of one owner, the survivor inherits the entire asset directly and automatically, without going through the probate court.

Even if you're married your spouse will not automatically inherit your property, or be able to manage your affairs in your absence, without proper ownership and/or legal documents.

Many times individuals enter into marriage after they have already acquired property. It may be appropriate for you to retitle individually held property into joint ownership with your spouse. Contact your military legal assistance office for guidance.

Beneficiary designations

A beneficiary designation is a formal way of declaring who you would like to inherit your property in the event of your death.

Beneficiary designations are available for:

- Life insurance policies
- Retirement accounts
- IRAs
- Bank accounts
- Brokerage accounts

You simply fill out a form provided by the insurance company, bank, or investment company, indicating your primary beneficiary or beneficiaries, as well as, any contingent beneficiary or beneficiaries. You don't have to name one individual to receive the entire balance of a specific account. You can divide an account among numerous people.

For example: You have a life insurance policy and desire to leave the majority of the death benefit to your surviving spouse; however, you would also like to repay a loan you received from your parents. You could indicate on your beneficiary designation that a certain dollar amount of the proceeds are to go to your parents and the balance is to go to your surviving spouse.

When you get that loan paid off with your folks you may want to revisit your beneficiary designation.

In some states you can obtain a transfer on death designation for personal and real property, such as a home or vehicle. However, if you own your home in joint ownership with rights of survivorship, no beneficiary designation is necessary. You may however wish to name a beneficiary on a vehicle or other type of property, such as a motorcycle or boat, if that is available in your state. Check with military legal assistance services or your county's registrar of deeds office for more information.

Keep a copy of all of your account applications as well as your beneficiary designation forms for safekeeping. Review these beneficiary designations periodically and make certain that they remain current with your wishes.

All assets registered in joint tenancy with right of survivorship already have the equivalent of the beneficiary designation. The surviving joint owner will automatically inherit the asset or account upon the death of the first joint owner.

When you're young, healthy, and invincible, it's so easy to postpone thinking about death or incapacity. And if it costs money, that's another good excuse to postpone something that you don't think you'll need for decades. However you've got a family who depends on you.

Get your affairs in order. Utilize the military legal assistance services. Give your family one of the most important gifts you can. After something happens to you is not the time for your spouse or family to deal with figuring out what you would have wanted. Tell them in writing just exactly who is to receive what assets, who you want raising your children, and taking care of their money. Also put in writing who you want making decisions regarding your healthcare or financial affairs, and under what extraordinary circumstances you want your life prolonged, through the use of the estate planning documents listed in this section.

Revisit your estate planning documents and beneficiary designations periodically to make certain that your wishes are documented fully and appropriately.

Chapter 10

Housing Options for the Military Family

*I*t's not uncommon for a military family to move every two to three years. So, figuring out the best housing arrangements for your family is a major consideration. Fortunately, you have many options. Choices are a wonderful thing, if you know how to evaluate the options available to you.

On-base housing might be very appropriate for your family especially during the early years. Living on-base provides you with community, convenient access to all the installation's facilities and programs, and enables you to save money for other things you'd like to accomplish in your lives.

In this chapter, we explore the variety of housing options and benefits available to you and your family, and give you guidance on which options may make the most sense for your family, depending on your specific situation.

Understanding the Basic Allowance for Housing

All servicemembers receive free (or almost free) housing. If your spouse is a servicemember and you live together, regardless of whether you have dependent children living with you, you will either live in on-base housing, or be given a Basic Allowance for Housing (BAH) to live off-base.

Military families receive the housing allowance, even if your servicemember is staying in the barracks (along with single servicemembers) for basic training or technical school. Your family receives this allowance because the military requires servicemembers to provide adequate housing for their dependents. And a spouse is considered a dependent for this determination. Regardless of how dependent you may feel — when it comes to receiving extra compensation — most military spouses have no problem being classified as a "dependent."

Basic allowance for housing — CONUS

Servicemembers and their families who live off-base are provided with a Basic Allowance for Housing (BAH). This extra cash is provided to help offset the additional costs of living off-base. Of course, if you choose to live on-base, the military covers your housing expense. However, at certain duty stations there may not be on-base military housing available, or adequate accommodations for your family's needs, so living off-base is your only option.

The basics of BAH

The actual amount your family is eligible for is based on the local rental housing market and your servicemember's pay grade. Also, your BAH is *not taxable* income. So, to compare apples-to-apples, if your family were to receive $800 per month in tax-free BAH, that may be equivalent to more than $1,000 a month in additional taxable basic pay.

BAH is a set amount per month. Your actual housing expense could be substantially higher. The allowance is determined based on the average costs in the area, and is designed to provide you with *appropriate* housing for your servicemember's rank and family status.

For example, if your spouse is an E-5, your family qualifies for the minimum acceptable housing allowance that should enable you to acquire a two-bedroom townhouse or duplex. If your spouse is an O-5, your family receives a housing allowance that provides for a four bedroom single-family residence. The number of dependents is not taken into consideration in determining the amount of BAH.

Visit `http://www.military.com/benefits/military-pay/basic-allowance-for-housing-rates` for current rates by geography, pay grade, and dependent status.

The housing allowance is paid out automatically when you apply for off-base housing. You may use this money to help cover your housing expenses whether you rent or purchase your home. We discuss the pros and cons of renting versus purchasing later in this chapter.

Military married to military

If you and your spouse are both employed by the military, each of you is entitled to the Basic Allowance for Housing benefit if you live off-base. If you live together, one of you can claim BAH with dependents and the other must register at the single rate.

Your family receives the highest total BAH pay if the servicemember with the highest pay grade claims BAH with dependent(s).

Overseas housing allowance

When you first report to a permanent duty station outside the continental United States (OCONUS), if you are unable to stay in government housing for some reason beyond your control, you may be eligible for up to 60 days of overseas temporary lodging allowance.

If your servicemember is stationed overseas and lives with you off-base, they don't receive BAH. Instead they receive a special Overseas Housing Allowance, or OHA. This allowance is intended to offset the actual cost of rent, utilities, and recurring maintenance expenses. Unlike BAH for your state-side counterparts, OHA is not a set monthly amount. It is recalculated every two weeks to address the potentially volatile housing costs in overseas markets.

However, if your servicemember is assigned overseas, and you elect not to accompany them, they can live in barracks on-base, and still receive BAH to assist you in obtaining adequate housing state-side. It's a servicemember's obligation — enforced and supported by the military — to provide adequate housing for their dependents.

If your family is eligible for Overseas Housing Allowance you also qualify for; a move-in housing allowance to cover the purchase of necessities, onetime fees, such as real estate agent fees or lease taxes, and reimbursements for required security expenses.

If you lease off-base housing while on overseas assignment, be sure that your lease agreement contains a *military clause*. This clause enables you to break your lease in case you are forced to terminate the lease before expiration in order for your servicemember to fulfill their military orders.

Considering On-Base Housing

Most installations have very limited on-base housing for married service-members and there is usually a waiting list. Sometimes the waiting list is as long as 12 months or more. To qualify for on-base family housing you must reside with your servicemember.

Unfortunately, you may not even know if housing is available until you arrive at your new installation. If housing isn't immediately available, the housing office will give you a rough estimate of how long you'll have to wait, which could be months.

Your installation may have contract housing available. Find out about contract housing through the housing manager. A waiting list may be available through your new installation's Web site.

Accommodations vary greatly from installation to installation. Units are typically unfurnished duplexes and sometimes fourplexes. The type of housing your family qualifies for is dependent upon the age of your family members and the rank of your servicemember.

Basic utilities are usually provided at no additional cost for on-base housing. Sorry folks — cable-television and telephone service is not included. Of course you can always subscribe to these additional services but you pay the cost. Kitchen appliances, such as stoves and refrigerators are usually provided and many times built-in dishwashers come with the unit. Clothes washer and dryer hookups are available in most units, and laundry mats are also available near the family housing area. It's very much like renting a home in the civilian world.

If you wish to make any "improvements" to your on-base residence, you usually can obtain permission, but you must agree to return the property to its original condition, if the next person to move in doesn't want to accept your "improvement." So, if you want to paint your daughter's bedroom violet, just keep in mind that in a few months you very likely may be repainting it a nice, bland off-white. You're encouraged to make it your home. But, just as you would with rental property, you need to obtain permission to make any changes or "improvements" to your on-base residence. Keep in mind that your commander may be considerably tougher than any landlord you've experienced in the civilian world.

Unlike military barracks, the inside of occupied on-base military family housing is not inspected, unless the commander receives a problem report. However, the outside of your residence is an entirely different matter. Each branch of the armed forces is pretty strict about the tidiness of the outside of your residence and yard. In fact, military personnel may cruise the family housing area regularly and write tickets to any resident who doesn't maintain the appearance required for the neighborhood. If you receive too many tickets in a short period of time you can be requested to move off-base.

Your on-base housing will definitely be inspected when you get ready to move out. Base housing is expected to be left in immaculate condition. Well, as immaculate as the unit can get. Some accommodations are very out-of-date, but they must be clean when you move out! Some families have gone so far as to hire professional cleaners to assist them. Many bases now have programs where the base itself hires professional cleaners for you.

Exploring Off-Base Housing

As a military family you have virtually unlimited options with regard to off-base housing. Well, the options are unlimited, but your resources and preferences will restrict which of these options make sense for your family.

One of the benefits of on-base housing is that your family can likely get along very comfortably with one vehicle. On-base family housing is close to all of the military community resources, the kid's schools, medical care, shopping, and so on. You can walk or there are shuttles available. However, living off-base may require you to obtain a second vehicle or utilize public transportation — either way it increases your costs.

Regardless of the many conveniences that come with living in family housing on a military installation, there are also many disadvantages. These disadvantages may include your inability to truly separate your servicemember's work from your private life. You may also have a strong desire to personalize your home, and if you plan to stay in an area for a period of time you may desire to purchase your residence. There are many valid reasons for your family to desire to live off-base. And even if you did want to live on-base, military housing may not even be available.

If you live off-base, the military is not providing you with housing; therefore, you receive a tax-free cash benefit to offset your cost to obtain housing elsewhere. You can use this benefit, also known as, Basic Allowance for Housing (BAH) to pay all or a portion of the monthly rental expense on a home, or to pay all or a portion of the monthly mortgage payment if you decide to purchase a home. Refer to the section later in this chapter for more on the rent versus purchase decision.

The amount of your allowance is dependent on the average cost of housing in your local market and your servicemember's pay grade. This tax-free benefit for married servicemembers typically ranges from about $800 a month to over $2,000 a month depending on rank and location. For more information about the Basic Allowance for Housing refer to that section earlier in this chapter.

This housing allowance can be used to rent or purchase any type of residence such as, an apartment, a townhome, a mobile or modular home, a condominium, a duplex, or a single family residence. The key considerations for your family should include:

- ✔ Location — proximity to work, schools, and public transportation, if appropriate
- ✔ Size of living quarters, including numbers of bedrooms and bathrooms
- ✔ Fenced-in yard, garage, basement, storage and so on
- ✔ Total cost

Of course there are many other important details in selecting your home, but these are the key criteria for most families. If you have kids or dogs you might want a good sized fenced in yard. That may not be an allowable or reasonable option, if you were to live on-base. Actually, having pets can limit your options for renting as well.

You may also find that you need more space than what is available with on-base housing. You might desire a private space for a home office, as well as separate bedrooms for your children. It is highly probable that you will need to augment your housing allowance to be able to rent or purchase a home meeting these criteria.

Leasing

Leasing a place usually requires no more than completing a rental application; paying a deposit and the first and last month's rent, getting a background check, and signing a lease.

No worries if you have to break the lease because your servicemember is assigned to a new duty station. See Chapter 7 for more information about your legal benefits and protections.

With leasing you retain the utmost in flexibility. That doesn't mean that things can't go wrong — but it sure limits the number of problems.

Typical problems with leasing include:

- ✔ Your landlord could raise your rent at the end of your lease term — and cause you to either pay up or move.

    However, if rents in your area go up rapidly after signing your lease you are likely going to be stuck with paying market rates when it's time to renew your lease. You can't move and reduce your costs without moving into a lower quality or less desirable location.

✔ The great landlord you signed the lease with could sell the property —
or worse yet — go bankrupt.

If they are responsible for paying your utilities, you could find yourself
without electricity or water and have very little recourse. Fortunately,
most landlords are reasonable business people and these potentialities
are highly unlikely.

Major positive benefits of renting include:

✔ You can obtain housing quickly and you can move out just as quickly —
if you receive orders to report to a new duty station. This flexibility is
very attractive and appropriate for most military families.

✔ Your level of commitment, as far as time to research the perfect location
and the amount of cash you need to secure a new residence, is low relative
to purchasing a home.

Buying

Purchasing your home has its own positives and negatives. You're probably
very familiar with all the positives that homeownership can bring. The pride
of ownership, the ability to play your music just as loud as you want; decorate
any way you desire, all the while hopefully building equity in your home.

But owning a home also means that when a pipe bursts in the wall behind
your upstairs bathroom and wreaks the ceiling below or your new washer
and dryer overloads your circuit breaker, it's your problem. (Actually —
those were one author's problems — just recently!) Ah — the joys of home
ownership! These joys do come with a price.

You also have to deal with the responsibilities of home ownership when your
servicemember is away. Is this something that you are prepared to deal with
alone?

The sections that follow go through some of the beneficial and not-so-
beneficial aspects of buying a home as well as financing and other factors
you should consider before purchasing a home.

Tax benefits

Don't overestimate the tax benefits of homeownership! Prospective homeowners, real estate agents, and mortgage brokers are eager to tout the tax
benefits, but they overestimate the actual tax savings. They don't adjust for
the fact that every taxpayer is entitled to a standard deduction.

The total of your mortgage interest, real estate taxes, and other itemized deductions may run about $13,000 per year. However, if you're married and file a joint tax return, you're automatically entitled to a standard deduction of about $11,000. So, the additional tax deductions you get from owning a home is only about $2,000 not $13,000!

Multiply the $2,000 in additional deductions times your tax rate to determine how much taxes you'll actually save by owning a home. Your tax savings is probably closer to $300 to $500 per year, which is a far cry from the $2,000 or $3,000 you might have been planning on.

Major considerations

Purchasing a home isn't a light decision. You have many things to consider, especially against the option of leasing. Table 10-1 gets you started by checking out some advantages and disadvantages to buying a home.

Table 10-1	Pros and Cons of Buying
Pro	Con
It's yours!	It's yours!
Building equity	Maintenance costs and responsibilities
Flexibility to make it *your* home	Inflexibility — you can't sell it in a hurry
Mortgage interest and real estate taxes are tax-deductible	Maintenance costs could wipe out any tax savings

Factors to consider when thinking about buying a home:

- ✔ How long do you expect to live in the property?
- ✔ If you relocate sooner than expected, would you want to keep the home and rent it out?
  - • If so, what is the rental market like in the area?
  - • What do you think you can get in rental income if you were to rent out the house?
  - • How do you feel about being an absentee landlord? (More on rental property ownership later in this chapter.)
  - • Are there any reputable rental property management companies in the area, and what are their charges?
- ✔ How much cash is needed to get into a house?

- Down payment?
- Closing costs?
- Required repairs?
- Desired repairs and remodeling?
- Utility company deposits?
- Furniture, furnishings, window coverings, light bulbs, and so on?

✔ What is the real estate market like in the area?

- Are there a lot of houses available for sale?
- How does this house "fit" within the neighborhood? Keep in mind that you never want to have the most expensive house on the block.

✔ Are you and your servicemember ready, willing, and able to provide the maintenance necessary to take care of the house, or pay to have people do this for you?

Check out *Home Buying For Dummies* for more information.

Buying versus renting

You have a lot of things to consider when deciding whether you would be better off purchasing or leasing your home. There are advantages and disadvantages to both approaches. A lot of the decision boils down to how long you plan to live in the home and what you anticipate the cost of rent and real estate prices to do during the time you own the property.

You can access a great calculator to help answer the question at `http://www.NYTimes.com/2007/04/10/business/2007_BUYRENT_GRAPHIC.html`.

If you have the option to purchase a home for $150,000 with no down payment, or pay $1,000 a month in rent — based on the assumptions in Figure 10-1 — you can see your breakeven point.

Annual Assumptions		Buying is Better than Renting by End of Year									
Home Price Appreciation	Rental Inflation	1	2	3	4	5	6	7	8	9	10
0%	6%									X	
1%	4%										X
2%	4%								X		
3%	3%							X			
4%	3%						X				
5%	3%					X					
6%	3%			X							

Figure 10-1: Buying versus renting.

Notice that even if rental inflation is quite substantial, if home prices do not appreciate, you're better off renting from a financial standpoint. If home values go down, you may never break-even financially.

Contrary to popular belief of the 1990's and early 2000's, houses don't always appreciate. In certain real estate markets home values got so excessively overpriced that it may take years for home values to stabilize and begin appreciating again. However, given enough time, a home purchased for a fair price does tend to be a good investment.

It doesn't make economic sense to buy a house if you don't expect to keep it longer than three years!

Given that most military families relocate approximately every three years, it may not be advisable for you to consider purchasing your residence. That is, unless you're interested in purchasing real estate to upgrade and resell in a short period of time (see "Rehabbing a property," below), or retain the home as rental property when you move on to your next duty station.

Rehabbing a property

You might be able to find a fixer-upper, remodel it yourself, and sell it for a gain — even if you have only owned the property for a year or two. This strategy is also known as flipping.

Keys to a successful flip include:

- **Buying right.** Find the ugliest house in a good neighborhood that has structural integrity. Some houses just need new owners with a vision, who are willing to invest some cash and a whole lot of elbow grease to bring them up to date. Many buyers don't have the interest or the desire to remodel a house. Due to this fact, homes requiring significant cosmetic work can be found at considerable discounts to competing properties.

- **Living in the property while you're going through the rehab.** This helps minimize your costs; however, you have to deal with the mess of an ongoing construction projects. This can be a deal breaker if you have young children.

- **Having the skills and desire to do a substantial amount of work yourself.**

- **Having the cash flow and/or cash reserves needed to complete the remodeling project.**

- **Having the cash flow and/or cash reserves needed to continue paying the mortgage on the property if you can't sell the house as you might hope.**

- **Planning out a detailed project list, timeline, and budget — and sticking to it.**

This is one strategy that may work if you're interested in putting in some sweat equity in an attempt to profit from a short-term real estate holding period. If you have the know-how, time, energy, and cash, you could turn short-term home ownership into a money-making opportunity.

This strategy can be extremely fulfilling and extremely frustrating. Make sure you do a lot of planning and research before diving into a real estate renovation. For much more information, read *Flipping Houses For Dummies*.

Becoming an absentee landlord

Maybe you've never heard the term absentee landlord. If not, you're not alone. An absentee landlord is a property owner who doesn't live in the same community or area as their rental property. This is a remarkably common phenomenon with military families. They purchased a home and for one reason or another still own it. Many times this is by design.

Possibly you made the conscience decision to accumulate a portfolio of rental real estate. Or maybe you buy a fixer-upper in a great neighborhood, do a wonderful job with the renovation, and yet find yourself holding the property long after you've moved away, but you can't sell it for the right price, so you rent it out.

Owning rental properties as investment can be a great wealth-building strategy. Real estate does tend to appreciate over time. It has historically been a great hedge against inflation. Someone else is actually purchasing the asset for you — your tenants. You are using leverage — a mortgage and very little of your own money. And there are tax benefits to owning investment real estate.

Real estate investing is a very legitimate strategy for the educated, informed, and prepared. There is no such thing as a legitimate get rich quick scheme! Making money in real estate takes time, skill, and patience.

Beware of late-night infomercials touting "systems" that teach you how to get rich investing in real estate with no money down. The only people getting rich off of these schemes are the promoters!

There are a lot of downsides to becoming an absentee landlord to keep in mind:

- Real estate is illiquid. In other words, you couldn't sell it in a hurry if you tried.
- Ongoing maintenance is required, which takes cash and energy, but you're not around to perform the maintenance.

As an absentee landlord it is smart to hire a management company. They advertise and process rental applications, collect and deposit rent payments, pay bills on the property, and arrange for service providers to perform necessary maintenance. Typical fees to a management company are about 8 percent of the rental income per month, subject to a monthly minimum fee of $100 to $150.

✔ If you don't have any or enough rental income coming in to pay all of your current costs, you could find yourself spending hundreds of dollars a month to supplement the rental income to make the mortgage payments.

✔ Tenants can be challenging, to put it mildly. An unruly tenant could cause hundreds, if not thousands, of dollars in damages to your property. If they don't want to vacate, you could find yourself in court trying to force them out of your property. And when they do finally pack up and move, it could take weeks or months to restore the property to its original condition so you can rent it again — hopefully to great tenants.

Evaluating your financing options

If after all of these considerations are taken into account and you decide that homeownership is right for your family — it's time to consider your best option for financing your home purchase.

VA loans

One option available to you and your family but not available to your civilian counterparts is a VA loan. VA guaranteed loans have a number of advantages over other types of mortgages, specifically:

✔ No down payment is required.

✔ Your credit score can be lower than that required for conventional loans.

✔ Interest rates are very competitive.

✔ No mortgage insurance is required.

✔ Fees for a VA–guaranteed loan tend to be very low and are added into the loan so there are no out-of-pocket loan closing expenses.

VA loans are not issued by the Veterans Administration. They are *guaranteed* by the VA, but issued by traditional banks, savings and loans, and mortgage companies. The guarantee means that the lender is protected if you fail to repay your mortgage. Traditional lenders require a down payment of 20 percent, however due to the VA guarantee you can obtain a VA home loan with no down payment.

To be eligible, your active-duty servicemember must have served in the military for at least six months. Guard and Reserve members must have served six years.

When applying for a VA home loan your servicemember will need to get a *certificate of eligibility* from the Veterans Administration that certifies they are eligible to participate in the loan program. Complete VA Form 26-1880, which is the certificate of eligibility request form. Or better yet, ask your lender to obtain the eligibility certificate for you through the ACE (automated certificate of eligibility) system. This online application can establish eligibility and issue any certificate of eligibility in a matter of seconds.

Your active-duty servicemember must also obtain a *statement of service* signed by the commander of their unit, or personnel officer, which shows their date of entry and their current active duty period.

For more information visit http://www.homeloans.va.gov.

To obtain another VA loan you must have repaid your first loan and sold the property. You can use a VA loan for your primary residence, but if you want to accumulate rental real estate you'll need to use other forms of financing.

FHA loans

The Federal Housing Administration (FHA) insures home mortgages offered through banks, savings and loans, and traditional mortgage companies. Unlike VA loans, an FHA loan requires a down payment. However, an FHA loan may be just the ticket for you if you are a first time home buyer or have very little cash to put down. FHA generally requires down payments of 3 percent of the home purchase price.

One of the main advantages of an FHA insured home loan is that your credit can be less than ideal and you can still obtain a mortgage — at a competitive interest rate. Due to the fact that the FHA is insuring the mortgage lender you're able to obtain financing, with fair credit, and a minimal down payment.

This insurance is not free! To obtain a home loan without having 20 percent of the purchase price for your down payment you will pay Private Mortgage Insurance (PMI) premiums. PMI can add $50 to $150 per month to your mortgage payment. You are required to continue to pay this private mortgage insurance cost until you have at least 20 percent equity in your home.

The mortgage interest on your home is tax-deductible; however, PMI is not!

VA loans are not subject to PMI insurance premiums. If you can qualify for a VA loan, that should be your first consideration, unless of course, you can afford a down payment of 20 percent or more. In that case, you'll likely get the best interest rate from a conventional loan. Ask your lender.

If you aren't eligible for a VA loan at this time, and you don't have 20 percent for a down payment, FHA can be a great way to go.

Choosing between a fixed-rate mortgage and an ARM

For the last several years home mortgage rates have been at or near forty year lows. However, you've likely also heard horror stories about families whose adjustable rate mortgages have skyrocketed and now they are struggling to make their house payments. What the heck is going on? Well, these folks didn't have fixed-rate mortgages — likely because they couldn't afford the monthly cost of a mortgage payment at the interest rates available for fixed-rate mortgages — and now they are finding their monthly mortgage payment substantially higher than it was initially.

The interest rate charged on fixed-rate mortgages is guaranteed for the life of the mortgage, typically 30 years. However, adjustable-rate mortgages may only be "fixed" for one, three, or five years. After that "fixed" period, the interest rate becomes adjustable annually. These mortgages are referred to as an ARM, or 3/1 and 5/1 ARMs.

Adjustable rate mortgages can go up as much as 1 or 2 percent each year after that initial "fixed" period, but under no circumstance can your total interest rate exceed the cap documented in your mortgage agreement.

By accepting the risk that your interest rate could go up substantially while you have this loan, the mortgage company offers you a lower initial interest rate. There is no reason to accept this uncertainty unless you are absolutely confident that interest rates are going lower or remaining constant during the time you have your mortgage, or you are absolutely confident that you will be paying off this mortgage prior to or shortly after the time that the rate becomes adjustable. Absolute confidence in the direction of interest rates requires a perfect crystal ball; however you very likely know how long you anticipate staying in this house.

If fixed-rate mortgages are available at 6½ percent and you could obtain a 3/1 ARM for 5¾ percent — and you know you'll be relocating in five years or less — you'd be better off taking the adjustable rate mortgage. See example in Figure 10-2.

$150,000 Mortgage	Monthly Principal and Interest Payment			
	30 Year Fixed-Rate	3/1 ARM		Net Difference
Monthly	$948.10	$875.36		–$72.74
Yearly (1st 3 years)	$11,377.20	$10,504.32		–$872.88
By End of Year 3	$34,131.60	$31,512.96		–$2,618.64
By End of Year 4	$45,508.80	$43,187.76	*	–$2,321.04
By End of Year 5	$56,886.00	$56,083.20	**	–$802.80

Figure 10-2: Comparison of fixed-rate versus adjustable-rate mortgages.

*Assumes 1% increase in interest rate in Year 4
**Assumes another 1% increase in interest rate in Year 5

Relocating

You better get used to it — PCSing is part of military life! You may relocate every two to three years. But how else are you going to see the world if you stay in the same place very long?

It's not uncommon to have mixed emotions about relocating. You've established yourself in one community and now you need to do it all over again at your new location. Fortunately, through the military community, you have a plethora of support available including your Family Support Center, your current and new installation's relocation offices, and friends or friends of friends who may have lived on your new installation or are living there now. Of course, this section lends a helping hand as well, offering advice and resources to check out when you're facing relocating.

Assessing relocation assistance

And just as you'd expect, the military provides detailed guidelines and procedures outlining everything related to relocating your military family. The following list gives you some great places to access this information:

- Military OneSource counselors are available 24/7 at 800-342-9647. If you prefer, you can access Military OneSource online at `http://www.militaryonesource.com`, click on the category on the left-hand navigation bar entitled *Moving*. From there you'll find a wealth of information on everything from organizing to-do lists and prioritizing what needs to be done, to who you need to contact, and how you get hold of them.

- To help prepare you for your first PCS assignment, check out all of the great resources available on the Military HOMEFRONT Web site at `http://www.militaryhomefront.dod.mil`.

Your current installation's housing or relocation office is the place to go for:

- A "welcome aboard" package for your new installation
- The amount of housing allowances and entitlements you may receive
- Information regarding the availability of government housing at your new location
- Assistance locating off-base housing at your new location
- Help with temporary lodging

PCS allowances change periodically, and it's not safe to assume that you'll automatically receive certain allowances or entitlements. Check with your finance office to determine the exact amount of your allowances and entitlements.

This list details some assistance resources you need to contact as soon as you get your new PCS orders:

✔ **Set an appointment with your installation's transportation office.** Transportation office counselors will explain all of your PCS move entitlements and answer all of your questions. One of your first decisions is whether to have the government move you or whether you prefer to move yourself. If you choose to have government assistance, the transportation office counselor will schedule your move. And the transportation office can also let you know whether or not you can move yourself using your own vehicle, hire movers, or rent a truck, and if so, how best to go about moving yourself.

✔ **Access a copy of the "Plan My Move — Checklist" from the Military HOMEFRONT Web site at** `http://apps.mhf.dod.mil/pls/psgprod/f?p=107:1:2092223026492119`**.** This checklist will enable you to orchestrate and execute your family's move with precision. Its nearly four pages long, with action steps and due dates, working backwards from the date of your move. You're not going to overlook critical details if you follow this checklist!

Contact the Department of Defense's Automated Housing Referral Network at `http://www.AHRN.com`**.** This will help accelerate the process of securing housing at your new location.

When you get a new PCS assignment a lot of things need to be accomplished in a hurry. Take advantage of all of the support resources available to you. And don't hesitate to ask for help, including help from other families on your installation. Friends and neighbors are happy to lend a hand to help you pack, clean, or watch the kids, while you take care of all the details. These folks have been through moves themselves, and everybody appreciates a helping hand when it's their turn.

Establishing community at your new location

If you didn't have an opportunity to check out all of the available resources in your community and surrounding area prior to PCSing, dive right into your new community at your earliest opportunity. You'll want to become familiar with the facilities, and find out who's who around the installation.

Drop by your Family Support Center. You may find that you need to borrow something from the lending closet until your household goods arrive, or polish up your résumé. The folks at the Family Support Center are a great resource to help you assimilate into your new community. They'll fill you in on what's going on around town including:

- ✔ MWR programs, services, and activities for you, your children, and your whole family
- ✔ The Fitness and Sports Center for classes and training sessions, intramural sports, and tournaments
- ✔ The Skills Development Center for arts and crafts classes for you and the kids
- ✔ The Child Development Center and the Youth and Teen Center

Get out and meet people. Join a group or take a class. Get involved. Remember, you're not the only new kid on the block. The sooner you start establishing community the easier your adjustment to your new installation will be for you and your family.

Keeping in touch as you move around in the military

Just as important as it is to establish community at your new location, you should also make a conscious effort to keep in touch with your old friends as you or they move. Moving is a way of life for military families, but that doesn't mean you have to lose friendships. Rather, you have the opportunity to have a lot more friends, from all walks of life, living all over the world. You'll likely cross paths with friends from former duty stations, and you'll meet friends of friends.

With the advent of e-mail and the Internet, it's much easier to stay connected with your geographically diverse group of friends. If you don't already have one, establish a free email account that you can access anywhere in the world — presuming you have Internet access. The three major players are Hotmail by Microsoft, Gmail by Google, and Yahoo Mail. With each of these providers you can set up private groups. For example, you could have a Yahoo group for all of your closest friends. Your group stays connected and is able to view each other's posts and communications in relative security. You can even add new friends to your group and friends can bring in their friends. You can share documents, photos, and even videos. This type of forum provides a wonderful online social networking community, and it's free!

As important as it is for you to stay connected with your friends, your children may also enjoy having the same type of online community to stay connected with their friends. You may end up participating in a number of online groups; military spouses, former classmates or coworkers, a couple's group, and so on.

Regardless of how private you may feel your communications are, never share any information with anyone that could jeopardize operational security, or anyone's personal security. See Chapter 19 for more information.

Chapter 11

Finding Employment and Educational Opportunities

In This Chapter

▶ Exploring your military education benefits

▶ Assessing which options may be right for you

▶ Tapping into spousal benefits

Military service provides access to a wide variety of benefits for you and your servicemember in the area of education and employment. Taking full advantage of these opportunities will enable you to truly leverage your military experience.

Remember to think beyond the paycheck. Total compensation includes all of the benefits available to you and your servicemember including the following: 30 days paid leave per year, healthcare, meals and housing, life insurance, travel, discounts, training and leadership development, money for school and education assistance programs, plus veteran's benefits. All of these add to the immense package of benefits offered to servicemembers and their families. In this chapter we focus on the educational and employment benefits available to you and your servicemember. Take advantage of these benefits, and you'll get the most value out of your time in the military.

Active-duty servicemembers may qualify for more than $50,000 in education benefits, which can be used to obtain an undergraduate college degree, specific vocational training, or graduate and post-graduate degrees. Many of the educational programs available today are designed to fit your military lifestyle. In this chapter we explore the variety of educational benefits available to you and your spouse, as well as employment assistance and opportunities that will benefit you.

Professional Military Education

Servicemembers' military careers provide them with on-the-job training, leadership skills, and opportunities for promotion. With each promotion they gain more skills, have more responsibility, and of course additional pay and benefits. Each branch of the service has its own process for advancing service-members. Regardless of the branch, promotions have the same objectives: to advance officers and enlisted personnel who possess the right qualifications and abilities to successfully perform the duties expected of the next higher pay grade.

How quickly your servicemember is advanced or promoted in the military sometimes depends on whether or not the next higher rank is understaffed. Basically it's the same as the civilian world. If there is a need to fill a position at a higher level, those people most qualified to fulfill that position will be considered first for promotion.

Many universities have established special partnerships with the Armed Forces and have programs available on some military bases. Programs are accessible to servicemembers *and their spouses* through independent study, distance learning, and on-base courses.

Finding Educational Funding

There are many ways to obtain and pay for a formal education. In the following section we highlight the plentiful options available to you and your servicemember.

Montgomery GI Bill

We have a saying in the armed forces, "join the military and see the world," and all on the military's tab! But a more likely financially significant benefit is the opportunity to obtain a college education, specific vocational training, or an advanced or postgraduate degree — all paid for by the U.S. government! The Montgomery GI Bill (MGIB) provides a very generous tax-free benefit to active-duty servicemembers and veterans. More than $38,000 per eligible servicemember is available that can be used to pay for tuition, books, fees, and living expenses while earning a college degree or certification from a technical school. The MGIB can also be used for professional licensing or cer-tification and on-the-job training programs. This benefit is paid directly to the student on a monthly basis.

All active-duty servicemembers are automatically enrolled in the MGIB unless they choose to "opt out" of this benefit. To "opt out" a servicemember must do so during the first three days of active-duty. You might be wondering why anyone would choose to "opt out" of this benefit. Well, two primary reasons come to mind: one, participation in the MGIB actually requires a contribution of $100 per month from the military pay for the first 12 months of service. Two, someone may choose to "opt out" of participation because he already has an advanced degree or all of the college or vocational-technical education he ever anticipates wanting or needing.

The benefit of the MGIB is so significant that we highly recommend service-members not "opt out" of the benefit. Yes, it costs money to participate, but in exchange for your $1,200 total commitment you could receive a benefit of up to $1,075 per month if you are enrolled as a full-time student whether on active-duty or within ten years after the completion of your service. And you don't have to attend classes on a full-time basis. You can receive a pro-rata share of this monthly stipend if you attend classes on a quarterly or half-time basis. In just a matter of weeks you can more than make up for the cost of participating in the MGIB program.

Your servicemember can get an extra $150 per month in MGIB benefits if he elects to contribute an additional $600 before leaving the service. This option is called the "GI Bill Buy-Up." The "Buy-Up" increases your total contribution to the Montgomery GI Bill program to $1,800, however, it will increase your total GI benefits by as much as $5,400. That's not a bad return on investment!

To qualify for the MGIB your servicemember must have completed high school or have the GED equivalency certificate and have completed at least two years on active-duty.

The MGIB is also extended to Guard and Reserve members. The Reserve GI Bill provides your servicemember up to 36 months of benefits, which is worth more than $10,000 tax-free and can help him pay for college tuition, books, fees, and vocational training expenses.

To qualify for the Reserve GI Bill your servicemember must:

- ✔ Have a six- year enlistment obligation
- ✔ Complete his initial active duty
- ✔ Have a high school diploma or GED
- ✔ Remain in good-standing

To access your Montgomery GI Bill benefits your servicemember must:

✔ Verify that the school where degree program is VA approved. Call 888-442-4551 for verification.

✔ Complete the application for VA educational benefits (VA Form 22-1990).

✔ Submit the completed form to your school's registrar's office.

Post-9/11 GI Bill

In July 2008, the Department of Veterans Affairs released details on the Post-9/11 Veterans Education Assistance Act of 2008. The new Post-9/11 GI Bill goes into effect on August 1, 2009 and is considered one of the most significant and positive changes to the GI Bill since World War II.

All members who have served three months or longer on active duty since September 11, 2001 are eligible for benefits under the new GI Bill, so long as they have not used other veterans' education benefits.

Some major highlights of the Post-9/11 GI Bill include:

✔ Benefits are free and you have up to 15 years after active duty to utilize your benefits.

✔ Benefits may be received for up to 36 months.

✔ Members with at least 36 months of service are entitled to

• Tuition and fees, paid directly to a public institution of higher education, not to exceed the most expensive in state undergraduate tuition. Benefits may be paid for undergraduate and graduate coursework, as well as, distance learning, vocational, and technical training. However, the new GI Bill does not cover apprenticeships, correspondence courses, flight training, and on the job training.

• Monthly housing allowance equal to your basic allowance for housing (BAH) amount payable to an E-5 with dependents. Not available to active-duty servicemembers.

• Annual books and supplies stipend of up to $1,000.

✔ Spouses and dependent children may be able to use the benefit.

✔ Servicemembers who are currently utilizing or have not yet begun utilizing their MGIB benefits received a 20 percent raise in their benefits beginning August 1, 2008.

✔ Officers who were ineligible for MGIB are now eligible with the Post-9/11 GI Bill.

✔ Guard and Reserve members who serve at least three months on active duty are eligible for the new GI Bill.

✔ Unlike the Montgomery GI Bill, a high school diploma is not required in order to qualify for the new Post-9/11 GI Bill.

For more information on the new Post-9/11 GI Bill visit http://www.gibill.va.gov/s22.htm.

Tuition Assistance

The Armed Forces Military Tuition Assistance (TA) program is available to all active-duty servicemembers, and in most cases members of the Reserve. Each branch of the armed forces determines the maximum amount of tuition assistance benefit provided to their servicemembers. The maximum benefit can be as much as $4,500 per year depending on the branch of service.

Tuition assistance is a benefit. It doesn't have to be repaid, unless your servicemember fails or drops out of the course or program for which they are using the tuition assistance benefit.

Tuition assistance is usually paid directly to the institution rather than to the servicemember. Active-duty members may elect to use their Montgomery GI Bill in addition to tuition assistance to cover more expensive programs.

Tuition Assistance must be used in the year it is allotted or it is lost. So, use your Tuition Assistance first and then tap your Montgomery GI Bill if additional funds are needed to pay for education.

Scholarships and financial aid

There are many sources for scholarships designated to servicemembers, veterans, and their immediate family members, to help cover the cost of tuition, fees, books, and in some cases living expenses. You may be eligible for thousands of scholarships or grants. Most of these awards go unclaimed each year because people don't know how to access them.

Servicemembers should check out www.military.com/scholarships for more information about scholarships and grants that are available to them. As a military spouse you should visit www.military.com/spouse to find out more about scholarships and grants that may be available to you.

If for some reason your educational program cannot be fully funded through the Tuition Assistance (TA) or Montgomery GI Bill programs, and military scholarships and grants, traditional federal financial aid is also available to you.

Tap into your Tuition Assistance program first, then the Montgomery GI Bill and military scholarships and grants before applying for traditional federal financial aid.

Continuing Education for Spouses

Nearly 90 percent of military spouses say that they would like to have the opportunity to pursue additional education. Moving every few years makes finishing a degree challenging to say the least — challenging, but not impossible.

Developing a plan that works

You don't have the luxury that other people have. Unfortunately, you're probably not going to be able to stay in one place to finish a degree program. And you're going to have to balance your schoolwork with your military lifestyle, which means taking into account deployments, moves, and other elements out of your control. It's possible to finish a degree while balancing the military lifestyle, but to get on the road to success, reassess the plan you have in place. Depending on your personal situation, it may not be practical for you to finish a degree straight through. Here are some things to remember as you plug away at your degree:

- **Don't get bogged down by numbers.** Who cares if it takes the average person between three and five years to finish an undergraduate degree? They probably don't have to deal with the situations and juggle the lifestyle you do. Take the time you need to finish the classes on your own terms while still taking care of your other obligations.

- **Find institutions with nontraditional venues so that you stand a better chance to finish a degree even through multiple moves.** An example of this is the University of Oklahoma that has multiple outlets at various military installations. The downside of these programs though is that the curriculum is limited, and you're hostage to the classes that are offered.

- **If your reason for pursuing higher education is ultimately to contribute to the family income, research high-growth and portable industries before you go shopping for a program.**

Tuition assistance programs

One of the biggest challenges of higher education is finding a way to pay for it. Refer back to Chapter 9 for information on saving for your college education.

Regardless of how much you're able to save, the skyrocketing costs of a college education almost guarantees that you're going to be looking for additional help. Fortunately, a great number of scholarships exist for military spouses. Start by looking at your installation. Your installation's education center will have information on potential scholarships and other sources of financial aid. Check out the spouse clubs as they often offer military spouse scholarships.

 If you're stationed overseas, you may be eligible for a special tuition assistance program. The Air Force's version is the Spouse Tuition Assistance Program (STAP), but other services have their own version. STAP provides enough funds to pay a portion of tuition costs and caps the maximum benefit to about $1,500 a year.

In addition to looking on base, you might also want to look off the installation for additional opportunities. Many military service organizations and associations offer military spouse scholarships. As with anything else, it's important to research the resources available to you. Start by consulting a military scholarship finder. You'd be surprised at the number of organizations that offer scholarships.

Don't limit yourself to military scholarships, either. Remember to consult reference books at the library to see what other opportunities might be open to you because of your cultural background or area of study.

 Some servicemembers are able to transfer their Montgomery GI Bill benefits to their spouses. Beginning August 1, 2009, the DoD is making available the opportunity to transfer MGIB entitlements to spouses and eligible children. The details of this transferrable benefit are not fully known at the time of this writing. Please visit www.GIBILL.va.gov for up-to-date information.

Finding Employment Opportunities for Military Spouses

More than 60 percent of all military spouses are either working outside the home or currently looking for employment. The transient lifestyles of military families makes finding and maintaining a job challenging — again, challenging, but not impossible.

Getting ready to work

If you're getting ready to transition from being a stay-at-home spouse or mom to working, take some time to do some assessment that in the end will help you find your ideal job. Take an inventory of your skills and interests. Find out what motivates you. These inventories will help you find a good fit in terms of a work situation.

Do a self-assessment. What do you like to do? What do you do well naturally? What tasks bring you a sense of satisfaction? And if you felt like you could not fail, what would you most like to do? Why do you want to work? Is it to make money? Do you want to make a difference? Do you just want to enjoy what you do regardless of how much money you will or won't make? Sitting down and taking a few minutes to figure what will make you happy will help you zone in on the type of work you might be interested in.

After you do a self-assessment, take an inventory of all your experiences. Include your volunteer experiences, your educational background, and any technical certifications you have earned. You're also going to want to include the professional and alumni associations you belong to. This inventory will serve as the basis of your résumé.

If you have the time or the interest, you might check into taking a personality test or type indicator test. These types of "tests" will teach you more about yourself, help you understand how you work, and the environments that might work better for you. If these surveys are not available at your installation family support center, you can find them online.

Now that you have an inkling of what areas you're interested in, start exploring the different careers out there. The U.S. Department of Labor puts out a great *Occupational Outlook Handbook* that is an invaluable resource for career information. Inside the book, you'll find information about different types of jobs and careers. If you've ever been curious about what kind of education it takes to be an entomologist, what you can expect to earn, and what your typical day might look like, then this is the book for you. You can find a copy of the book at `http://www.bls.gov/oco/`.

Cost-benefit analysis of working outside the home

Once you have an idea of what you'd like to do, it's important to put together a plan of action. Do a cost-benefit analysis of working outside the home. Figure out why you want to work. Is it to get out of the house? Meet other people outside of the military? Maybe it's just for your own self-esteem. If your motivation for working outside the home is any one of these reasons, then it doesn't really matter how much money you make.

However, if you're working to add money to the family coffers, then you're going to want to pay close attention to the costs associated with working. Some common things that eat away from your paycheck:

- ✔ Childcare costs
- ✔ Clothing costs and dry cleaning
- ✔ Dining out
- ✔ Commuting costs

There are calculators on the Web that will help you figure out what your anticipated cost of working will be. Try: `http://www.bizymoms.com/cart/careers/bizymoms_calculator.html`.

After you know where the challenges are, you can work toward formulating a good, workable plan of action. Look for creative alternatives to cut costs such as: flexible schedules, compressed work weeks, carpooling, childcare co-ops, and packing your own lunch. When you're researching potential companies, identify military-friendly employers and programs that will allow you to advance your career around the country. Do your research — talk to other spouses and gather information.

Knowing what the costs are will help you formulate a plan to make it work. The plan will also help you determine the dollar amount you have to make to work outside the home and still meet your financial obligations. Then, discuss it with your spouse so that he understands what kind of impact your working outside the home will have on the family. This conversation will help manage the expectation on both sides.

Bringing your spouse into the discussion of working outside the home is a very important step that many people choose to overlook. However, it's essential to maintaining harmony at home to have the difficult talk and discuss how you'll deal with issues that will crop up.

Strategic volunteering

If you find you can't work outside the home for the time being, there are numbers of ways you can still get work experience. The one that immediately comes to mind is volunteering. Because volunteers are key to the military lifestyle most of the organizations on base will have volunteer opportunities available. Think about where you hope to go with your career once you join or rejoin the work force. Try to look for volunteer opportunities to support your goals. That way you will continue to build résumé bullets. For instance, if you want to work in the accounting field, you might consider volunteering to keep the books for the thrift shop or volunteer to serve as the treasurer for the spouse club.

As an incentive to entice more volunteers, some base organizations (such as Family Support Centers and Thrift Shops) will actually reimburse childcare costs. Childcare is generally provided on a space available basis by the Child Development Center, and it is only available when funds are available.

Don't limit yourself to the volunteer opportunities available on base. Opportunities exist outside the gates as well. If you don't know what you want to be when you enter the workforce, volunteering gives you the chance to try out different jobs without making a huge commitment. Try out the different industries you think you might be interested in.

Employment support

Installation family support centers will offer services ranging from résumé critiques, counseling, and ongoing classes on different aspects of employment. You can learn everything from applying for a federal job to evaluating employee benefits. Consult Chapter 17 for more information on family support centers.

Military spouses are great at networking to find the best resources with every move. However, it is sometimes difficult to put this networking skill to use when looking for a job. For whatever reason, it's a difficult leap to make, which is unfortunate because between 60 to 80 percent of people will find their job through networking. It's important to let people know you're looking. Join networking associations to expand your pool of acquaintances. These associations will also give you access to additional services and tools to aid in your job search. They help you keep up to date in your field of interest. Active membership helps you strengthen your leadership, presentation, and communication skills. It provides you with a built-in support group and an opportunity to learn about employment and internship opportunities before they become public.

Even if you're self-employed, there are organizations out there for you:

✔ Home-based working moms (www.hbwm.com)

✔ American Telecommuting Association (www.yourata.com)

✔ National Association of Home Based Businesses (www.usahome business.com)

Department of Defense and Department of Labor Initiatives

Help for military spouses looking for careers comes from the joint initiatives of the Department of Defense and the Department of Labor. In addition to launching a Web site to support military spouses (www.milspouse.org), the DoD and DoL have been very proactive in launching a series of programs to promote military spouse employment.

Portable careers in the military have traditionally meant a career in nursing or education. However, recently, other programs have been initiated to introduce spouses to other fields such as real estate and medical transcription work:

- ✔ **Operation ReMax** provides military spouses and others who have a military connection access to mentoring, ongoing education, and coaching in the highly portable career field of real estate.

- ✔ **Medical transcriptionist** is another portable career choice for military spouses because of the nature of the work. Most of the data is submitted electronically, so you can work from anywhere. Additionally, it's highly flexible as you control the hours you work. Most employers will give you a 12-hour block of time to complete your daily work, so if you can be efficient in allocating your time, you'll be able to easily balance work and family obligations. There are educational requirements associated with the field, but there are many schools that offer military spouse discounts for this field of study. Check out www.aamt.org/script content/MilSpouses.cfm for more information.

In an effort to train more spouses in portable careers, the DoD and DoL have recently launched a Military Spouse Career Advancement Account demonstration. The program is currently available at 18 installations in 8 different states. Eligible applicants are offered $3000 a year (max $6000 over 2 years) to go toward education costs. Originally, the program was only open to spouses of E-1 to E-5 and O-1 to O-3, yet it has already been expanded to include *all* active duty military spouses. The industries have also been expanded to be more inclusive. For more information on the program, consult the Frequently Asked Questions (FAQs) that can be found at: http://caa.milspouse.org/Advance/FAQs/.

Self-employment

You may require a lot more flexibility than working for someone else will afford you. Luckily, a multitude of self-employment options are out there. Providing a service or freelancing will allow you the flexibility of picking your hours while still working your passion.

Are you talented in decorating rooms? Then perhaps you should look into interior decorating or helping people organize their homes. Maybe you have a degree in biology or language skills. How about tutoring? Maybe you have young children and wouldn't mind taking in a couple of other kids for some extra money. Are you a writer, photographer, web designer, or proofreader? All these skills lend themselves nicely to freelancing. Take writing as an example. Local news is everywhere. Start by writing query letters to editors and you can find a way to turn your interest into a paycheck.

For the ultimate in flexibility, how about direct sales? Perhaps you've been purchasing those kitchen items, pottery, or baskets. Now you can work the other side of the table and sell them. In addition to providing you with a discount on the items you were purchasing anyway, direct sales allow you to make your own hours and determine your paycheck based on how much you want to work. If you want to work part time and/or work on your own terms, you still have options open to you.

Military spouse preference program

The Department of Defense has a ***military spouse preference*** (MSP) program. The purpose of the program is to give military spouses a leg up in applying for jobs within the ***Department of Defense*** (DoD) by providing employment priority to those spouses who are accompanying their active duty sponsors on a PCS move. The hope is that military spouse preference will lessen the impact that multiple military moves could potentially have on a spouse's career. Here's the lowdown on the program:

✔ The program is open to spouses of active duty servicemembers, Coast Guard, and full-time National Guard troops.

✔ Spouses PCSing with their servicemember to another installation are able to register for military spouse preference at the installation up to 30 days before the sponsor's report date.

✔ If you're moving to an overseas location, you need to wait until you arrive before you can register. You can register at any number of locations within commuting distance of your sponsor's duty station.

✔ Military spouse preference cannot be used in conjunction with a move where the servicemember is either separating or retiring.

✔ Not all jobs are open to military spouse preference. Examples of some that aren't are: positions in the excepted service, positions filled from Office of Personnel Management (OPM), certificates or under agency Delegated Examining Unit or Direct Hire Authority procedures, and nonappropriated fund (NAF) positions.

✔ Preference generally ends once you accept a permanent position or decline an interview for a valid job.

✔ More information can be found at installation family support centers.

✔ Military spouse preference does not mean you're guaranteed the job. You still have to be the best qualified applicant.

For more information on military spouse preference, consult: `http://www.defenselink.mil/mapsite/spousepref.html`.

Putting it all together

If you know where you want to work, it's time to get out there and find a job. So where exactly do you look? Don't worry — we've got that covered for you in the following list:

✔ **The installation:** Family Support Centers are a great place to start. In addition to leveraging the spouse employment program for access to extensive programs and services, you can also tap into the job listings they keep on file.

✔ **The Web:** The Internet is also a great tool in your job search. Don't limit yourself to the traditional search engines and company Web sites. Some organizations also have Web sites with jobs databases for their members/users. Two examples of these Web sites are the Military Officers Association of America (`www.moaa.org`) and the Military Spouse Corporate Career Network (`www.msccn.org`). Many specialized Web sites such as `www.usajobs.com` for federal employment and `www.idealist.org` for non-profit jobs are also available.

✔ **Military spouse–friendly companies:** While you're searching the Internet, you should take some time to check out companies that have been identified as "military spouse–friendly employers" through programs, such as the Army Spouse Employment Partnership, and lists, such as the annual Military Spouse magazine's Top 10 Military Spouse Friendly Employers.

✔ **Staffing companies:** Register with staffing companies such as Kelly Services. It's usually free of charge, so register with several of them. In addition to the regular temp jobs, they often list temporary to permanent jobs. If you're unsure what you want to do when you grow up, temp agencies might be a good place to start out. Benefits of the staffing companies include the freedom to try out lots of different jobs without a huge commitment. Registering with multiple companies also increases the probability of finding a job quickly.

✔ **Job fairs:** If you want to check out lots of different companies at the same time, check out job fairs. You can check out industry focused or military-friendly job fairs. Before attending a job fair, do your research. If there is a Web site with all the participating companies listed, you might want to take a look. Find the companies advertising the jobs that most closely match your interests and figure out what booths you'll visit. Chances are good that if you pick a good job fair, there will be far too many booths for you to visit all of them. Be strategic about it. In addition to doing adequate research, here are some additional pointers:

 • Dress professionally and carry copies of your résumé and reference sheets.

 • Develop a 30-second "elevator speech" that speaks to your professional accomplishments and capabilities in an organized manner.

 • Take notes, write on the back of business cards to distinguish between representatives.

 • If you spend a significant amount of time speaking to someone, send a thank you note.

✔ **Classified ads:** Ads are particularly useful for finding local jobs. Sunday is usually the first day that ads are run. Respond to the ad immediately as employers utilizing the classified ads are generally looking to hire right away. Many newspapers now have companion Web sites to go with the job listings that are updated more frequently than once a week.

✔ **Network:** Reconnect with your alma mater and use the alumni career services. In addition to taking advantage of special job fairs and possible job listings, it's a great opportunity for networking. Believe it or not, even in today's high tech world, 60 to 80 percent of all job seekers will still find their next job through networking. Everyone is a contact. This includes family members, friends, social contacts, mentors, church members, and service providers (doctors, dentists, hairdressers, realtors). So get out there and meet people. You never know where your next lead is going to come from.

✔ **Professional associations:** Expand your network by joining a professional association tailored to your industry. As an example, if you have a lobbying background, you might want to think about joining an organization such as *Women in Government Relations* (www.wgr.org).

State initiatives to support military families

Despite all the efforts being made to remove the impediments to military spouses being able to finish their education and/or maintain a viable career, no one can dispute that the constant moves begin to wear on spouses. Transferring credits from one university to another, moving from state to state every few months, or even overseas impacts a spouse's ability to finish a degree or continue moving up in a chosen career path.

Some of the issues are: the high cost of out-of-state college tuition rates, the expense associated with military spouses having to pay for certification and licensure every time they move, and the lag time it takes for spouses to find a job once they move into a new area. Over the past few years, significant gains have been made at the state level to remove the impediments to a higher quality of life for military families.

As an example, understanding the cost of out-of-state could potentially cost up to four times the price of the in-state tuition rate, the Department of Defense State Liaison office has made much headway in getting states to sign on to providing in-state tuition for servicemembers and their dependents in the state where they're stationed. Many of the states have also agreed to extend the in-state tuition benefits after the servicemember has PCS'ed.

Spouse employment issues also present a burden to many military benefits. Every time a family moves, spouses who work in professions such as nursing or teaching have to pay for another state certificate or license. These differences in certification requirements can hamper a spouse's re-entry into the job market after moving to a different state. The State Liaison Office is pursuing alternative certification through the American Board for Certification of Teacher Excellence (ABCTE) program that is portable from state to state (of participating states) and would allow spouses who achieve the certification to teach without a break in service. They're also going after states to adopt the Nurse Licensure Compact or to make similar provisions for military spouses who are transferring from one state to another.

Some states now assist spouses to become certified teachers through the "Spouses-to-Teachers" program. More information can be found at: http://www.spousestoteachers.com/.

Finally, despite all the great programs, spouses will inevitably be faced with a PCS that will force them to leave their job and spend some time out of the work force while they're looking for employment. Many states have now acknowledged that military spouses are being forced to move in support of their servicemember. Many states now provide unemployment benefits for military spouses. More information on this and other initiatives of the DoD State Liaison Office can be found at: www.usa4militaryfamilies.dod.mil.

Part III:
Supporting the Military Family

The 5th Wave   By Rich Tennant

©RICHTENNANT

I think it's really important for you to learn how to bounce back from life's setbacks.

In this part . . .

You'll be happy to know that you're not in it alone. There are a multitude of resources and organizations out there to support military families. In this part, you'll learn more about the official resources as well as the community assistance available to you. You'll also learn critical skills to building a strong military marriage and raising a family in the military.

Chapter 12

Raising a Family in the Military

Military brats (as we fondly call our kids) have the same needs as any other child. They crave independence but count on the unconditional love and support of their parents at the same time. Where they differ from their civilian counterparts is that they often grow and develop in the absence of their servicemember parent. Due to crazy work schedules and a frenetic op tempo, you could possibly end up being a single parent for a good percentage of your children's formative years.

In homes where both parents are currently serving, inevitably, a family faces times of being geographically separated. Unless the two servicemember parents can always get assigned to the same installation, chances are good that in addition to the occasional deployments, they may also be given different assignments.

Kids sometimes have a difficult time understanding why one parent keeps missing the milestones or why they always seem to get the short end of the stick when it comes time to pick room parents or team managers. A servicemember enlists and willingly chooses the military as a way of life. Military spouses for the most part know what they're getting into when they marry a servicemember. Children, on the other hand, have no choice. Raising happy, well-adjusted children in the military can be quite the challenge, but in this chapter, we tell you about the realities of raising children in the military as well as how to overcome the obstacles.

Finding Childcare

The military is filled with families. And many military families in which both spouses work, list childcare as the highest expense associated with one spouse working outside the home. When you think about the challenge that families face as their childcare needs change in the face of deployments, you can only imagine what a huge deal affordable and/or flexible childcare is for military families. And unless you're fortunate enough to be stationed near your family, you can't count on family support for childcare like your civilian friends can. So, you're going to have to be a lot more independent and look to other options.

To get started, figure out what your childcare needs are. Are you looking for hourly drop-in slots or are you looking for full time care with flexibility in case you need to drop your child off early and pick up late? Perhaps you work part time and you're looking for something more than drop-in care but less than full-time care. Regardless of your situation, determine your needs and take stock of all the alternatives available, which we just happen to discuss in the following sections.

Occasional or part-time care

You can check out several options if you only need occasional or part-time care. Try looking at the following:

✔ **Childcare co-ops** operate where a number of families get together and decide to share childcare duties. Members of the co-op earn "points" by providing childcare. They spend "points" by redeeming them for childcare.

Everyone's kept straight by the "secretary" who is either elected or appointed. This person keeps track of all the points. When a family needs childcare, they will call the secretary with specifics such as date and time. The secretary will then try to locate a sitter within the co-op who is willing to take the "job," After the care is provided, both parties agree to the number of points and report it to the secretary.

The secretary can be "paid" for her service with extra points, or the co-op might decide that the position of secretary should be shared by everyone in the co-op on a rotational basis.

Advantages to co-ops include:

• You don't exchange money because families trade childcare duties.

• Children get close to different families.

• Children interact with each other and develop social skills under the watchful eye of parents.

✔ **Volunteering** might be a good, free option available to you if you're searching for childcare so that you can get out of the house and be around other adults. Many organizations on the installation will pay day care expenses for their volunteers. And getting out of the house and volunteering will give you valuable experience to add to your résumé. Refer to Chapter 11 for more information.

✔ **Go to your installation's gym** and check to see if it has free childcare. If you're tired of being cooped up in the house and the weather's just not going to allow you to go running around with the jogging stroller, maybe you're looking for some time at the gym and wondering what to do with your child. Some installations actually offer some type of child minding at the gym.

✔ **Some gyms in town** also offer inexpensive classes for children that will allow you to squeeze in a workout while they're occupied and socializing. Places such as the YMCA sometimes even offer very reasonably priced pre-school classes for children that allow you to get in a regular workout right on site. The sessions are also long enough to give you time to run errands on your own. An added advantage of the preschool classes is that the kids have an opportunity to socialize and learn skills in an educational environment, which helps them prepare for kindergarten and give you some time to yourself.

✔ **Many churches** also offer some types of preschool classes, if you're not hung up on having the kids on site where you're working out.

Comparing on-base vs. off-base options

Now, if you're looking for full-time childcare because you both work outside the home, then part-time and occasional solutions are probably not going to work for you. However, this complication doesn't mean that you don't have options. We discuss your options in the following sections.

CDC (child development center) on-base childcare

In Chapter 3, we discuss that every effort is made to ensure that high-quality, affordable childcare is available to military families. Most every installation has a child development center (CDC). Some installations are even large enough to warrant more than one facility. The centers generally provide care for children between the ages of six weeks and 12 years old. Although the majority of CDC users are under the age of five, the centers also run a school-age program known as school-age care (SAC). SAC programs are offered for children (ages 6 to 12 years) before and/or after school and during holidays and summer vacations.

The child development centers follow a priority ranking system that ranges from facility to facility, but top priority tends to go to people stationed to the installation in the following order: single/dual active duty military; single/dual DoD civilian employees; active duty military with a working spouse and DoD civilian employees with a working spouse.

Childcare costs at these facilities are subsidized, determined on a sliding scale, and based on a family's total income so the CDCs are a relatively affordable option. The facilities also open a little earlier and stay open a little later than comparable places off base to accommodate military schedules. Unfortunately, because the child development centers are so affordable and convenient, there is usually a long waiting list.

It's never too early to start planning. Get on the waitlist at the CDC as soon as you know you're pregnant.

FCC (family childcare) — on-base childcare

For those who cannot get into the CDC, other options are available to you. For the convenience and price most comparable to the installation CDC, check out the family childcare (FCC) program on base. Through the FCC program, certified day care providers living in government housing provide flexible childcare options to include night, weekend, and hourly care. These types of slots fulfill about a third of military childcare requirements, but even with these additional spots, not everyone is going to be able to be accommodated on the installation.

Getting help for off-base childcare

Because it's impossible to meet 100 percent of the childcare needs on the installation, the resource and referral (R&R) programs are critical to the DOD's ability to refer families to quality childcare off the base when care is unavailable on base. That's where the resource and referral (R&R) programs pick up. Available at most military bases, these programs offer referrals to childcare in the local community. Because it's impossible to meet 100 percent of the need on the installation, R&R services are critical to the DOD's ability to refer families to quality childcare off the base when care is unavailable on base.

In addition to the referrals you can get from the CDC, you could also be eligible for some additional resources. The Department of Defense (DoD) has entered into a partnership with the National Association of Child Care Resources and Referral Agencies (NACCRRA) to help servicemembers and their families find affordable healthcare in their community. Along with the locator services, NACCRRA also has some programs in place that subsidizes the cost of childcare for certain demographics. The programs differ from branch to branch, so you need to check out the Web site and research the options open to your sponsor's specific branch of service: www.naccrra.org/MilitaryPrograms.

Some families have a difficult time finding childcare because they live too far away to tap into base resources. Our Military Kids (OMK) is a NACCRRA program geared to families who don't live on or near a military installation, helping them to find affordable childcare and in some cases to subsidize it. While the program is open to everyone, it's intended for families of deployed Guard/Reserve members.

Educating the Kids

It's hard enough making friends in school. Factor in a move every two to three years and you begin to understand the challenges facing our military kids. Typically, military children move between six to nine times over the course of their parent's typical 20-year military career.

Your children's anxiety of having to start all over again is compounded by the fear of being behind because they're possibly starting a new school months after the official first day. We show you in the next sections all the resources available to support military children, and simply by understanding what's available, you can mitigate some of your children's fears and anxiety.

Regardless of what type of schooling you choose for your children, military children have a difficult time of maintaining continuity throughout their school experience because each state has different graduation requirements. There is movement afoot to get an Interstate Compact signed that will standardize the high school requirements from state to state. To read more about this, go to www.usa4militaryfamilies.dod.mil/portal/page/mhf/USA4/USA4_HOME_1?current_id=22.60.30.0.0.0.0.0.0&content_id=242181.

Making smart decisions

When you start looking at schools, you can find many options to choose from. Regardless of whether you choose to send your children to a parochial school, other private school, the base school, or decide to forego all these options in favor of homeschooling, you can find many helpful tools to take advantage of:

- **Military families:** Your best resource is going to be other military families, particularly other spouses. I'm sure you already know someone who either just came from the base you're moving to or who could get you in touch with someone still at the base. If they have kids who are around the same age as yours, all the better. It is from these other spouses and friends that you will get the inside scoop on who the best teachers are, what schools are better for sports, band, or other activities your children might be interested in. Having the information going through the filter of someone who knows you and your kids will give you some valuable insights into what might work well for you and your family.

✔ **Internet:** If you don't have the luxury of knowing someone from the installation, try the Internet. Regardless of what options you're researching, tons of Web sites can help you make your decision.

- **Homeschool:** Because of the constant moving or a perceived lack of quality, affordable educational options, many military families choose to home school their children. If you're looking into it, check out your state Web site for information on how to get started and issues specific to military families. As an example, Alaska has a great Web site www.homeschullinginalaska.com that not only answers Frequently Asked Questions, but also has links to homeschooling resources in other states when it's time for you to move on.

- **Public schools:** If you want to go the more traditional route and check out public schools, Web sites such as www.greatschools.net can compare schools within the area you're moving to. This specific Web site rates schools based on criteria such as: principal leadership, teacher quality, extracurricular activities, parent involvement, safety, discipline, and overall quality. It also allows you to compare schools in the same school district or narrow it down to compare schools within a certain mileage radius from a home you might be considering. While not absolutely scientific, the Web site will give you a good picture of the schools in the area you're moving to.

- **On-base school:** If you think your kids might be headed to a school on a military installation, check out: www.dodea.edu/home/index.cfm. This is the main Web site for the Department of Defense Education Activity and from the home page, you can link to your specific school. You're going to be amazed at all the information you can find online at the site. You'll like knowing what type of checklist you should follow for your child to transfer into the school and more information about transportation. Your kids will appreciate knowing what types of activities are offered at each of the schools, what school supplies they'll need, and even what they're serving for lunch. Your kids' needs aren't so different than your own. They want the most information available to allay some of their fears.

These are only a few of the Internet resources available to you, but you get the idea. If you can imagine it, you can find it on the Web. Once you have an idea of what you're looking for in terms of an education solution for your kids, start your research by consulting the Internet.

Department of Defense schools

Chances are good that your kids will have the opportunity to attend a DoD school, so you need to catch up on the following information:

✔ The umbrella of Department of Defense Education Activity (DoDEA) consists of the 199 schools around the nation and worldwide. Overseas, DoDEA operates the Department of Defense Dependents Schools (DoDDS). DoDEA also operates the Department of Defense Domestic Dependent Elementary and Secondary Schools (DDESS) located in the United States and its territories and possessions.

✔ DoDEA provides education to eligible DoD military and civilian dependents from pre-kindergarten through grade 12.

✔ Not knowing what they can expect, some parents worry about the quality of education their child will be receiving. They worry needlessly. One hundred percent of DODEA schools are accredited. On average, DODEA students score above the national average on standardized tests, and the schools maintain a high graduate rate of nearly 99 percent.

✔ Outside of the fact that half the audience of the PTA meetings will likely be wearing a uniform, it would be hard for you to discern any big differences between DODEA schools and other great schools you may have attended. They have gifted and talented programs as well as academic and extracurricular activities.

Leaving the nest

Just when you begin to wonder how many more schools your kids will have to transfer into or how much more you all can take, you turn around and it's time to start visiting those college campuses.

The nomadic lifestyle of military families is not terribly conducive to making those college visits. Keep this in mind: It's never too soon to start visiting those schools and combining those visits with trips home to the extended family or other travel near the schools your child is considering. The years fly by and before you know it, the kids will be headed off to college, and you'll be left wondering where the time went.

Because the years can fly by, it's never too soon to start saving for a college education. Refer to Chapter 9 for more information on saving for college. Fortunately, military children have many scholarship opportunities available to them. Consult a scholarship finder to narrow down your choices. The different types of scholarships out there will amaze you. Scholarships can be as specific as available only to children of people who graduated from a service academy.

In addition to going to the Web to find scholarships, look in your local community. The spouse clubs, commissary, and officers/enlisted clubs all offer scholarships for military children. You just need to know they're out there.

Like everything else, although the scholarships and grants are available, they're just not going to come knocking on your door. You're going to have to go seeking them out. Get your kids involved. Make it part of the whole college application process. Get them started early, take notes of what programs they're eligible for, and mark down significant deadlines on a calendar so you don't miss anything.

Moving Around

One of the biggest challenges of being a military family is the constant moving. As soon as you begin to put down roots and get to know people, it's time to pull up stakes and move again. Imagine how potentially difficult this is for kids who may not always understand why they have to say good bye to their friends yet again. It never gets easier to leave your friends behind, but by checking out the tips we provide in the following sections, you can support your kids through these transitions so that their adjustments will occur faster and with greater ease.

Sometimes the fear of the unknown can make kids cling harder to what they're comfortable with. Not knowing what they can look forward to at the next installation makes it hard for them to say good bye to the familiar and their current friends. It's going to be a stressful time for your kids, so take that into account when they're acting a little more unreasonable or surly than usual.

Focusing on the positive

With all the nuisances attached to moving around, it's easy to lose sight of the fact that moving around also affords you some tremendous opportunities. Your children are going to get to visit the places that most other children will only be reading about in their textbooks. Other children will be admonished to be tolerant and culturally literate. Your kids will live it.

If you're fortunate enough to get stationed overseas, they'll get to visit countries and meet people that will serve to expand their horizons. With a few steps, you could help them maximize their experiences:

- ✔ Visit the DoD link created just for children in transition at `http://www.defenselink.mil/mtom`.

- ✔ Help them look up or point them to the Web to check out information on the new installation.

- ✔ Figure out what's worth seeing and make plans to go.

- ✔ Find out if your new installation offers the youth sponsorship program.

✔ If you're moving overseas, encourage your children to learn a second language. They might enjoy trying it out in real world situations.

✔ Remind them that these are opportunities being afforded to them that many other children will never experience.

When it is time to move, don't sneak out of town — make a big deal out of it by hosting a get together. Depending on the age of your kids, let the older ones have their friends over for a get together where they reminisce and lament with one another because one of the bunch is moving. For the younger kids, have a party and invite all their friends. Regardless of the age of your children, they need closure. Here are some ideas to help your children prepare to stay connected with their friends:

✔ Circulate an address book of sorts so that your kid's friends can provide their contact information.

✔ Have extra change of address cards made up so that they can hand them out to their friends if they feel like it.

✔ Take lots of pictures.

✔ Cut your kids a lot of slack. Transitions are never easy. For kids especially, leaving friends and the familiar is always difficult.

Joining in sports and recreational activities

One of the easiest ways to get kids out of their funk and out there meeting new people is to keep them involved. If your child is passionate about a sport or an activity like dance or music, then research the options at the new base or community. Make this part of the house hunting process. Just as you'll visit schools, visit the community centers and find out about the youth sports available.

The common interest of a sport or activity will help draw your kids out of their shells. It serves as another avenue for your kids to make new friends. Plus, it's great for them to have something to jump right into.

If you're moving from a warm place to a cooler one, you may find a whole slew of new sports for your kids to get into. Moving from Hawaii to Idaho, maybe they want to check into skiing and winter sports they may never have tried before. You know your kids best. If they get excited about sports, make the effort to find activities for them to take part in.

If you're coming in during the summertime, make an effort to find some summer camps your kids can take advantage of. If they like the traditional camps where they're canoeing and hiking and spending lots of time outdoors, go through the parks and recreation departments of your town. The youth centers on base will also have options. Whatever their interests are: writers' workshops, drama camps, or maybe a robotics camp, you can help them find something that works. If your child is into scouting, find a new troop for them to join.

Get the kids involved as soon as possible. Facilitate their involvement by doing some of the legwork for them. Consult community resources such as the installation Youth and Teen Center to find out what's out there. Making a concerted effort to get kids involved is particularly important if you move over the summer. It'll help for them to have some friends on that first day of school.

Making sure that your kid's best friend comes along

With all the turmoil associated with a PCS, the last thing you need is to be surprised by the pet quarantine requirements at your new overseas location. Imagine how upset your kids are going to be when they find out that they're going to be separated from their best friend for weeks to possibly months. Don't let this happen to you. If you have a family pet and have received orders to move overseas, start figuring out how to make the move smoother.

Most installations in locations where they have quarantine in effect have fact sheets or Web pages dedicated to the topics. For example, if you're moving to Misawa AFB in Japan, you can check out the following Web site for information: `www.misawajapan.com/pcs/petsin.htm`. Keep in mind that you're going to have to fill out forms and make arrangements both for shipping your pet overseas as well as kenneling them once they arrive in the country. This could potentially be a very time-consuming process, so crank this into your checklist of things to do when you receive your orders for that overseas tour.

It's undeniable that quarantine is highly inconvenient and stressful for families, but up until a few years ago, there was a mandatory six-month quarantine in place for pets arriving in the United Kingdom, which has since changed to a minimal quarantine period. Just a reminder that although a nuisance now, quarantine used to be a lot worse!

Staying in touch

When you're moving around so much, it's challenging enough bonding as a family. Expand the circle to include grandparents, aunts, uncles, and cousins and the notion of staying in touch can quickly become somewhat daunting. Do yourself the favor of acknowledging that you can't be everything to everyone. You'll be tempted to keep everyone happy. You'll be pulled like a wishbone to accommodate everyone's needs and desires to have you travel to visit them, but remember that travel works both ways. Your relatives can just as easily make the trip to come see you.

While it's important for you to stay connected to your extended family and make some of the milestone events if possible, it's even more important for you to balance that with the needs of your immediate family. Remember that you are your child's best advocate. Be selfish with their time and schedule. Take care of their needs first and accommodate others when and where you can.

In addition to your extended family, you should both make an effort to stay in touch with friends throughout your military career and encourage your children to do so as well. Chances are high that you will run into them again and if your kids are friends, those relationships serve as another support system for them. It's just as thrilling for your kids as it is for you to find out that they're going to be stationed at a new base with their old friend from a couple assignments ago.

Remember that April is Month of the Military Child. Web sites such as www. monthofthemilitarychild.com provide ideas for crafts and activities to celebrate with your kids. Our military kids don't have an entire month dedicated to them by accident. It's an acknowledgement that they serve too.

Chapter 13

Maintaining Strong Military Couples

*I*f you were one of the lucky ones who married with a full military wedding complete with dress uniforms, sabers, and the arch, you probably left the church with stars in your eyes. All the pomp and circumstance that surrounds a military wedding can be quite heady. The men are so handsome in their uniforms; they exude a presence that is larger than life. And going through the rituals of a military ceremony with the grand finale of leaving the church under an arch of sabers, you get a sense that you're getting a taste of something steeped in tradition. Then as you're just about to clear the arch and your exit is barred by a pair of crossed sabers and you feel someone playfully slap you on the rear with a saber before you're allowed to leave, you begin to realize that you've become part of the family, the tradition.

But, as with all fairy tales, there are ogres, dragons, and difficulties as you travel your road to happiness. Extended separations, an incredibly stressful job, and being on call 24 hours a day, 7 days a week, 365 days a year can wear down any relationship. Add to that the type of focused person who tends to gravitate to the military, and you run the risk of ending up in situations where one spouse has a hard time engaging in meaningful conversation. You begin to get the idea. A strong relationship in the military does not happen by accident, and in this chapter, we take you through some ideas that can help make your military marriage a great one . . . as long as you're willing to put in a little work!

Communicating Effectively

If you're not good at communicating with each other, you may as well roll up the carpet and call it a day — your marriage is headed down a long and bumpy road. Servicemembers' jobs are like none other. They stand a much greater chance of walking out the door one day to go to work and possibly never coming back. That's not meant to be a scare tactic, that's just the reality of the situation. Take the following sections to heart and put the ideas we provide to good use in your marriage to keep effective lines of communication open consistently. You'll not only end up enjoying each other's company much more, but you'll also enjoy an increased level of mutual respect and feel more prepared for anything that comes your way.

Dealing with your long-distance relationship

Even under the best of circumstances, extended absences and stressful work situations complicate communication. You as a reasonable human being will have reasonable expectations that your spouse will always want to be with you and at home. You will want to believe that every minute that he is apart from you thousands of miles away, he's miserable. Most of the time, that'll be true. But some of the time (actually, most of the time), you'll resent the fact that while you are dreading the deployment and the separation; he seems to be skipping out the door. You're not imagining it. That probably is a smile on his face. He has the nerve to be excited about leaving.

Don't take this personally. It's no reflection on you or your marriage. You married someone in the military, that rare person who generally loves what they do. Well, there's got to be a trade off. And that trade off is that in addition to love of country and patriotism, they genuinely love what they do and are miserable when they are sitting behind a desk and not doing what they love. So, love them enough to let them go and do what they do best. However, first be proactive and talk about issues that might come up. The time to talk is well in advance of a pending deployment or TDY. More about this in Chapter 16.

Now here's the trick. Communication doesn't just mean the words you speak out loud. Read the nonverbals. It is possible for him to love you, dread leaving you, and still anticipate the adventure ahead. Look for the non-verbal signs that communicate that he cares about you and worries about your well being while he's gone. If he's taking the cars in for maintenance right before he goes and checking all the various hoses, valves, and what-nots that could leak or break, he's doing it because he cares about your safety. Remember that communication extends beyond the spoken word. Sometimes it's the actions that speak volumes.

Career military members are not generally conflicted between leaving the family behind and doing their job (if they were, they would probably separate from the military). To them, it's not a choice. They're just really good at compartmentalizing their emotions and they need to be. Once they're out the door, they turn off the family compartment and concentrate on the mission. And trust me; you want them to be that way. Being able to take for granted that you will be perfectly fine on your own allows them to focus on the task at hand and contributes to their situational awareness. Don't resent the time that they're away from you. Just try to make the most of the time that you're together by doing the following:

- **Develop the friendship.** Remember it's just as important to like your spouse as it is to love him. Take the time to figure out the things that you enjoy doing together and develop some shared interests that you can do as a couple.

- **Approach military life as a partnership.** You're in it together and should approach things as a team. As with any other marriage, it's a give and take, but military marriages are unique in that there will be times when your service member's career will take the lead and require you to make the bulk of the sacrifices. If you aren't approaching this challenge hand in hand and managing expectations on both sides, then the road ahead will surely be a bumpy one.

- **Lavish praise, support, and encouragement.** Just because he comes across as a self-assured professional doesn't mean he doesn't have his moments of insecurity as well. He needs to know that you believe in him. Be each other's best cheerleaders. A side effect will be the positive example you set for your kids. If they see that you can be positive and supportive of one another even in the face of some tremendous challenges, they will develop a healthier ability to power through difficult times with grace under pressure.

- **Take time to talk to one another, and not just when you have a problem.** One of the biggest perks of being married is having that person to talk to who won't judge you. Your spouse is the ultimate "safe" person to talk to. You should be sharing your feelings, dreams, and concerns.

- **Agree to disagree.** Sometimes, you're not going to see eye to eye on an issue. Approach it reasonably; be respectful in listening to your spouse's side; and really hear what he's saying. At the end of it, you may still not be able to reach a consensus, but if you come to it with an open mind, you can continue the conversation and perhaps reach a compromise.

- **Touch base with one another through e-mails, phone calls, or notes to let your spouse know you're thinking of him.**

- **Be flexible and understand that some things are out of your spouse's hands.** He can't control everything and it's generally not his fault when he gets called in unexpectedly to work or is sent off on a no-notice TDY.

> ✔ **Continue to build the trust.** Building trust is very important to surviving the long separations. If you can't trust your partner, the absences will just exacerbate those seeds of distrust.

Like anything else worth having, a strong relationship is a lot of work to maintain, but don't just look at it as working toward a goal. Think of it as a journey and imagine all that you'll learn about one another along the way. Remember that you're both learning and growing every day, so there's always something new to talk about. Take the time to listen to one another and you'll have no problem communicating.

Managing expectations

The challenging part of a military career is that it doesn't really leave much room for the nonmilitary spouse to have much of a separate life, which is particularly true if you have children.

For many military couples, the expectation is that the nonmilitary spouse will be the one who makes the sacrifices. When the call is made and the military member has to deploy or go away on a TDY, not a second thought is paid to whatever responsibilities are left behind. You are left holding the proverbial bag. So, if you want some help, it's in your best interest to make sure you manage expectations on both sides. Figure out what you're each responsible for so that neither of you gets your feelings hurt nor is disappointed when something is overlooked or is forgotten.

Most military members do a great job at putting their affairs in order before they leave. Perhaps that means generating automatic bill pay, getting powers of attorneys, getting the cars serviced, replacing the broken faucet, or any of the other tasks that will help make your life a little easier while they're gone. But you share the responsibility of making sure things are done ahead of time. Otherwise, the responsibility will be *all* yours when they're gone.

Operate on the assumption that it's going to be very difficult for the service-member to take care of issues that might crop up during a TDY or deployment. Try to get things as organized as possible so that when you are alone for months on end and acting as the single parent, you won't have the additional stress of having to take on your spouse's responsibilities. If you don't do a good job of managing expectations, you could likely start resenting having to take on the extra responsibilities. Once you start down that slippery slope, it's hard to come back without making some changes in your life. More about coping with deployments in Chapter 16.

When you talk about managing expectations, an array of topics immediately spring to mind when it comes to decisions you should probably have to make at some point or another:

✔ Does your servicemember plan on staying in?

✔ Are you considering overseas assignments?

- If kids come along, is there an expectation that one parent will stay home? If so, for how long?

- How many kids?

- Where will you live once you retire?

- How will the finances be handled? Will there be a dedicated household account?

- Is there an expectation that you will visit parents on a regular basis? When? Who gets what holidays?

These examples are just a few of the decisions you may face, but you get the idea. These topics aren't any different from topics all married couples would address, but what sets you apart is that being married to a servicemember takes away some of the flexibility in the answers. All expectations have to stem from the basic premise that one of you will be out of the picture for big chunks of time. Additionally, regardless of what you collectively decide, the needs of the service will ultimately determine where you go. However, it'll be good to know that neither one of you is interested in going overseas in case that's an option that finds itself on the table one day. And the only way you would know that is by having the conversation.

Expectations are a funny thing. They shift constantly. If you don't loop in your spouse, you're setting him up for failure. He can't read your mind. Just thinking you told him about something isn't enough. Slow down and really talk things over. If you can both go through how things will impact your family and come up with a plan of action to mitigate the possible fallout, then you stand a better chance of getting what you want. And if you approach everything with a team mentality — that you're in it together — you stand a better chance of succeeding.

Respecting one another

Just as with any other successful marriage, you're going to have to respect each other as individuals with individual needs. You don't stop growing and learning when you get married, and it's important that your partner recognizes your need to have your own life. Just as you respect your military spouse's decision to serve in the military, he needs to respect your choices as well.

This list contains some of the major issues that can disrupt the level of respect in a marriage:

- ✔ **Finances:** The issue of finances comes laced with landmines and a number of opportunities for disagreement. However, just because you're worried about having uncomfortable and potentially contentious discussions doesn't mean you shouldn't talk about them. It's important that you both work off the same sheet of music. Be interested and ask for an explanation of what's coming in and what's going out. When your husband is deployed or TDY, chances are good that you'll have to handle the family finances, so it's a good idea to have the conversation well in advance. Prioritize where you want the money to go and discuss the big purchases. Important decisions should not be made in a vacuum and you should both respect one another enough to take into account each of your points when discussing.

- ✔ **Raising the children:** Child rearing is another area where mom and dad might have differing views on right and wrong. For so many reasons, it's important to present a united front. Respect your spouse enough to not naysay him in front of the kids. Because your spouse will be out of the house for extended periods of time, it's going to be challenging enough trying to keep him involved in your children's lives without encouraging insubordination.

  Each parent is going to come to the table with definite ideas about how the kids should be raised, but ultimately, you're both going to have to decide what's in the best interest of your child. Some questions to ask yourself and to discuss with your spouse include:

  - Public school or private?

  - What's a fair allowance?

  - What types of chores should kids be expected to do?

  - How should they spend their summer vacations?

  - What types of activities should they be allowed to participate in?

  - What type of religious education will the kids get?

  - How often are they supposed to see their grandparents?

- ✔ **Military spouse employment:** While the servicemember will recognize that it's great to have that second income to enhance the family's quality of life, it doesn't always make it easy to accept the fact that the dynamics of the family will change when both parents work. Who's going to stay home if one of the kids has to be picked up from school with a temperature? Who's going to sit at home and wait for the plumber because your toilet's leaking? I'll give you a hint — it's not going to be the servicemember. Or if it is, you need to know what the expectation is right off the bat. Unless you're both working off the same page, opportunities are rife for disagreements and disappointments.

Spouse employment is a tricky subject, and the adjective was carefully chosen. We all want to develop our own professional life, but if you are on a career track and married to a currently serving member, something's going to have to give. Faced with moving every two to three years, it is nearly impossible for spouses to maintain a career while their servicemember spouse is still serving. Someone's career is going to have to matter more, which leaves the other spouse making all the sacrifices. As the servicemember only has so much control about where he goes next, it's going to be up to you to find (or make) a portable career.

Often, the spouse has very few options and might start to resent the servicemember for putting her in that position. Keep in mind that this situation is not forever. Your time will come. Find ways to grow in your chosen career path while still supporting your servicemember. And keep talking openly about your expectations. Temper these discussions with the reality of military service and what you can and can't control.

Spouse employment is a very contentious topic that hits close to home for many people. This desire to have something of your own is one reason that DoD is so focused on this issue. We all understand that quality of life issues such as spouse employment, transferability of credentials, and licensure impact the issues of recruiting and retention, decisions that are made around the kitchen table.

If you keep the lines of communication open and constantly running, you can both enjoy each other's respect. To enjoy mutual respect, try out these ideas:

- **Once you establish the ground rules, stick to them.** If you need to change something that has already been decided, bring it back to the table. Don't deviate from the plan without looping in your partner.

- **Don't let things spiral out of control — consult one another.** Although you may have to compromise while your servicemember is still in, your time will come. It is possible to have it all, just not all at once.

- **Continue to learn and grow throughout your life together.** If your spouse can't support and respect you, that's going to cause problems. So develop good rituals that allow you to visit on a regular basis so that nothing comes as a surprise. Your spouse won't receive a nasty surprise when you want to go back to school, if you've kept him in the loop the entire time. Allow him the opportunity to be your best advocate.

Unplugging

We're all very good at the daily grind, but we get so intent on checking the squares that we often forget to stop and smell the roses. Unfortunately, we're all good at putting ourselves last. Life sometimes gets in the way of our best intentions of working toward our own goals and interests. It's entirely too easy to be consumed by your life in the military to the extent that your identity becomes wrapped up in the unit or the service. Find ways to balance that with other interests or activities that will help you develop some clarity and keep things in perspective. Along these same lines, it's helpful to cultivate friendships outside of the circle of the military. Think of your church, school, or clubs. Having civilian friends opens the circle of support you have available to you.

The unfortunate thing about the military lifestyle is that you essentially live in a fish bowl. That's especially true if you live on base. There's a general feeling that you're constantly being scrutinized, that you're always "on." Feeling as if you're living under a microscope can start to wear on a person. The stress of trying to maintain a strong and united front doesn't always leave you a lot of time to take care of yourself. The stress can also start to wear on your relationship if you don't take the time to regroup every once in a while.

To maintain your equilibrium, you need to unplug from time to time and get reacquainted with one another away from the hustle and bustle of the base and the demands of the job. Here are some ideas:

- ✔ **Try to inject some romance into the equation by making the effort to set up a date night (without the kids) for just the two of you.**

- ✔ **Go out with other couples or stay in and have a game night with a babysitter on site for the kids.** It's important to hang out and make friends as a couple.

- ✔ **If your servicemember is working ridiculously long hours, see if you can set up a lunch date.** Bring him lunch or meet him on base somewhere. Find time where you can steal a half hour or so in the middle of the day.

- ✔ **Find a hobby you both enjoy and can do together.** This hobby can be anything ranging from running together to entertaining. It's great to have common interests to talk about outside of your military life.

- ✔ **Volunteer together as a family.** Doing something for others together will help instill in your children the importance of being involved and spending time together on philanthropic pursuits helps you develop other common interests.

Accessing Help to Make Your Marriage Healthier

Sometimes talking it out isn't enough. The stress can start to get to you and you might need a little extra help. Needing help is no reason to be ashamed. In today's world with the crazy op tempo, we're all working hard to hold it together. But, if you feel like things are getting a little out of control, fortunately, you can go to many places to get help.

If you're comfortable speaking to your chaplain, the base chapel should be the first place you start. Most base chapels offer pre-marriage and marriage counseling. The programs help you develop good, solid tools in approaching problem solving and will enhance your communication skills. There is no shame in being pre-emptive and searching out education and additional resources to nurture your relationship.

In addition to faith-based initiatives, the different services also make marriage enrichment programs such as retreats available to troops and their families. Consult the chapel and the base Family Support Center to learn more about the resources available to you.

If you're not comfortable going to the chapel, you can call Military OneSource directly for referrals and additional assistance. Along these same veins, if you work outside the home, your employer may have an Employee Assistance Program (EAP) that provides access to confidential counseling sessions free of charge. Find help where you can and make an investment in your marriage.

If your problems stem from abuse, contact Family Advocacy immediately. They can provide the assistance you'll need to remove yourself from the situation in a safe manner. They also have preventative classes in topics such as: anger management, conflict resolution, and parenting. See Chapter 17 for more information on Family Advocacy programs.

Divorcing

Sometimes, try as you may, things just don't work out. Whether it's because you've grown apart or the stress of the lifestyle is just too much, you're not alone in not being able to work through it. It's going to be hard to sever your ties to the military, but at some point, you're going to have to start looking out for your own best interests.

As a military spouse, you are used to having to take care of yourself and not asking for help, but this is one thing you shouldn't try to handle on your own. You'll need the following help:

- **Get yourself a civilian lawyer who is knowledgeable in the area of military law and divorce.** With any military divorce, it is important to retain the services of an attorney who understands the Uniformed Services Former Spouse Protection Act (USFSPA). USFSPA allows the courts to treat military retirement pay as they would any other marital asset or property. It also grants the Defense & Finance Accounting Service (DFAS) the authority to make direct payments to the former spouse under certain conditions.

    Do not sign anything without first having your attorney check it out.

- **Educate yourself on military law and policy.** An attorney is helpful, but be your own best advocate. Don't let someone else decide what is best for you.

    Depending on how long you've been married and how long your servicemember spouse has been in the military, you may be entitled to keep some of your military benefits. The general rule of thumb that you hear bandied about is 20-20-20. For those married at least 20 years to a servicemember who has served at least 20 years and for whom there is an overlap of at least 20 years of marriage with 20 years of service, they get to keep their military ID card and are eligible for all benefits (except Space-A) unless they remarry before the age of 55.

    For those who meet the 20-20-15 rule, they get to keep only their medical benefits for one year after the divorce at which point they become eligible for the Continued Health Care Benefit Program (CHCBP) which they must pay for.

    Regardless of what you think you're entitled to under USFSPA, it is ultimately the decision of the state court that decides the division of property. Some states are more military friendly than others. In all cases, stack the deck in your favor by getting yourself an attorney who is well versed in divorce and military law.

- **Get counseling.** Divorce is not an easy process. Depression and anxiety will likely come along with the territory. Seek professional help. Getting counseling and/or other help will give you the objectivity and calm that you need to make rational decisions for yourself and your children.

- **Keep your children's teachers and administrators up to date.** Chances are good that the divorce will also be tough on your kids. They're going to feel conflicted, their loyalties torn between two parents. Get their teachers and administrators looped in to what's going on. And if you notice any red flags, get your kids the help they need.

In addition to getting the help you need to get through your military divorce, you also need to keep in mind the following:

- ✔ **Remove your rose-colored glasses.** Your instinct will be to trust your ex, but remember, he will protect himself first and foremost, and you need to do the same.

- ✔ **Think long term.** While you're going through the process of divorce, it can be taxing just trying to get through each minute, but you need to look past it and see the big picture. In addressing the issue of property settlement, think about what you will need to take care of yourself and your children. Take into account what you're going to need to get the kids through college, think about what your earning potential is, think about sudden medical emergencies.

- ✔ **Be honest with yourself.** No matter how much you might want it, no one can tell you what to do; not even your attorney. When it's all said and done, you have to be able to look at yourself in the mirror and know that you did the right thing.

Remember that the Survivor Benefit Plan (SBP) deemed election is in play as well. If you're already the beneficiary, you have only one year from the divorce to contact DFAS to change the election from spouse to former spouse. If you don't do this, you miss out.

Military divorce brings with it some other challenges — all of which are individualized to each situation. In some cases if there are children involved, your children will retain their military ID cards (if you share custody), and it could be difficult for you to access your children's benefits if you no longer have a military ID card. You should keep all of these things in mind when going through the property settlement.

Chapter 14

Tapping into Community Support

. . . .

. . . .

*W*hile you can find a wealth of programs and support services on the installation (see Chapter 3), you may be surprised to find the array of programs offered off the installation as well. You can take advantage of a vast number of organizations and nonprofits outside the official channels that are looking to provide support to military members and their families. Whether you're talking about programs being offered by state or federal governments, non-profits, or grassroots initiatives, half the challenge is in figuring out what type of support is available to you and your family. Although finding these organizations requires a little more work on your end, with the info we provide you in this chapter, your workload just got a little lighter.

Starting at Square One

This section could also be called: *not overlooking the obvious.* The resources that exist to support servicemembers and their families are great, but don't narrow your options right off the bat. Start where everyone else does — at square one.

Regardless of what you're looking for, don't limit yourself to the services and resources that are available on the installation or to those services specific to the military. Looking around at more traditional resources available to everyone, you might find better programs to suit your needs. The Internet opens up your world and leaves you with little excuse as to why you can't find the type of support you need. But if you discount traditional research and focus solely on military resources, you could miss out on some helpful sources. Here are some examples:

✔ **Business:** If you're interested in starting a business of your own, take a look at the Small Business Administration (SBA). The SBA is currently running a special program called the Patriot Express Pilot Loan Initiative geared directly to eligible military members, veterans, and their spouses who want to start or expand an existing business.

For more information on this program, check out the information at: http://www.sba.gov/patriotexpress/.

✔ **Education:** If your main focus is the quality of your children's education, start by understanding the resources available to you through the school, the county, and the district. You'd be amazed by the number of programs available to supplement the education they get during the regular school year. Many districts offer summer school not just for students who require extra assistance, but also for other students who are looking to get a head start on the school year by taking a class over the summer. While not free of charge, these programs are a good way to help your kids meet other children over the summer if you happen to PCS to a new area outside of the regular school year.

Before moving to a new state, try to familiarize yourself with the educational climate. Figure out if there are considerations such as in-state tuition benefits for military dependents and any other programs to support your family.

✔ **Home:** If you're looking to buy a home in your new location, don't discount affinity programs with real estate companies that might garner you a discount on your realtor's commissions. And definitely don't overlook the Department of Veterans Affairs when looking for your loan. Information about the VA home loan program can be found at: http://www.homeloans.va.gov/. More about financing a home in Chapter 10.

Getting Support for the Guard and Reserve

Because Guard and Reserve members and family are not always on active duty, there is more of a challenge in providing support to Guard and Reserve families when they are activated. Unlike their active-duty counterparts, they are generally not used to self-identifying as members of the active-duty force and may not necessarily understand the benefits available to themselves or their dependents. There's a very good readiness guide that gives a broad overview: http://www.defenselink.mil/ra/documents/BenefitsGuide0929.pdf.

One of the great things about our Guard and Reserve families is that they are very adept at finding community resources. Since they are tied to the states until federally activated, their moves are not generally predicated by their military service. It is more the norm rather than the exception that they are not located near a military installation. Thus, their thoughts do not necessarily go right to the installation for family support. With the advent of the war, we are using our Guard and Reserve components of our military services as we have never before in history, and it's starting to show in the wear and tear on the families and the employers. Therefore, the services, the Department of Defense, and other interested parties have made a conscientious effort over the past five years to beef up family readiness for the Guard and Reserve. Check out www.guardfamily.org for information on resources available to you state by state as well as an overview of your military benefits.

The biggest issue facing Guard and Reserve members with the current deployment tempo is ensuring that their jobs are still there when they return. The Uniformed Services Employment and Reemployment Rights Act (USERRA) is the biggest source of employment support for activated Guard and Reserve members (find out more about USERRA in Chapter 16).

When issues arise between Guard and Reserve members and their employers and the parties involved are unable to reach a mutually acceptable solution, the servicemember should turn to the Employer Support of the Guard and Reserve (ESGR). ESGR is a group within the Department of Defense that exists to promote understanding and cooperation between guard and reserve members and their civilian employers. They assist in resolving conflicts that arise between servicemembers and their employers during periods of activation and can be found at www.esgr.org.

Finding Support at the State Level

Outside of the federal military benefits you and your family are entitled to, don't forget to check out the benefits available to you at the state level. This is particularly relevant to the Guard and Reserve population. Each state provides widely disparate benefits to all military servicemembers and veterans, such as:

✔ Some do not have a state income tax.

   However, remember that military dependents have to pay income tax for the state in which they reside and work.

✔ Some allow you to not have to renew your driver's license while the servicemember is actively serving in the military. (Check on your state's DMV Web site to understand the rules that govern their regulations for military personnel and dependents.)

However, military personnel who come into the military as residents of one state and want to transfer their residency to another need to consult their installation legal office. Generally speaking, you have to physically reside in a state before you're able to claim residency. However, in most cases, if you intend to return to the state after leaving the military, you can maintain your residency even after you have PCSed. This usually only applies to the servicemember.

✔ Even the benefits afforded to military dependents vary greatly:

- Depending on what state you reside in, you may be eligible for different benefits. A majority of states grant in-state tuition rates to the dependents of military personnel stationed within the state. Of these, most of them allow for the continuation of these in-state tuition rates even after the servicemember has PCSed to their next duty assignment.

- Another benefit offered by states to support military families is the unemployment benefit. Depending on which state you are PCSing to, you may be eligible for unemployment benefits.

✔ With the advent of the DoD State Liaison office, the Department of Defense has gotten much more adept at working with states to remove the impediments to a better quality of life for military families. They have identified ten key issues and have been working diligently to address them with each of the 50 states. The issues are:

- Care and support of the Guard and Reserve

- Assistance to severely injured servicemembers

- In-state tuition

- Military children during school transitions and deployments

- Spouse employment

- Unemployment compensation

- Predatory lending

- Voting

- Foreign language requirements

- Accessible support for military families

They have made remarkable progress in getting states to come on board with in-state tuition. Now they're pushing the military children, during school transitions and deployments, by trying to get states to come on line and sign an interstate compact that would make it easier for children to transfer schools from one state to another by standardizing requirements. The issues they work are significant to all of us, and you can check on what your state is doing to support these initiatives by referencing the DoD State Liaison Web site at www.usa4militaryfamilies.dod.mil.

There are several maps throughout the Web site that show where each state stands in supporting the proposed initiatives. You'd be surprised by how quickly the state liaisons work, so check back often for updates and news on how things are going. There is also information on the site on how to get involved in case any of these issues resonate with you and move you to take action. More about the DoD State Liaison office in Chapter 11.

Supporting Military Families

When you talk about organizations that have historically supported military families, few organizations stand out from the pack. The USO and the Fisher House Organization are two examples of organizations that are steadfast in their support of the troops. However, with the advent of the war, many more people and organizations have heeded the call to serve and have done some tremendous work. In the sections that follow, we focus on the two with a great historical record of support: the USO and Fisher House.

The United Service Organizations (USO)

Since before the United States entered World War II, the United Service Organizations (USO) has been providing support to our servicemembers and their families. Although their mission may have expanded, the USO primarily still serves to link the American public with troops stationed overseas and to bring a taste of home to the troops. The USO is probably best known for their service of bringing celebrity entertainers to the troops out in the field. Everyone from singers, comedians, and athletes has participated in USO tours to visit the troops. This practice goes back decades to World War II when the Bob Hope Christmas shows became a USO tradition for over three decades.

Nowadays, the USO has expanded its mission to support the troops through a myriad of other programs to include: United through Reading, Operation USO Care Package, Operation Enduring Care, Gifts from the Homefront, and many other programs. You can learn more about all these programs and more by visiting the USO Web site at www.uso.org. Regionally, the different USOs also participate in other programs to support military families. As an example, in the metropolitan D.C. area, the USO has partnered to sponsor a Military Spouse Career Expo. Take the time to check into your local USO and find out more about the programs and services they offer in support of military families.

Fisher House Foundation

Another organization that stands out among all the others is the Fisher House Foundation. The Fisher Houses were founded by Zachary and Elizabeth Fisher as a "home away from home" for families who are visiting their wounded servicemembers at military treatment facilities. There are dozens of Fisher Houses around the country and overseas (in Landstuhl, Germany) where family members can stay at absolutely no cost. Information from the Fisher House Web site (www.fisherhouse.org) tells us that, since their inception, the Fisher Houses have served more than 110,000 families, provided over 2 million lodging days, and saved families more than $90 million in lodging costs, plus savings on subsistence and transportation costs.

And the houses are just the start. Among many other programs, the Fisher House Foundation also runs a Heroes Mile program. Through this initiative, the foundation has partnered with numerous airlines to allow people to donate their frequent-flier miles for use by wounded servicemembers or their families who may want to fly to their bedside. So far, they have provided over 13,000 airplane tickets.

Although Zachary Fisher was unable to serve in the armed forces because of a leg injury, he still found an admirable way to serve his country and support the servicemembers and their families whom he respected so well.

Growing Grassroots Military Support

The media reports that the military is at war while America is at the mall. That may be true to some degree, but all around the nation, schoolchildren, grandmothers, and other regular citizens are seeking to help by doing what they can and contributing their talents to support the troops in meaningful ways that defy this ideology. It seems that anywhere people see a need, homegrown groups are rising to the challenge, looking to fill a niche and provide a service.

Checking out grassroots efforts

After discovering a need, various types of resources and organizations have been founded to support the military, and the following list provides you with a sample of what they offer:

✔ Those looking to support military children have founded organizations that allow the children to apply for "grants" that go toward paying for homework assistance or fees for extracurricular activities. Also a number of groups have stood up to provide scholarships for military children as well as free camps to children of deployed servicemembers. Other camps are geared toward the children of wounded warriors. Even more programs such as Snowball Express (`www.snowballexpress.org`) allow children who have lost a parent in the line of duty to forget their cares for a weekend and just be kids. Understanding that there is no greater therapy than being amongst their peers, all these camps share the common goal of letting kids bond with other children who are facing the same situation.

✔ Stories of families being stuck at military medical facilities for months on end at their servicemember's bedside because they either don't have private vehicles or the money to wander off the facility prompted other groups to act on their behalf. Some organizations started collecting gas and phone cards as well as restaurant coupons for the family members and caregivers of the wounded.

✔ Stories of wounded warriors laying in hospital beds without appropriate clothing because their prosthetics wouldn't allow them to wear the clothing issued to them prompted even others to start sewing adaptive clothing. Many people remembering the way soldiers were treated when they returned from Vietnam wanted to make sure that today's soldiers understand that they are coming home to a grateful nation. The desire to provide these wounded warriors with a tangible token of their gratitude prompted thousands of quilters to begin a movement to sew handmade quilts for servicemembers.

✔ The families of servicemembers deployed overseas often fall prey to Murphy's Law. If it can go wrong, it will go wrong and usually when your husband is TDY or deployed and always all at once. Several organizations have sprung up to provide emergency funds for families of deployed servicemembers. These organizations generally pick up where the service aid societies leave off.

✔ Once the warriors are out of the hospital and the military, there are even more organizations standing ready to provide help with life rehabilitation and employment assistance.

Definitely look outside the box for your resources and support, but don't forget the more traditional forms of support as well. The service aid societies exist to provide emergency aid to servicemembers and their families, so don't overlook them.

Getting to know America Supports You

Since the advent of the war, the number of charitable organizations that have stood up have exceeded anybody's wildest expectations. Some of the frustration stems from the fact that many of these organizations overlap one another in terms of the support and resources they seek to provide. It can be frustrating trying to find what you need. Fortunately, America Supports You gives you a good starting point.

America Supports You is the brainchild of Allison Barber, Deputy Assistant Secretary of Defense for internal communication and public liaison and military spouse. Recognizing that communities, individuals, and corporations were looking for ways to support military members, Ms. Barber established America Supports You in 2004 as a means of matching needs with resources. The Web site can be found at www.americasupportsyou.mil. When you visit, you will find hundreds of groups interested in providing support to servicemembers and their families. Servicemembers and their families who are seeking help or assistance can then go to the Web site and search under the different categories for programs that may match their needs.

In the event that you're looking for a good cause to donate to, many of these organizations accept donations through the Combined Federal Campaign.

The organizations and programs are listed under categories that include:

- ✔ Receive computer donation
- ✔ Get frequent-flier miles
- ✔ Receive gift certificates
- ✔ Get help for the wounded
- ✔ Get help so you can help others
- ✔ Learn about entertainment for the troops
- ✔ Learn about homes for disabled troops
- ✔ Receive letters and messages
- ✔ Receive military family support
- ✔ Scholarships
- ✔ Receive and send packages
- ✔ Service aid societies
- ✔ Training and placement for veterans
- ✔ Tragedy assistance

The Web site also serves as a great opportunity for anyone to get involved. Individuals wanting to support the troops or just help out can read about the different organizations in their area and reach out to those that appeal to them if they have time or donations to offer.

Every year, America Supports You also sponsors Freedom Walks across the country. This tradition was born out of a desire to honor the victims of 9/11. In communities around the nation, individuals join together to walk and pay tribute.

Searching the Web for Support

Regardless of whether you choose to use the more traditional forms of family support or tap into the newer technologies, the advent of the Internet ensures that military spouses don't have to feel like they're alone in their situations anymore. In the next sections, we describe two ways you can find online support with military spouses who are either in or have been in the same situation as you.

Connecting through online communities

It seems like since 9/11, any number of online communities have popped up. Spouse community Web sites such as www.spousebuzz.com, www.milspouse.com, and www.cinchouse.com have really picked up with the ops tempo. These communities are generally moderated by more experienced bloggers and posters, but outside of that they're a free for all. By logging into these forums, spouses are able to post questions and ask for advice from other spouses and "experts" who have gone through or are going through the same experiences.

It's great to get advice on handling deployments with the kids or what to do when you haven't heard from your spouse in a while. Social networking through these venues can fulfill your need for that connection with other adults while sharing information.

You should be cautious about posting on these sites and always be conscientious of operational security. Do not post information that you would not want your mom or employer to read. And most definitely resist sharing any information about troop movement or other details pertaining to the deployment.

Faced with having to take one more of the household duties and responsibilities during a deployment, people with questions about their benefits have started using these forums to bounce things off of other people. Think of thousands of your friends and acquaintances available for you at all hours of the day. Regardless of what you throw out there, chances are someone's gone through it and is ready to offer some advice. A lot of family members are turning to these forums as a means of venting and support.

The disadvantage of utilizing these forums to cull information is that they are not generally monitored by experts on military pay and benefits, so you have no way of knowing if the information being given is 100 percent accurate. Think of this as a starting point, and make sure you always verify the information you receive through official channels.

Burning up the airwaves

In addition to online spouse forums, there are a number of military spouses who have taken to the airwaves to share their stories and experiences. Some such as www.militaryspouseradio.com are centered around work and career topics while others such as www.armywifetalkradio.com and http://navywiferadio.wordpress.com/ take on more of the lifestyle issues. The shows regularly highlight military spouses and what they're doing in their little corner of the world as well as subject matter experts on issues of interest to military spouses and families. The shows are a great way to feel connected to the military spouse community through the airwaves and to stay abreast of new programs that may be of interest to you. It's a relatively new phenomenon for family members to have information that speaks directly to them presented in this format.

The shows come and go quite rapidly, but there are always others coming up behind them to fill the void. As always, Internet search engines will help you keep up to date with the newest offerings out there.

Tapping into The Military Coalition (TMC)

All around you, you'll find organizations working on your behalf. Getting involved and finding support is easy enough if you know where to look. The Military Coalition (TMC) is a great place to start.

While the currently serving demographic generally steers clear of all things legislation, perceiving a conflict of interest with military service, it is absolutely alright to join a military association. They are "your" professional association and look out for your best interests on Capitol Hill.

In the sections that follow, we introduce you to TMC, its organizations, and what it can offer you.

Discovering what TMC is all about

The Military Coalition (TMC) is an umbrella organization for a group of 35 military, veterans, and uniformed services organizations that includes (in alphabetical order):

Air Force Association (AFA)

Air Force Sergeants Association (AFSA)

Air Force Women Officers Associated (AFWOA)

American Logistics Association (ALA)

AMVETS (American Veterans)

Army Aviation Association of America (AAAA)

Association of Military Surgeons of the United States (AMSUS)

Association of the United States Army (AUSA)

Chief Warrant Officer and Warrant Officer Association of the United States Coast Guard, (CWO&WOA)

Commissioned Officers Association (COA) of the United States Public Health Service, Inc.

Enlisted Association of the National Guard of the United States (EANGUS)

Fleet Reserve Association (FRA)

Gold Star Wives of America (GSW)

Jewish War Veterans of the United States of America (JWV)

Marine Corps League (MCL)

Marine Corps Reserve Association (MCRA)

Military Chaplains Association of the United States of America (MCA)

Military Officers Association of America (MOAA)

Military Order of the Purple Heart (MOPH)

National Association for Uniformed Services (NAUS)

National Guard Association of the United States (NGAUS)

National Military Family Association (NMFA)

National Order of Battlefield Commissions (NOBC)

Naval Enlisted Reserve Association (NERA)

Naval Reserve Association (NRA)

Navy League of the United States (NLUS)

Non Commissioned Officers Association (NCOA)

Reserve Enlisted Association (REA)

Reserve Officers Association (ROA)

The Retired Enlisted Association (TREA)

Society of Medical Consultants to the Armed Forces (SMCAF)

United States Army Warrant Officers Association (USAWOA)

USCG Chief Petty Officers Association (CPOA)

Veterans of Foreign Wars (VFW)

Veterans' Widows International Network (VWIN)

The goals of the Military Coalition are to:

- ✔ Maintain a strong national defense by recruiting and retaining skilled and highly capable personnel in the seven uniformed services

- ✔ Maintain fair and adequate compensation and benefits in order to attract and retain professional uniformed servicemembers for careers of service to the nation

- ✔ Represent the interests of the entire uniformed services community, including families and survivors

- ✔ Respond to assaults upon the compensation and benefits earned by members of that community through years of service

- ✔ Educate the public on the extraordinary demands and sacrifices associated with a career in uniformed service and the need to maintain a system of compensation and benefits to recruit and retain the high-quality personnel needed to meet the nation's defense requirements

Figuring out how you fit in

Even though they commonly work together under the umbrella of The Military Coalition, the organizations do not always fall on the same side of every issue. They all act autonomously, and not all the organizations have the same platforms. Find one that resonates with you. Organizations such as the Air Force Association (AFA) and the Association of the United States Army (AUSA) focus more on hardware, while organizations such as the Military Officers Association of America (MOAA) and the National Military Family Association (NMFA) focus strictly on the softer personnel issues.

Making the case on Capitol Hill

While the TMC organizations maintain their own membership rolls, together under the umbrella of the Military Coalition, they represent over 5.5 military members and their families. This equates to quite a punch on Capitol Hill. Thus, the TMC has been instrumental in a number of legislative wins for military and military families to include:

- ✔ TriCare for Life healthcare benefits

- ✔ Increased Servicemen's Group Life Insurance (SGLI) benefits

- ✔ Increased Montgomery GI Bill education benefits

- ✔ Pay raises for the currently serving exceeding those proposed by the administration

- ✔ Improved PCS reimbursement rates

- ✔ Phased out SBP/SS offset (Widow's tax)

- ✔ Won major restrictions on predatory lenders

When added to the 5.5 million other voices, your voice does matter. Regardless of whether or not you choose to be actively engaged, you are providing a proxy for the associations to work on your behalf. It's hard to argue with testimony from an organization that represents so many people.

In addition to their advocacy, a number of the organizations are full-service associations. So when you're looking for an association to represent your best interests, don't discount the other benefits and services that these associations offer. Some are more robust in their offerings than others, but here is a sampling of what they can provide for you:

- ✔ Offer scholarships to military dependents
- ✔ Sponsor award programs
- ✔ Hold national conventions

In addition to general offerings, check out the details of what these two organizations can provide:

- ✔ **The National Military Family Association (NMFA),** originally begun by a group of military spouses, provides free summer camps for children of deployed servicemembers (Operation Purple Camp) as well as scholarships for military spouses (www.nmfa.org). It has a regular legislative newsletter that goes out and regularly testifies on Capitol Hill on quality of life issues for military families.

- ✔ **The Military Officers Association of America (MOAA)** is the largest association of military officers and their surviving spouses with nearly 370,000 members. MOAA is also a co-chair of the TMC. They have an award-winning Web site and monthly magazine. They gave out over $8 million worth of interest-free loans and grants to military children in 2008 alone. Their Officer Placement Service runs at least two career fairs a year and provides members and their spouses with career counseling, a jobs database, and network contacts to help with their job search. They also hold several signature events each year that allow them to bring in subject matter experts to discuss topics of interest to military members and their families. They maintain a suite of publications addressing every stage of a military career and life as well as many other products and services for their members. Check them out at www.moaa.org.

Outside of The Military Coalition, there are other associations who are working on behalf of military families. An example of this is the Military Spouse and Family Legacy Association. Started by two friends, this is a young organization working to have a monument built in Washington, D.C., recognizing the contributions and sacrifices of our military spouses and families. The idea that they came up with during a cross-country trip quickly evolved — within months — into legislation with the help of Representative Thelma Drake (VA). See more at www.militaryspousemonument.org.

Chapter 15

Dealing with the Disability or Death of a Family Member

Coping with the loss of a loved one or adjusting to life after disability will take a toll on even the strongest people. The death of a spouse is considered the most traumatic life event people encounter. Severe disability, both physical and mental, can at times be more challenging for a military family than the loss of their servicemember. Due to the nature of service in the Armed Forces, premature death and disability are all too common for military families.

In this chapter we discuss the many support services provided families and surviving spouses.

Dealing with Disability

Disability is often viewed as the inability to see, hear, speak, or walk, and so on. The medical profession has made great strides in helping people to adapt as best as possible to loss of sight, hearing, speech, and mobility. That's not to say that these disabilities are any less challenging to you or your servicemember; however, medical treatments and technological advances can reduce some of the burden faced by veterans with physical disabilities. And our society at large is more accepting of individuals with visible disabilities, as opposed to those disabilities not easily recognizable, such as traumatic brain injuries and with individuals challenged with other mental disabilities, such as post-traumatic stress disorder (PTSD).

Traumatic brain injuries

A traumatic brain injury can have lingering effects. These impairments may affect communication, hearing, sensory perception, and motor functions, along with subjective symptoms that adversely affect your servicemember's quality of life.

The Veterans Administration proposed changes in early 2008 as the number of cases of traumatic brain injury in veterans increased. The reason for this increase in traumatic brain injuries is due largely in part to the types of weapons used in combat today.

You might presume that a brain injury is something visible. However, many traumatic brain injuries received by servicemembers of the Iraq and Afghanistan wars are severe, but invisible. Some traumatic brain injuries are hard to detect and go undiagnosed for months, if not years. Due to this fact, your servicemember or veteran may not be receiving the medical care and treatment that he needs.

If in doubt — check it out! Start with your local medical treatment facility.

Post-traumatic stress disorder (PTSD)

PTSD is an anxiety disorder affecting thousands of combat veterans. If your servicemember is experiencing persistent frightening memories, has trouble sleeping, startles easily, or feels emotionally numb, especially towards those he is close to — like you — he may have post-traumatic stress disorder.

Other symptoms of post-traumatic stress disorder include increased:

- ✔ Irritability
- ✔ Aggressiveness
- ✔ Violence
- ✔ Inability to be intimate
- ✔ Avoidance of situations and anniversaries that remind them of the incident

Here are some things you may notice about your servicemember:

- ✔ You may be experiencing events when your servicemember loses touch with reality and believes that the traumatic incident is happening all over again.
- ✔ Your servicemember may lose interest in things he used to enjoy.
- ✔ Families of servicemembers that are affected by PTSD say their veterans seem like *different people.*

Most combat veterans don't develop full-blown or even minor PTSD. However, you should be aware of the symptoms and recognize that symptoms usually begin within weeks of the traumatic event, but they can also take years to emerge. Servicemembers may experience symptoms lasting a few weeks, or their illness may be chronic.

Effective treatments for post-traumatic stress disorder are available. Medication and psychotherapy are usually prescribed to treat the symptoms and are very effective. Improving therapies are helping most people with PTSD lead fulfilling lives.

The Department of Veterans Affairs provides free counseling sessions, as well as inpatient and outpatient care, to servicemembers with PTSD. For more information, visit http://www.ncptsd.va.gov. The VA website is a great resource to help you better understand PTSD, find a health care provider and learn more about the benefits available to your family.

Medical review boards

If your servicemember has a medical condition, including mental health conditions, which makes him unable to perform his required duties, he may be *separated* from the military for medical reasons. However, before he is separated from service his Medical Treatment Facility (MTF) must refer him for review by the Medical Evaluation Board (MEB). The MEB is comprised of high-ranking military physicians. The MEB examines medical records and determines whether or not the medical condition will render your servicemember unable to perform his military duties. The MEB also refers the case to a Physical Evaluation Board (PEB) for a determination of *fitness-for-duty*.

The review boards can recommend:

- Return to duty
  - With no assignment limitations
  - With assignment limitations
  - With medically required re-training
- Placement on military disability or retirement
- Separation from active duty
- Medical retirement

The recommendations of the MEB and PEB are then reviewed by a central medical board. If you and your servicemember feel the recommendations are inappropriate, your servicemember can appeal at a formal hearing and may have legal counsel assist them in their appeal.

For legal assistance regarding an appeal, contact your legal assistance office.

Medical retirement

Permanent disability retirement occurs if your servicemember is deemed medically unfit to perform his job. If the disability is determined stable, permanent, and rated at a minimum of 30 percent, your servicemember is eligible for permanent disability retirement benefits.

If your servicemember is declared *unfit* to perform the required duties of his job due to a medical condition, the Physical Evaluation Board (PEB) assigns a disability rating in accordance with the VA's schedule for rating disabilities. Although the Department of Defense and the Department of Veterans Affairs both use the VA's schedule for rating disabilities, all of the general policy provisions do not apply to the military.

The military rates only medical conditions determined to be physically unfitting and compensate for the loss of a military career. The military's rating is permanent upon separation from service. Benefits are calculated based on years of service and basic pay.

The VA ratings, on the other hand, may fluctuate over time, depending on the level of disability. The VA may rate any disability which occurred or was aggravated by service and compensate your servicemember for loss of potential civilian earnings. The VA compensation is a flat amount based upon the percentage rating assigned.

Your servicemember may qualify for temporary disability retirement benefits if his condition is considered *not stable* for rating purposes. In other words, the extent of disability may change over the next five years. In this case, your servicemember may be separated from service and receive temporary disability retirement benefits. Your veteran must undergo periodic medical reexaminations at least every 18 months and receive PEB reevaluations.

Servicemembers on permanent or temporary disability retirement receive the higher of the following two retirement pay computations:

> disability rating × retired pay base
>
> or
>
> 2.5 × years of service × retired pay base

Temporary disability retirement benefits shall not be less than 50 percent of your servicemember's retired pay base.

Veterans Administration benefits

If disabled while on active duty, your servicemember may be entitled to VA disability compensation if he is at least 10 percent disabled as a result of his military service. The VA also provides vocational rehabilitation to recipients of VA disability compensation to assist eligible veterans in obtaining lasting, suitable employment.

If your servicemember is permanently and totally disabled, or age 65 or older, and your family income is very limited, you may also qualify for a VA disability pension.

For a great reference on all issues related to veteran's benefits, check out *Veteran's Benefits For Dummies*. Also, visit the VA Web site at http://www.vba.va.gov/bln/21/index.htm.

Other disability resources

In addition to the resources listed earlier in this section, if you want to increase your understanding and awareness of living with disability, the adjustments to expect, and the support services available, check out the following resources:

- ✔ **General**
  - http://militaryonesource.com: Military OneSource offers a variety of resources to assist with disabilities.
  - http://www.milspouse.org/Job/Jobs/disab: MilSpouse.org
  - http://www.disabilityinfo.gov/digov-public/public/DisplayPage.do?parentFolderId=53: Disability Info.gov provides quick and easy access to comprehensive information about disability programs, services, laws and benefits.
  - http://www.copingwithdisability.com/: This is a website about coping with all different kinds of disabilities and health issues.
- ✔ **Teaching children about disabilities**
  - http://www.parenthood.com/article-topics/article-topics.php?Article_ID=9931: Everyday Etiquette: Dealing with Disabilities by Diane Gottsman
- ✔ **PTSD (post-traumatic stress disorder)**
  - http://www.ncptsd.va.gov/ncmain/ncdocs/fact_shts/fs_coping.html: Coping with PTSD and Recommended Lifestyle Changes for PTSD Patients by Joe Ruzek, Ph.D.

- `http://ptsd.about.com/od/selfhelp/PostTraumatic_ Stress_Disorder_SelfHelp.htm`: Coping skills, relaxation exercises, and other strategies for managing anxiety and stress associated with PTSD.

✔ **Military disability compensation and medical separation**

- `http://www.defenselink.mil/prhome/docs/rand_ disability_sum_1005.pdf`: An Analysis of Military Disability Compensation

- `http://usmilitary.about.com/od/theorderlyroom/a/ medseparation.htm`: Medical Separation and Retirement

- `http://www.military.com/benefits/military-pay/va- disability-compensation`: Veteran Disability Compensation — Military Benefits — Military.com

- `http://www.gao.gov/new.items/d064.pdf`: Report to Congressional Committees — United States Government Accountability Office — Disability Benefits

- `http://moaaonline.org/moaa_email_center/notice- description.tcl?newsletter_id=16426287`: MOAA helped the Senate Veterans Affairs Committee sort out multiple proposals to revise disability and medical programs for the wounded and their families.

- *An Analysis of Military Disability Compensation,* by Richard J. Buddin (RAND Corporation, 2005)

Surviving the Death of a Servicemember

The longer your spouse stays in the military, the higher the chance of know-ing someone who is killed in the line of duty or someone who dies of natural causes while still on active duty. Not only might your friends need support, but you and your family may also end up on the receiving end of condolences as well. Regardless, death of a family member can be a confusing and difficult time for anyone and everyone. So in these sections, we do what we can to guide you through the tide of challenges you may face after the death of your servicemember.

Giving and receiving friendly support

You or someone you know may end up dealing with the loss of a servicemember, but you may find it hard to know how to help or how to let yourself be helped through such a difficult time. The following sections give you some ideas on what to say or do whether you're on the receiving or giving end of support.

Helping your friends cope

You're probably going to be in the position to support a close friend or fellow spouse from the unit and having a general idea of what to say or do will help.

First of all, understand that it's going to be a very confusing time for your friend. There are going to be lots of people pushing her to make decisions during a very traumatic time in her life. Try to do the following helpful things instead of adding to her grief and confusion:

- ✔ Offer to help with the kids.

- ✔ Deliver meals so that she doesn't have to cook. Maybe start your meals later into the process when everyone else is starting to taper off and get on with their own lives.

- ✔ Be there to help with whatever she needs. Whether it's rides to and from the airports for visiting family or just sitting quietly together so she doesn't have to be alone.

Letting your friends help you

If you're the one going through the loss, understand that though it may be annoying and somewhat distressing to have people around, they mean well and are just trying to help. During traumatic times, people tend to rally. Let them. Lean on them when you need to. This is a terrible time in your life, and there will be people around who can take bits and pieces of the responsibilities you need to take care so you have less on your plate and can concentrate on what really matters — taking care of yourself and the kids.

You may want to consider designating someone to be your spokesperson so that you don't have to deal with more people than is absolutely necessary.

Have someone pick up a disposable cell phone for you and one for your kids. People are going to be jamming your phones with caring calls and the last thing you need to worry about is missing important calls and not being able to reach your children. Be judicious about who you give this phone number to. The point is to keep it private so that you can stay in contact with your immediate family and those people who are helping with your affairs.

Working with the Casualty Assistance Officer

Within 24 hours of a servicemember's death, the service branch will assign someone to notify and help the family. The Army refers to these people as casualty assistance officers; the Air Force refers to them as a Casualty Assistance Representatives; the Navy, Marines, and Coast Guard, refer to them as Casualty Assistance Calls Officers. Regardless of what you call them, they are responsible for notifying the next of kin. Following notification, they will also stay with the family and help them through the process of filing for claims. They will also assist the family in beginning the process for funeral or memorial services. It is the responsibility of the casualty assistance officer to mitigate the delay in settling claims and paying survivor benefits. You are free to tell the Casualty Assistance Officer that their services are no longer needed whenever you feel that you no longer want or need their help.

Recently, there have been cases of fake Casualty Assistance Officers (some in uniform) propagating scams against military spouses while their servicemembers are deployed. This has to be the most despicable form of identity theft out there. If there is any doubt in your mind about the person standing in front of you, don't share any information until you contact your family readiness officer or other official personnel to verify someone's identity.

Filing for benefits

Your Casualty Assistance Officer will assist you in filing for benefits, but it doesn't hurt to know what you should be doing. The following are just general guidelines of items that need to be taken care of and should not be considered a comprehensive list:

- ✔ Obtain multiple (about two dozen) copies of the death certificate that you will need to submit with the applications for benefits that you will be filling out.

- ✔ If your servicemember spouse was killed while still on active duty, file for the Death Gratuity Payment (DD397).

- ✔ If your servicemember spouse died on active duty, you're also covered under the Survivor Benefits Plan (SBP).

- ✔ Contact the Social Security office to find out what benefits you might be eligible for. For more information, consult www.ssa.gov.

- ✔ Chances are good that you are also covered under the Serviceman's Group Life Insurance (SGLI) unless your spouse declined coverage. You'll need to file Form SGLV 8283.

- ✔ You may also qualify for Dependence and Indemnity Compensation (DIC) from the Department of Veterans Affairs. Call the nearest Department of Veterans Affairs (VA) center by calling 800-827-1000.

- ✔ Contact your other insurance companies.

- ✔ Change the information on all shared property (cars, house, stocks, and other mutually owned items).

- ✔ Meet with the executor of your estate. You may or may not need to meet with a lawyer depending on the complexity of your estate and the number of people involved.

As good as your Casualty Assistance Officer may be, filing for and understanding all the benefits available to you is not for the faint of heart. Understanding this, the service relief societies entered into a partnership with the Armed Forces Services Corporation to provide assistance to surviving spouses of servicemembers killed on active duty. The AFSC Lifetime Membership for surviving spouses and children of servicemembers killed on active duty is sponsored by the Army Emergency Relief (AER), Navy Marine Corps Relief Society (NMCRS), Coast Guard Mutual Aid (CGMA), and the Air Force Aid Society(AFAS). Under this program, AFSC staff utilizes a sophisticated software program to project a survivor's benefits throughout her lifetime. This knowledge and assistance will help the survivor craft a good, solid financial plan. The AFSC benefits are meant to augment the work of the Casualty Assistance Officer and not to replace it. Those interested in reaping the benefits of this special offer need to apply for sponsorship through their service relief societies. Links to all of them can be found at: `http://www.afsc-usa.com/societies.html`.

Understanding your military benefits

Remember that as a survivor, you are still eligible for many of your military benefits. As long as you have not remarried, you continue to be eligible for commissary and exchange benefits. You are able to stay on base in temporary lodging based on the discretion of the installation commander. If you live on the military installation, you'll have a limited period of time (generally up to 180 days) before you have to vacate your base housing. Surviving spouses are also entitled to a no-cost final move for up to one year after the death of the servicemember occurred.

Your medical benefits will continue after the death of your spouse, however, at different rates:

- **For the first three years** following your spouse's death, you are considered a *transitional survivor* and are eligible for the same benefits as a family member of an active-duty person.

  Children are considered transitional survivors and will remain eligible for medical benefits equal to a family member of an active duty service member until they turn 21. If they are full-time students at an accredited institution, they have until age 23.

- **After the first three years,** at three years and one day, you are considered a *survivor*. At this point, you remain eligible for medical benefits, yet you pay the same costs and are eligible for the same level of benefits as those of a family member of a retired servicemember. For more information on your medical benefits, consult: `www.tricare.mil`.

Here are some things worth noting about benefits for survivors:

- ✔ Space-A travel is one of the benefits that you lose as a military survivor.
- ✔ When it comes time to search for scholarships and grants for college, the children of servicemembers who are killed on active duty are often eligible for many programs that are earmarked specifically for them.
- ✔ Your spouse's death changes your status so you will have to apply for a new military ID card for yourself and your kids.

Moving on

Dr. Elisabeth Kübler-Ross wrote a book on the different stages of grief called, "On Death and Dying." According to the Kübler-Ross model, the five different stages are: denial, anger, guilt, depression/sadness, and acceptance. There's no rhyme or reason as to how long each stage will last or which stage you'll go through when. There is no right or wrong way to grieve. Give yourself the latitude to do it your way, and make sure you get the help you need to make it through.

When you start to come out of the fog, you might notice that other people may have moved on. While they want to include you in the activities you may have done before you lost your servicemember spouse, things will have changed for you, and you may not have as much in common as you did before. It may be time to expand your circle and make new friends. In dealing with death and grief, it may be helpful for you to go out and find people who have gone through the same things you have. They will have more in common with you and understand where you're coming from without you having to fill in any of the back story.

Support groups

Since 1994, the Tragedy Assistance Program for Survivors (TAPS) has provided survivors with assistance in rebuilding their lives through comprehensive support systems and resources. They run a Good Grief Camp for Young Survivors that allows children who have lost a parent in the line of duty to connect with other children who are going through the same experience. While the children are going through the camp, the surviving spouses have the opportunity to meet their peers and take advantage of a day of workshops geared toward their issues of grief, surviving, and coping skills. To learn more about TAPS, go to www.taps.org.

In addition to TAPS, there are other organizations that provide camps to grieving children. One of these groups, Comfort Zone Camps provides bereavement camps for military children. More information about their organization can be found at: www.comfortzonecamp.org.

Sometimes, survivors just want to get away from the grieving for a time and just hang out with other kids or adults just like them and engage in some escapism. One of the newer organizations out there to support military families is called the Snowball Express. Serving children who have lost a parent on active duty, they bring these children and accompanying parent or guardian out to Orange County, California, for a weekend of fun. Again, it is great for the kids to be around other children who are going through the same experiences that they are. To learn more about Snowball Express, go to: www.snowballexpress.org.

These organizations are just a sampling of resources out there to support surviving spouses and family members. As discussed previously, America Supports You is a great clearinghouse of other organizations that exist to provide support to servicemembers and their families. More about America Supports You in Chapter 14.

Planning ahead

We all harp on the need of planning ahead and yet none of us are very good about heeding our own advice. When we're talking about worst-case scenarios, and look back in hindsight, it's inevitable: We will wish that we had taken advantage of more pre-planning. Don't let this be you. Don't fall prey to poor planning. Go ahead and have the difficult discussions ahead of time so that if the unimaginable happens, you already have some plans laid out.

The transient quality of the military lifestyle guarantees that a lot of things that most people take for granted are going to cause you some confusion when you have to think about them. This doesn't negate the importance of addressing them:

✔ Where do you consider home? You're entitled to a final move on the military, but have you ever considered where home is for you?

✔ Make sure you know where to find the information for all your bank accounts, investments, and insurance policies.

✔ Make sure you understand what your assets are.

✔ Some preparation documents require that you each put down on paper how you would like to be buried and where. They also require you to write down how you would like your possessions disposed of. The more hard core will also have you write your own obituary to give everyone a starting point. You probably don't have to do this level of planning, but it doesn't hurt to talk about it.

✔ Understand all of your benefits that you will be eligible for so that you don't have to rely so heavily on the kindness of others.

✔ Consider what your financial needs will be for different times in your family's life so that you can make sure they're funded correctly.

✔ Ensure that your important documents are up to date and that each of you knows where they are located.

It's important to plan ahead and keep your information up to date. Regardless of whether or not you have children, everyone should have a will and it should be updated every time you have a significant life event. Don't be that ill-prepared person. If the unimaginable happens, you'll feel better knowing that some things have already been taken care of.

Part IV:
Mastering Deployments

The 5th Wave
By Rich Tennant

"Remember men, when you're out there, be ready for the unexpected — booby traps, snipers, CBS camera crews..."

In this part . . .

If deployments could come with a how-to guide, this would be it. In this part you'll learn everything, from what you need to prepare for a deployment to tips on how to utilize special financial deployment programs available to you. You'll also learn how to stay connected and anticipate the pitfalls by understanding the cycles of deployment.

Chapter 16

Prepping for Deployments

. . . .

. . . .

Deployments are inevitable in the military. The more you learn about what to expect, and the more you prepare in advance, the easier military life will be for you and your family. We're not saying that it will be easy! Being separated from your partner definitely makes life more challenging. But, this is his job. Your job is to hold down the homefront, and it's a big and sometimes overwhelming responsibility. In this chapter we help you prepare as best you can for the inevitable deployment.

Separating the Truths from the Myths

People tend to have preconceived notions or beliefs when facing the reality of deployments, but we give you the truth:

Myth: Deployments are governed by the life-is-fair principle.

Truth: Nothing could be further than the truth. There is no grand plan at play. It's the needs of the service first and foremost, and it doesn't really matter what your personal situation is. Depending on their specialty code or unit, your spouse could feasibly be sent more often than others.

Myth: If there are seven cycles of deployment, you'll have time to go through all seven before you start all over again.

Truth: Unfortunately, with today's operations tempo, the cycles of deployment are starting to overlap. Before a family has had an opportunity to get reacquainted, it's time for the servicemember to leave again. And if the deployments weren't bad enough, you still need to make allowances for regular TDYs and training requirements. It is all too normal these days for military families to be living simultaneously in different cycles of deployment.

Myth: They won't send my husband because I'm eight months pregnant.

Truth: This is almost too easy. I know you've seen the pictures of gangplanks and airplane hangars full of mothers with infant children born while their dads were deployed. Unfortunately, pregnancy and other family planning issues don't generally play into deployment decisions.

Myth: It gets easier every time.

Truth: It doesn't ever get easier. You'll still lament every missed milestone and worry as much with the last deployment as you do with the first one. The difference is that you'll become a pro and the planning will get easier.

Myth: It doesn't matter what happens, there will always be someone there to take care of me.

Truth: In a worst case scenario, there will likely be someone there to help you through your ordeal. However, how well you survive depends on how well you plan. If you don't put certain things into place before the servicemember deploys, even the most well intentioned folks can't help you.

In addition to the myths, try to remember a couple of things when it comes to deployments:

- Sometimes, people do so much for us and do such a great job of taking care of us that we begin to take it for granted. It's easy to begin feeling like such great care is something that is owed to you. This could not be further from the truth. Please be gracious and do not adopt an entitled stance.

- Being well prepared for a deployment will help you in the long run. Having everything in place and knowing where everything is will give you the peace of mind that will be so elusive to you in the other areas of your life while your spouse is deployed.

Preparing for Deployment

Your servicemember may be deployed with little or no notice. Sometimes you may get notified a few weeks in advance. In any case, your family will not have much time to prepare for deployment after receiving notice. Your servicemember's life gets very hectic once the deployment notice is issued. He may be too busy with his work to take care of essential family life issues during that time. These responsibilities fall on your lap.

Deployments are inevitable, so work with your servicemember *now* to take care of all essential family life matters. In the following section we highlight the major issues you need to consider when preparing for deployment.

The military provides pre-deployment briefings for you and your servicemember after a deployment notice has been issued but prior to deployment. These sessions are scheduled to provide you with additional information, clarification, and the opportunity to ask questions regarding your servicemember's entitlements and your family's benefits during deployment.

Powers of attorney

Possibly the most important document that you have in place prior to deployment is a power of attorney. There are actually a couple different kinds of power of attorney documents that you need:

- A ***financial power of attorney*** document is critical when your spouse is on deployment. This document enables your servicemember to appoint you to make financial decisions and manage his affairs while he's away. You may think that just by being married you will be able to transact business on behalf of your spouse. This is not necessarily the case, such as; signing a joint tax return for your spouse, managing real estate and business interests, or any individually owned assets or debts that your servicemember may have.

    Make sure that you provide an official copy of your *financial power of attorney* form to the person you have named to act on your behalf. Also, provide a copy of your official health care power of attorney document to your family physician and to the people named as your healthcare agents. Keep another set of these documents in a safe place, such as in your important documents file in a fireproof safe, or with an online secure document storage service.

- A ***durable power of attorney for health care*** is also an important document to get in place when preparing for deployment. This document enables you to name a person or, better yet, a couple of people, to make healthcare decisions if you are unable to make them for yourself. Of course, the same goes for your servicemember.

    Due to the fact that military couples are often separated geographically, it is especially important to have a durable power of attorney for healthcare, naming each other as your primary agent, but also name a successor who can step in if healthcare decisions need to be made and your spouse is away.

    Often *healthcare power of attorney documents* are packaged together with a *living will*. These documents are also known as called *healthcare directives*. A *living will* spells out under what circumstances, if any, you want your life prolonged should you have no reasonable chance of recovery. Both you and your servicemember should also have living wills drafted by qualified legal professionals. Consult with the legal assistance office on your installation. They can provide you with the legal documents you both need.

An excellent online secure document storage service is Executor's Resource. Online document storage services are a great option for your mobile military family. Executor's Resource provides you the opportunity to upload all your important documents, paperwork, and even photos, videos, and voice messages. You can provide different levels of access to your spouse, family members, friends, and even financial advisors, clergy, or physicians. For more information visit `http://www.executorsresource.com`.

Financial planning

Financial planning is all about preparing in advance for all of life's inevitable events. You may be tempted to procrastinate with your financial planning because you're thinking that there are no impending events or issues with which you have to deal right now. Not the case! Deployment is inevitable!

Financial planning involves thoughtful consideration of all potential inevitable events in your financial life. For more information on doing your own financial planning, check out the *Personal Finance Workbook For Dummies* (Wiley).

Getting organized

Getting your financial household organized can be one of the greatest gifts you give yourself and your loved ones. On the day you get that deployment notification, you can spend quality time with your spouse and family, rather than running around taking care of last-minute financial arrangements.

To get your financial household in order and prepared for deployment, organize your financial records into *one* place using an organizational system, such as a three-ring binder with divider tabs, or actual file folders in a portable file box. Include sections for:

- **Contacts:** Name, address, and contact information of financial, legal, and tax advisors, and people to contact in the event of emergencies, such as, back-up baby-sitters, child's teacher, next-door neighbor, and so on.

- **Official documents:** Legal documents, birth certificates, adoption papers, marriage certificates, divorce decrees, copies of your family member's individual military ID cards, Social Security cards and passports, copies of orders, tax returns, medical and dental records, net worth statement, credit report, warranties, and so on.

- **Assets:** Car titles, registration forms, proof of insurance, and maintenance records; privately-owned residence; deed, mortgage, insurance, and maintenance records; bank accounts, investment account statements, retirement plans, and IRAs.

> ✔ **Liabilities:** Credit card statements, school loans, copies of loan agreements, and most current statements for any other debts other than home mortgage and automobile.
>
> ✔ **Expenses:** Monthly budget, annual and periodic expenses, and lists of payees, addresses, and account numbers.
>
> ✔ **Other:** Online account login information and pass codes.

Keeping your information safe

The information contained in your financial planning binder, or file box is extremely private and important to your family. You do not want this information to fall into the wrong hands. Keep this information locked up in a safe place, scan it, and store it on an USB drive or consider utilizing a secure online document storage service.

Being the Chief Financial Officer of your military family can be a daunting job. You'll often need to pay bills, make inquiries, check your account balances, and so on, while your spouse is on TDY. Your family also moves frequently. This makes online investment account access, online banking, and online document storage the most convenient way to manage your personal finances, and provide access to your spouse should they want or need to do something in this area.

Having everything online requires you to maintain a list of all of the Web sites, login information, and passwords because every site has slightly different rules about how many letters, numbers, and symbols can or must be used in login names and passwords. Plus, it is safer to use different passwords on different sites. Be very careful not to write this information down because it can be lost or stolen. A great option is to utilize a software tool such as RoboForm to store this information.

RoboForm is an inexpensive software program that enables you to save all of the information on Web sites you visit frequently; including the URL addresses, login information, and your passwords, all in one place — either your hard drive or a UBS jump drive. You might consider using both for convenience and as a backup. To access your RoboForm data you'll need *one super-secret password* and then you can get into all of your secure accounts online with just a click of a button. No more remembering Web addresses, login names, and passwords. RoboForm also enables you to store all of your personal information such as driver's license numbers, Social Security numbers, military ID number, family information, contact information, and so on. It's really an incredibly convenient device. You can find out more about RoboForm at their Web site at `http://www.RoboForm.com`.

Budgets

You might think of this as a money diet, but I encourage you to think of a budget as a disciplined approach to help your family reach your financial objectives in life. You only have a certain amount of money coming in each and every month, and you have many required expenses, as well as some desired expenditures that you would like to cover out of this cash flow. Budgeting enables you to get the life out of your money.

Focus on the amount of net income you have to work with and establish automatic withdrawals from your servicemember's paycheck, as well as your bank account, to cover your family's required expenses, and the balance that lands in your checking account after all of your required expenses are met can be spent on those things that provide your family the most enjoyment.

It's kind of an inverse way of budgeting. Rather than keeping track of every cent that you are spending:

- Make a list of all of your required monthly expenses.

- List all of your periodic and annual expenses.

- Pay all of your required monthly expenses automatically.

- Set up a high-yielding money market account and direct one 12th of the total of your annualized periodic and annual expenses in to this escrow spending account.

- When periodic expenses arise, you simply tap in to your high-yielding money market account to cover those expenses.

- Whatever is left over in your checking account may be spent on any discretionary items that you and your family determines most appropriate.

  - Remain very conscious of the amount of money your family has available for discretionary expenditures each month. Your net income may vary somewhat month to month, however desired expenditures can gyrate wildly. This is where cash flow planning comes into play.

    For example, in three months you want to take a family trip and you anticipate spending $1,500. Allocate $500 per month into your high-yielding money market account so that you have this money available in three months when you need it for your trip. Otherwise, you may be tempted to charge the expense on a credit card.

  - Avoid charging things on your credit card that you cannot pay off the following month out of your discretionary cash flow. Credit cards should be used exclusively for convenience and in the rare occasion that you have a true financial emergency. Sorry, the annual sale at Macy's does not constitute a financial emergency!

Emergency fund

What constitutes an emergency? Well, life happens and sometimes it takes money you hadn't planned on spending to deal with it! You might have a fender-bender, your brother-in-law needs a helping hand, or your son has the opportunity of attending a special, yet expensive, summer camp program.

Having money readily available that you can get your hands on in the event of such an emergency, or opportunity, is the purpose of an emergency reserve fund. The amount of money you should have on hand varies on your family's circumstances. If you are currently living comfortably on your servicemember's net paycheck, you may be fine with a minimal amount of cash reserves. $2,000 to $5,000 in your savings or money market accounts may be sufficient.

On the other hand, if you currently have earned income that could abruptly terminate because of deployment, or due to PCS, you should have substantially more readily available cash reserves to cover your family's needs until you regain employment. A minimum of three to six months worth of required living expenses should be maintained in a high yielding money market account.

A great resource for high-yielding money market accounts and savings accounts in your area is BankRate.com (`http://www.Bankrate.com`).

One of the most consistently competitive high-yielding accounts is offered by ING Direct (`http://www.INGdirect.com`). They offer extremely competitive interest rates, no minimum to open an account, and online money transfer to and from your checking account, free of charge.

Taking Advantage of Special Deployment Benefits

It is imperative that you recognize and take advantage of the many special benefits provided to your family due to your spouse's deployment. These benefits help to simplify your personal financial management, provide for tax-free income on combat pay, and insure that your servicemember will be able to return to their civilian employment if they are activated Guard or Reserve.

Getting direct deposit

If you aren't currently signed up for direct deposit of your servicemember's paycheck, upon deployment direct deposit becomes mandatory. Contact your bank and ask it for the specific instructions needed for direct deposit of employer paychecks. That information will be needed by the accounting office.

If you have questions contact the Defense Finance and Accounting Service (DFAS) at 800-390-2348 or visit them online at www.dod.mil/dfas.

Saving in the best plan available

Servicemembers deployed in combat zones and certain contingency operations may take advantage of the DoD's Savings Deposit Program (SDP). While deployed in these areas, your spouse can contribute all or part of their net pay into a DoD savings account earning 10 percent (taxable) interest. That's an extraordinary rate of return and it's safe and accessible when you need to tap these funds for your family's financial goals. There is no reason not to participate in the SDP. Your spouse can contribute as little as $5 per pay period. And you've got extra pay coming in due to the preferential tax treatment of combat pay, and your servicemember is likely also receiving additional pay, so this may be the best time ever to sock some money away. It's easy, safe and you'll get an outstanding interest rate.

Getting started in the SDP is easy. Visit your local finance office and ask to deposit money into the fund. Information can be accessed online at www.defenselink.mil.

Note: the DoD limits the amount members can contribute to $10,000 per deployment. Also, the account will stop earning interest 90 days after a member returns from a combat zone and funds should be withdrawn at that time and reinvested to compliment your family's financial plans.

Receiving tax-free combat pay and benefits

Your loved one receives extra compensation for combat, and this extra compensation is both state and federal income tax free. This additional pay could be about $300 to $500 per month tax free. Their basic and any special pays are also tax free during the time they are deployed in combat.

If at any time during the month your servicemember is deployed in a combat zone, the income for that entire month is excluded from taxable income. Plus, if your servicemember is deployed for more than 30 days, you may also be entitled to the Family Separation Allowance of $250 per month. (Refer to Chapter 5, Hazardous Duty Pay section, for details on the amount and types of compensation paid due to combat.)

Ensuring reemployment: USERRA

One of the major provisions of the Uniformed Services Employment and Reemployment Rights Act, also known as USERRA, is a law that requires employers to reemploy Guard and Reserve members when they return from deployment, under most cases. Not only is the employer required to reemploy the servicemember returning to the civilian work force, but they must also reemploy your servicemember in a position comparable to the one they had prior to going on active duty.

For additional information refer to Chapter 7.

Understanding the Emotional Cycles of Deployment

The cycles of deployment used to consist of three different stages: pre-deployment, deployment, and post-deployment. However, more recently, the deployment cycles have been divided into seven stages:

- Anticipation of Departure
- Detachment and Withdrawal
- Emotional Disorganization
- Recovery and Stabilization
- Anticipation of Return
- Return Adjustment and Renegotiation
- Reintegration and Stabilization

With just a few clicks, you can download the entire fact sheet. Go to http://deploymenthealthlibrary.fhp.osd.mil, and click on "View Product List." Use the on-screen scroll bar to scroll down to and click on "Coping with the Deployment of a Spouse or Partner," then "Emotions," and then "Emotional Cycles of Deployment."

In the following sections, we take you through these cycles in layman's terms.

Preparing for them to go

The first cycle: *Anticipation of Departure* deals with getting ready for service members to leave. You have a huge checklist of things you should do in preparation for a deployment, and this is the time in the cycle when you're rushing around trying to get everything taken care of.

This period is loaded with opportunities to make each other mad. As if there weren't enough things on the checklist to do, you'll each find other things that have to be done before he leaves. All of a sudden, you'll remember that both cars need tune-ups, the gutters need to be cleaned, and, of course, in the midst of it all, the hard drive on your computer has just crashed. And since he's going to miss the holidays, the garage needs to be cleaned out so that you can pull the Christmas stuff out of the attic so that it'll be more accessible to you when you need it. This will remind you that you really want him to be involved with buying some of the Christmas and birthday gifts for the kids so you'll spend precious time sprinting through the mall trying to check things off your list.

Now, here's the interesting thing about this cycle: On one hand, you have a lot of obligations, things you need to get done before he leaves. On the other hand, when faced with the reality that your best friend and partner will be leaving for many months to a year, you're trying to cram memory-making opportunities into each and every minute of the day. So, how do you reconcile the two? How do you work down the ridiculously long "honey do" list full of things you're both trying to accomplish before the deployment and balance it with the desire to spend as much quality time together as possible? You don't. If it seems as if these two conflicting goals set you up on a path to ultimate failure, then you get the gold star for being insightful because they absolutely do.

Every time you sit down to a "romantic" meal, you will be preoccupied by thoughts that you have a lot to do and no time to waste. Or worse, you'll realize that this is the only time you guys have had all to yourselves without any kids in tow and will seize the opportunity to talk about worst case scenarios and what ifs. Over salads and shrimp cocktails, you'll find yourself talking about where your spouse would like to be buried in case the unspeakable happens, what he would like you to do with the children, where you would move, and so many other less-than-pleasant topics. Is there a way to solve this? Probably not. And maybe solving it isn't necessary because these are important conversations to have and when you're dealing with a time crunch, there's not necessarily going to be a convenient time to have the discussions.

Rather than feeling badly that you're "squandering" the time you have left together, accept that this difficult period is an inevitability and just enjoy the time you have before the deployment without loading it down with expectations of what an "ideal" pre-deployment period should look like.

Creating walls before they leave

The second cycle of deployment is *Detachment and Withdrawal*, which also deals with preparing for your servicemember to leave. This is the time when the servicemember begins to withdraw and focus on the mission at hand while the spouse starts to create a wall to protect herself from the hurt of the servicemember's impending departure. You start to compartmentalize your emotions and begin to pull away from each other, thinking that that will help make the departure easier to take. Very strange rationalization, and yet, we all find ourselves going there.

The servicemember starts to transition from spending time with the family in the pre-deployment stage to looking forward to the mission and the deployment ahead. Your nerves are somewhat raw and sensitive at this point, so you mistake this for him being excited to leave, but *this is not the case*. He is a trained professional about to go out in the field to do what he spent the rest of the year training for. Of course this is going to bring out some excitement. Don't confuse this with thinking that he's excited to be leaving you behind. This is not the case. He is just compartmentalizing and focusing on the mission ahead.

If you're honest with yourself, you'll look inside and realize that you're guilty of the same thing. Faced with the imminent departure of your best friend and helpmate, you have probably started withdrawing to try to steel yourself against the pain of him leaving. You're probably both withdrawing and pulling away from one another, trying to protect yourselves from the pain and hurt you'll feel when he leaves. You'll find yourself picking fights about the silliest things. It's almost as if you think it'll be easier on you if you're mad at one another when he leaves so that you don't care as much when they're gone. Perhaps you think it will almost be a relief when he's gone because he was behaving so poorly. Who knows what the rationale is. Just know that this is a difficult period for the marriage as you're both emotionally withdrawing from one another when intuitively, it seems like you should be clinging onto one another for dear life.

Don't be too tough on yourselves. Find comfort in the knowledge that you're traveling down the same path as multitudes of others who have also gone through the same stages of detachment with many of the same outcomes. There aren't any guidelines pointing to what emotions are and aren't acceptable to feel during the pre-deployment period. It's enough to understand that these types of reactions are normal, and if your spouse leaves in the midst of arguments and hurt feelings, it's not out of the ordinary.

Establishing your new normal

As soon as your spouse leaves you begin going through the *Emotional Disorganization* cycle. First, you'll stumble a bit as you struggle to figure out how you will balance everything. You'll begin to figure out what responsibilities you need to redistribute as you try to fill the void that your spouse left behind. Particularly if you're a parent, you'll figure out how to live up to all the expectations so that everything will continue much as it did before one parent left the picture. It can be overwhelming to try to figure out how to keep things as normal as possible for your kids.

This is the same stage when you'll start to come to grips with the loneliness. You're responsible for everyone's calendars and obligations in addition to taking on all the household duties. If anything breaks down or stops working altogether, you have to deal with it. Even on a regular day, life as a "single" parent can be exhausting. By the time night rolls around, you realize it's been a few days since you last engaged in any adult conversation. It can become somewhat overwhelming dealing with everything yourself without the benefit of a sounding board. You begin to feel like you're missing out on one of the greatest benefits of being married — having that safe port in the storm, your other half who listens to you without judgment.

Getting settled

Fortunately, the Emotional Disorganization cycle is followed by *Recovery and Stabilization*. During this cycle, you start to find your center of gravity again. You've had some time dealing with things on your own and while you don't prefer that your spouse is gone, you've begun to feel like perhaps you can handle this. You're on your way to discovering your new normal. You develop new routines and being alone gets a little easier.

You're feeling your way around the new responsibilities and have found ways to manage your new duties and take care of everyone.

Anticipating their return

While in the *Anticipation of Their Return* cycle, you get ready for the service-member to come home, which is generally a happy time. You start making plans for the homecoming and imagining the family back together again. You can finally see the light at the end of the tunnel, and it's fun imagining the moment when you see him again and what it'll feel like. You dust off the cookbooks and start planning those Sunday family dinners again anticipating the day when things get back to normal and you're back on your regular schedule.

Don't get too caught up in the fairy tale of what a homecoming should be like. The biggest way you can be disappointed is by building up your expectations to the extent that no homecoming could possibly live up to the scenario you've built up in your mind.

Anticipating and planning for the servicemember's homecoming is laden with hidden landmines, especially for kids. Prepare yourself for these potential pitfalls:

✔ **Delayed gratification:** People get delayed all the time. Planes are late, plans change, and before you know it, your spouse has been delayed by a few days, weeks, or months. As adults used to dealing with life's uncertainties, we are more likely to be resilient and flexible. Kids are a lot less so. Don't let them put all their eggs in one basket. Manage their expectations and help them understand that everything doesn't always happen on schedule. For example, creating and hanging a welcome-home banner is a great family bonding exercise, but make sure you have an alternative plan or an explanation when you have to take it down and re-hang it a few days later.

Help your children with the impending homecoming by discussing it with them. This can be done in conjunction with a family activity that you take on to prep for the homecoming. This might be shopping for your spouse's favorite foods, picking up some balloons to decorate the house, or any number of little activities your kids can come up with to make the homecoming more special. Let the kids determine how the discussion goes. They may have some anxieties that you'll want to address about how mom or dad may have changed during the deployment. They may feel guilty that they're not more excited that mom or dad is coming home. They may be nervous about how things will change in the home. Regardless of what they come up with, validate their emotions and make sure they understand that whatever they're feeling is normal and okay.

✔ **Overplanning:** Remember that when your servicemember returns from deployment, it's going to take him a little while to get acclimated to being at home again. Don't plan too many activities or try to cram too much into the first few days that he's home. Give him a chance to work himself back into the home and all of you a chance to get reacquainted. More about staying connected in Chapter 19.

✔ **Filtering in the family:** Extended family and friends are also going to want to play a part in the homecoming. Discuss this with your spouse who is deployed and see how he would like to handle the situation. Who does he want involved in the first few days of the homecoming? When does he want to see his other family and friends? By understanding what everyone's expectations are, you can all get on the same page and try to put a plan in place that takes into consideration the wants of the servicemember. Don't be surprised in the last few days leading up to a homecoming if you're surprised by an influx of family who want to join you at the terminal to welcome home your spouse. Have that discussion earlier on. If you know what to expect, you can at least plan for it. Much as you would like to count on a private homecoming with just your immediate family, that doesn't just happen automatically. Other members of the family are going to be clamoring for the servicemember's time and may have their own ideas of what should happen. Manage the expectations on all sides to help ease the transition back for the servicemember.

Coming back together as a family

During the *Return Adjustment and Renegotiation* cycle, families are feeling their way around, redistributing the responsibilities, and negotiating roles and duties within the household post-deployment. Under the best of circumstances, tempers will be short and everyone will get on each other's nerves. Unfortunately, during this period, you'll find yourself engaging in some emotional tug-of-wars as you reassess everyone's role in the home. This is tough and not made any easier by today's ops tempo because in the back of your mind, there's always the nagging thought that why bother getting it right when they're just going to leave again?

As you figure out what your roles should be at this point, you'll feel yourself bouncing around as you experience the following (they don't call it "adjustment" during this cycle for nothing!):

- ✔ **Guilt:** You're going to feel some guilt over the fact that you've embraced being in charge since your spouse was gone, not having to ask anyone's permission or facing anyone second-guessing you on every little detail. While your spouse was gone, you probably lived up to the challenge and developed a certain level of independence. Admit it, you enjoyed being the authority figure and not having to consult your spouse on every little decision you wanted to make. It was probably nice knowing that when you made a decision, you were the final word. Despite what they say about marriage being a cooperative sport, sometimes doing everything your way can be refreshing. However, what works when one spouse is deployed is not necessarily going to work well when you're both under one roof. Come to grips with the fact that you're going to have to share the authority again and the transition time will be much smoother.

- ✔ **Trouble giving up the reins:** You've taken on more of the chores while your spouse was gone, so you've probably also developed some routines and protocols for the way you like things done. When your spouse returns, understand that he's going to do things differently, and if you want him to continue taking on those responsibilities, you're going to have to let him do things his way. You're going to be loathe to give up your authority and possibly try to continue to do things your way. Of course it's a good thing to develop some more independence while your spouse is deployed, but when they get back, letting them back into the decision making process doesn't necessarily make you dependent. In a healthy marriage, you're interdependent on each other, and it should be a give and take with room for both spouses to share in the decision making process.

✔ **Sending the wrong signal, unintentionally:** In anticipating the next deployment coming up soon, some spouses choose to keep the responsibilities instead of going through the drill of reintegrating the other person into the household fully and then having to go through the other cycles of redistributing the chores and responsibilities again when they leave. While this may be more efficient in the long run, it could also have the unintended outcome of making your spouse believe that things run so smoothly when he's gone that you just don't need him anymore. Illogical, I know, but the ego is a fragile thing. Everyone likes to think they're needed.

Finding your family groove again

The *Reintegration and Stabilization* cycle is probably the trickiest of all because there's the temptation to rush things along and not wait for things to play out on their own. Regardless of how long you've been married, the time after a deployment is always awkward. Everyone's feeling their way around one another. When the servicemember deployed, the family dynamic shifted around to redistribute the responsibilities. The children are used to going to you for everything. This can make the spouse who was deployed feel as if there's no longer a place or a role for him in the home. Getting back into the family fold takes time and the servicemember is bound to feel some frustration because as far as he's concerned, when he left home, everything was a certain way, and he's returning thinking that everything will still be as he left it.

To help everyone fall back into place as comfortably as possible, remember that

✔ **Everyone changes.** After being gone for months (up to 15 months), the deployed servicemember has missed some milestones, kids have grown, and you've all grown in different ways. No one exists in a bubble and it's inevitable that you have all changed in some manner. It would be hard to take on all the new responsibilities without developing more independence. You're going to become more confident in your abilities to take care of things in your spouse's absence. You may have even developed a different network of friends and acquaintances while your spouse was gone. It'll be difficult for your spouse to imagine that life has moved on without him and to figure out a way to ease himself back into life at home. Trust that it will be just as strange for all of you to try to figure out the new family dynamic.

✔ **Don't force things.** Take some time to get the lay of the land and figure out what everyone's roles are. It's especially important to allow the children to accept the deployed parent back into the family fold on their own terms. They may have gotten used to going to mom for everything and it'll take them some time to get used to having two parents sharing the parental responsibilities again. Don't make them choose between you. Act as a parenting team and everything else will follow. The children will feel more confident that things are getting back to normal as soon as the parents start getting back to normal.

✔ **Let the kids make the moves.** Encourage your spouse not to force things with the kids, let them take the lead on when and how they want to get reacquainted. Encourage your spouse to make the effort to spend some one on one time with each of them. Let them choose the activity they would like to do with your spouse and encourage him and take a backseat to their needs and timetable. Depending on how well you stayed in touch while the servicemember spouse was deployed, the period of time it'll take for the family to reintegrate will vary. More about staying in touch with kids during deployment in Chapter 18.

Prioritizing with the golf ball theory of life

I'm sure you've heard about the golf ball theory of life: A professor stood before his philosophy class with a very large and empty mayonnaise jar in front of him. He proceeded to fill it with golf balls and then asked the students if the jar was full. They agreed that it was. Then the professor poured a box of pebbles into the jar and they rolled into the open areas between the golf balls. He again asked the students if the jar was full and they agreed it was. He then picked up a box of sand and poured it into the jar. The sand filled up the areas between the pebbles. He then asked once more if the jar was full and all the students responded "yes." Then the professor produced two cups of coffee from under the table and poured the entire contents into the jar, filling the empty space between the sand. What the professor wanted his students to recognize was that the jar represents their life. The golf balls are the important things such as: family, children, health, friends, and things in life that they're passionate about. If everything else was lost and only the "golf balls" remained, their life would still be full. The pebbles are the other things that matter like: jobs, house, car, and other material things. The sand is everything else, the small stuff.

The point: If you put the sand in first (the small stuff), there's less room for the pebbles and no room for the golf balls. In life, if you worry about the small stuff, then you'll never have time for the things that really matter to you. In addition, never forget that the professor did note that the two cups of coffee in his example had significance: Regardless of how busy or full your life is, you always have time to take a moment and share a cup of coffee with a friend.

Smoothing out the rough spots

All the different cycles of deployment last for varying amounts of time, and people will blow through some of the cycles easily while getting bogged down by others. In fact, the last cycle of reintegration and stabilization can take up to six months.

In a perfect world, a family would have the opportunity to go through all the cycles before starting over again with another deployment. Unfortunately, in today's world of increased ops tempo, families could feasibly be going through different cycles of deployment at the same time. Since redeployments are coming closer together, some of the cycles are starting to overlap. In addition to this, there are the other possible stumbling blocks of ongoing professional military education and training that requires servicemembers to be away from home on a temporary basis. As these are considered career-broadening opportunities, no consideration is made to the servicemember's deployment schedules. This significantly impacts the family in that the servicemember is being taken away from home again before they've had a chance to get re-acclimated to one another.

Another potential stumbling block is a PCS. Already an emotionally charged time in a military family's life, a PCS could become more stressful when done in conjunction with a deployment. The key to success is maintaining open lines of communication. Because there is so much that is out of the control of military family members, it's helpful for them to have as much information as possible to formulate better plans of action. Impress upon the servicemember the importance of keeping you in the loop. Nothing is insurmountable if you're working as a team (find out more about becoming and continuing to be a strong military couple in Chapter 13).

If you do find yourself faltering, there's no shame in asking for help (more about this in Chapter 17). There are also going to be times following a deployment when you're not going to be able to manage things on your own.

If you notice that your spouse is emotionally numb or withdrawn, experiencing sleep disorders such as insomnia, or prone to excessive bursts of anger or depression, he may be experiencing post-traumatic stress disorder (PTSD). While it is normal for any or all of these symptoms to occur a month to three months after a deployment, if they persist, you may want to seek additional help.

Managing Stress

To make it through a deployment and take care of your family, you're going to have to take care of yourself and keep your stress level at a minimum. Considering that you're already taking complete control of the family, tacking on care for yourself and your stress level sounds like a tall order. But if you break your life down and remember the following, you can manage like a pro:

- ✔ **Recognize that you're not going to do it all yourself.** You're no longer going to be able to do it all. Regardless of whether or not you work outside the home, you're still going to find that there are not enough hours in the day.

- ✔ **Don't sweat the little things in life, especially during a deployment when you're trying to be everything to everyone.** Learn to differentiate between what you *have* to do and what you'd *like* to do. You may want to volunteer to serve on your child's PTA board because you'd like to be involved, but you can't make it to the meetings because you have to be available to squire the kids around to their activities. It may seem callous, but you are going to have to draw a line in the sand and decide what you will and won't do while your spouse is deployed.

- ✔ **Obligate yourself to the bare minimum, knowing that other things will come up that need your time and attention.** Emotionally speaking, you'll be more drained than you would under normal circumstances and perhaps you won't be able to take on as much as you normally could. Remember that it's easy to get overwhelmed when your plate gets too full. When you find that you've signed on for too much, there's not that other person to come to your rescue by picking up some of the duties.

- ✔ **Find more hours in the day by figuring out what you can afford to pay other people to do.** If you work full time or have other obligations that take you away from home for extended periods of time see what tasks you can afford to have others do for you. The two most commonly outsourced jobs are housekeeping and the lawn care, both of which suck hours out of your day.

- ✔ **Take shortcuts to gain more hours.** We give you a few ideas in the following list:

  - • **"Something" doesn't always mean homemade.** If you're used to sending homemade baked goods for your children's various bake sales, class parties, and PTA events, you don't have the time or energy to put into it, but you'd still like to participate, find another way. Bake from a mix and ask your children to decorate the baked goods to give them the personal touch. Or, buy the baked goods and send them in. The people in charge of the event will just appreciate that you made the effort to send something in.

- **Start combining your outings.** If you're going out to the installation to take your kids to the MTF for their sports physical, use the time to get their prescriptions filled and combine the visit with a commissary run, or a visit to the exchange and gas station. Less time spent in transit is more time spent with the family.

- **Plan and get your kids involved in the planning.** Schedule those weekly calendar meetings to figure out what needs to be done that week. Understanding where everyone needs to be and when will help you lay out your obligations and then fit in the fun stuff.

- **Get help with meals.** It's not fun cooking for a small number of people and if you take the time to cook a nice meal, you don't want to eat it over the entire week because no matter how much you love beef stew, after three days of it, you just don't want to see it again. Considering participating in a meal co-op with some other spouses where you each cook meals in bulk, package them family style and then trade meals. That way, instead of just cooking lasagna for a small family, you can cook two or three trays of lasagna, trade them with your friends, and end up with three to four different entrée choices for the entire week.

- **Check out those places that allow you to put together dinner on the premises to be frozen until you're ready to cook them.** Nationwide there are any number of chains such as Let's Dish (www.let'sdish.com) that run sessions in their stores where people pick the entrees and side dishes they would like and then put them together on site. The dishes then get refrigerated or frozen until you're ready to eat them. The appeal of these places is that all the ingredients are prepared for you, so there's no menu planning, shopping, chopping, or prepping. All you do is pick your entrees and then show up to assemble them. Don't like a certain ingredient? Leave it out. Outside of the advantages already listed above, one that can't be overlooked is that after you're done putting the food together, someone else cleans up the mess.

- ✓ **Don't obsess about the things you can't control.** Everyone — deployment or not — could stand to keep this in mind. To find out more about managing your anxiety, check out Chapter 19.

Multitudes of resources are available to help you weather the deployment more effectively. Do what you need to do to take care of yourselves and remember: Your spouse has a mission while he's deployed. Yours is to maintain the homefront so he doesn't worry about what's going on back home. Sometimes, it can get to be a bit much to handle. The news reports are coming too frequently, or you've just been doing it for too long. Remember that you're not in it alone.

Chapter 17

Accessing Traditional Family Support

*O*ne of the most difficult aspects of the deployment is that your best friend and helpmate is out of the picture for months on end, and it can start to feel like you're in it alone. To stave off these feelings of isolation, you should look around at ways to get involved. Perhaps support groups are not your thing and you're looking for some help. Have no fear — you can find just what you want and more with relative ease.

Finding Support on Base

Look around the base and you'll find that many of the buildings house offices and programs designed specifically to help and empower military families. Just as you would do your homework before starting any new endeavor, take the time to research the resources you have available to you on base. That way, when you need to access a specific program, you'll already have an idea of what's out there to support you and your family.

FSC — Family support center

Regardless of what stage of deployment you may be at, the Family Support Center will be one of your best resources. You should get a strong start to the deployment by taking advantage of the pre-deployment briefings. As a matter of fact, go ahead and plan on attending any and all briefings you are given access to. Every deployment's different. Even if you've been through multiple deployments, it's always a good idea to have the refresher course. This way you'll be forced to sit down with your spouse and go through the paperwork each time. Here are some of the points you need to check out:

- **Will:** It doesn't matter what stage in life you're at, everyone needs a will and it needs to be updated with every significant life event such as: a marriage, birth, or change in finances. Currently serving members can generally utilize legal services on base for free. See Chapter 9 for details.

- **Powers of attorney:** You should also go through the different powers of attorney that are available and figure out which ones you need. When it comes to being prepared for a deployment, there's no such thing as too much information. See Chapter 9 for details.

- **Deployment benefits:** The personnel at the family support center can also help make sure you understand your deployment benefits to include the financial ones. Regardless of how long you've been in the military, the benefits are constantly changing, and it can be challenging keeping up with them. There's no shame in asking the experts. It's their job to know what the new programs are. A lot of the benefits can only be taken advantage of while the servicemember is deployed, so it's important to know what all your options are right from the start. No one wants to feel like they missed out on a good deal. Refer to Chapter 16 for more information on deployments.

  Depending on your branch of service and what's available on your specific installation, you may be eligible for deployment benefits ranging from free respite childcare to free oil changes. Check your installation for programs available to you and your family.

- **Financial readiness:** One of the greatest sources of contention for military families particularly during deployment is the state of the family finances. If you have the time and inclination, you may want to think about taking the financial readiness classes at the installation family support center. Chances are good that while your spouse is deployed, you'll be responsible for some, if not all aspects of the family finances. Understanding your financial management and investment options will make you all feel better. Servicemembers shouldn't have to worry that the family is undergoing money troubles while he's away.

- **Installation support:** In addition to the classes and individual services available, some family support centers also maintain lists of families of deployed servicemembers and will use this information to push information out to you. Don't underestimate the value of this little touch. It's nice to hear about what the installation is doing to support the families of those who are deployed. And who knows, maybe you want to try that spouse support group or attend the holiday potluck and party that they're having for the families. Just consider it another resource available to you. More information can always be found at the base family support center or on the official installation for the installation.

Turning to faith-based solutions

Base chapels are a tremendous source of support. Many people are used to turning to their chaplains for confidential faith-based counseling and support. If you've been attending the church for awhile, you're probably used to speaking openly with your chaplain about different issues, so it's a natural extension to go to him/her about sensitive issues dealing with marriage, deployments, and communication. What many people don't realize though is that you don't have to be a member of the congregation to seek help. The door to the chaplain's office is always open to everyone on the installation.

Military chaplains are also deployable so chances are good that they have had personal experience with some of the things you're going through.

Many of the programs available through the installation chapels are open to everyone regardless of your religious beliefs. A lot of the marriage and relationship enrichment classes run through the chaplains even though they are not faith-based solutions. Depending on the service branch and installation, you can find anything from classes and seminars on communication skills, marriage enrichment, weekend retreats, and other programs developed to help with relationship skills and maintain strong military marriages.

Participating in Family Readiness Groups (FRG)

When your spouse is deployed and you're responsible for your entire household on your own, sometimes the thought of getting out there and taking on more responsibility or helping anyone else seems ridiculous. You need to change that way of thinking. Don't think of it as a burden. Think of it as an opportunity to expand your network by getting involved with a group of people all pulling for a common goal — supporting the servicemembers and the families within the unit.

Even though you're not going to want to add another event to your calendar and sign on to attend yet another meeting, it's important that you go to the official FRG and unit events. This is when you'll get the official information from the unit. Instead of relying on second-hand information for your updates, go to the meetings yourself and find out what's going on. The purpose of FRGs is to foster the camaraderie and well-being of unit members and their families. FRG activities also serve the dual purpose of giving you the opportunity of meeting other servicemembers and family members in the unit. It's always helpful to be able to put names and faces to the people who are going through the same experience you are.

Even if you're fortunate enough to be stationed near your family, there's no such thing as too much support. The people in your Unit and by extension, the Family Readiness Group, will function as your extended military family. And unlike your birth family who may or may not understand or relate to your military lifestyle, your extended military family understands because they're going through it too. You don't have to fill in any back story because your reality is theirs as well.

Aside from the servicemembers who are tasked with responsibilities for the FRG and the recent advent of the paid *Family Readiness Assistants*, everyone else involved in running an FRG is a volunteer. These are family members from the unit who have the same stressors you do and have stepped up to fill a role and provide a service to their peers. Maintain reasonable expectations on your part and remember that they are taking care of the entire unit. Their sole purpose in life is not to be your beck and call girl. Remember, they're dealing with their own deployment and family issues. Let them know that you appreciate all they do on your behalf.

It is possible for volunteers to get compassion fatigue and burn out. This can be prevented by sharing the load. If you have the time, think about taking on a task for the FRG. Maybe you can lead a support group or take charge of one of the children's parties. If everyone understood the importance of giving back and being part of the solution, the burden would be shared more evenly and unit morale would remain strong and steady. Everyone would always know where to go for information and support.

If you decide against being actively involved with your FRG group, at least do the bare minimum and keep your contact information up to date. This will allow them to send you official communication and keep you in the loop.

During normal times, you'll appreciate having other spouses to hang out with and vent. Your children will enjoy having other children to pal around with whose family dynamic is similar to their own with one parent missing. But in worst case scenarios, you will truly appreciate the support and organization of your FRG. It's when something goes wrong that the strength of a unit and the FRG really come into play. If for no other reason, this in itself is reason enough to develop those relationships and get involved.

Having some fun and giving back

Recently, spouse clubs have gotten a bad rap. They're viewed as archaic bastions of a bygone era. This is unfortunate because nothing could be further from the truth. Becoming involved in a spouse club provides you a great opportunity to meet other spouses. The luncheons and other events are a great escape from the daily grind and a wonderful way to get that adult conversation in a civilized setting that doesn't include an overgrown mouse or plastic ball pits. Treat it as a form of escapism. Where you may be involved with your FRG, with a spouse club, you'll actually meet spouses from other units around the installation. This is a good opportunity for you to expand your circle of friends.

You can get as involved as you want. Sometimes, it's enough to just pay your dues, receive the newsletter, and attend some of the monthly events. There's generally a theme to each of the events. Sometimes it's an activity and other times it'll be a popular speaker or scholarship luncheon. Regardless of who you speak to, one of the most popular events remains Bingo. In the past, the theme was generally Crystal/Silver Bingo, but more recently, this has been replaced by Basket, Pottery, or International Bingos.

In addition to the social aspects associated to belonging to a spouses' club, you'll be part of a grand tradition of philanthropy. The clubs' activities are centered on raising money to give back to the installation and to military families. This is done through donations to various organizations and scholarships for military dependents. These funds are sometimes generated through the operation of a Gift Corner or Thrift Shop staffed mostly with volunteers. The viability of these shops depends on the club members who volunteer their time.

A small club can raise a few thousand dollars for charity while the larger clubs such as the ones overseas with large Gift Corners can raise and give out several hundred thousand dollars.

If you feel like you want to go beyond just attending the events and would like to take on a more active role in your club, volunteer for one of the available board positions. Depending on your level of interest, you can do anything from putting together the programs, making arrangements, or planning scholarships for the club. It's a great way to give back while having fun.

Participating on spouse club boards also provides great résumé bullets. It's transparent to many employers whether you were a volunteer or a paid volunteer. Experience is experience.

Getting Support Online

As great as the programs on base may be, sometimes after a full day of work or running the kids around, the last thing you want to do is leave the house again. Many people find that when they finally get a chance to wind down and possibly chat with some friends or visit with some counselors, it's late into the night. Fortunately, lots of support systems are available at all hours of the night.

If you just can't make it into the offices on base during regular work hours and need to talk to someone, you have a free resource available to you online called Military OneSource. Through a secure web portal providing free services to currently serving members and their families, Military OneSource (www.militaryonesource.com) compiles all of the best resources available to you and provides links to official organizations. Regardless of what you're looking for, this site is a good jumping off point for you.

One of the features of Military OneSource is that they will try to bring together special military discounts available to you and list them monthly based on their availability, so it's a good place to look if you're looking for discounts on products and services.

In addition to the information, Military OneSource also provides servicemembers and their families access to counselors through either in-person or telephonic consultations. If you find that you are stressed beyond your means and require outside help, this may be a good starting point for you. To schedule a counseling session, call 800-342-9647 (CONUS), or 800-3429-6477, or 484-530-5908 (OCONUS). They will start by having you answer some questions during an assessment process to decide the best course of action for you. At that point, the consultants will likely refer you to a counselor within a 30-mile radius of your home. If you are too far away to take advantage of this, they may refer you for telephonic counseling sessions. These sessions are provided to eligible servicemembers and dependents absolutely free of charge.

If you go past the six sessions per issue per consultant, then you will have to pick up the rest of the charges.

If Military OneSource is too purple for you and you're looking to access more service specific information, check out the family support Web sites sponsored by the different service branches:

- ✔ www.myarmylifetoo.com
- ✔ www.afcrossroads.com
- ✔ www.lifelines.navy.mil
- ✔ www.usmc-mccs.org

Sometimes, talking to a friend is exponentially more helpful than talking to a counselor. Unfortunately, by the time you get all the kids to bed, pick everything up, and catch your breath, it's well past a decent hour to call one of your friends. People have started turning to online forums for support and the opportunity to vent. Find out more about online support forums in Chapter 14.

Looking Outside the Fishbowl

All the support on base is great, but sometimes, you can start to feel like you're living in a bubble. It's military life 24/7 with no break in between. At least when your spouse is home, you can vent to him without the fear of judgment. You don't have to worry about being judged and found wanting because you aren't weathering the deployment as well as everyone else. The multitudes of meetings can start wearing you down, and sometimes you just want to visit with someone who's far removed from your reality on base. You may want to just get away from it all.

This is when those other networks of family and friends outside your unit or installation really come in handy. It's nice to engage in some escapism and pretend like you're just a normal family and that your sanity isn't determined by what's being reported on the news that day. Even though it would be so much easier to cocoon yourself at home and not deal with the outside world, having that connection with lots of other people will actually help make the time go by faster. Sometimes over the breaks, it's nice to make a little pilgrimage to visit grandparents or aunts, uncles, and cousins. It's a nice break to the monotony and allows you the chance to share the parenting load for a time.

With all the options available to you, there's no reason you should feel like you're in this alone. The help is out there for the taking. Just make sure you maintain open lines of communication with your friends and family so they know what's going on. Don't sequester yourself away from everyone, and take the time to be a good friend. Just as you're looking for ways to weather the deployment, many of your friends are in the exact same situation. More about finding community-based support in Chapter 14.

Chapter 18

Helping Children Cope with the Absence of a Parent

*W*ith the current operations tempo, it seems like servicemembers are spending more and more time away from home. Even if the servicemember isn't deployed, in the course of regular duties and TDYs, it seems like he's still spending more time away from home. This makes for a lot of missed moments with family. Unfortunately, the kids seem to bear the brunt of these separations.

Understanding the Effects of Deployment on Children

Depending on the age of the children, their stress and anxiety at the prospect of a parent deploying will manifest itself in different ways. Preschool students might start sucking their thumbs, wetting their beds, or withdrawing into their shells. They may become clingier to the parent who is left behind. Older children might become agitated or irritable more easily. They may have a difficult time concentrating on tasks at hand and may also have recurring nightmares. All these are pretty normal reactions to a deployment. However, don't be complacent. Look for the following warning signs that your children may be having an extraordinarily difficult time and may require some additional help or attention:

✔ Persistent lack of appetite

✔ Poor sleep habits that go on for an extended period of time

✔ Lack of interest in activities they normally enjoy

✔ Withdrawal from family and friends

✔ Long-term behavioral problems that are out of the ordinary for the child

Some of these issues will crop up in most children in the face of a parent's deployment. Red flags should be waving if any of these issues persist for a long period of time. Know what your resources are and use them if you need them. You don't need to handle everything on your own. It's okay to ask for help. You will be of no use to your children if you are unable to take care of your own needs first (you can find out more about handling deployments in Chapter 16).

Maintaining Routine

When a parent deploys, it might take some time to fill the void in terms of redistributing the chores and responsibilities. However, the sooner you can get a routine down, the better. Children can only manage so much change before they start to feel off balance. There is so much that is out of their control that they really do relish the routines in their life whether they admit it or not.

If you order Chinese food every Friday night and eat in front of the TV on tray tables, then stick to that during the deployment. For your kids, it's comforting knowing that even though dad is out of the picture for a little while, some things still remain the same. They count on that little bit of fun and family bonding at the end of the week remaining constant. This doesn't mean that you need to be inflexible. If they want to change the routine a little, then roll with it. However, *you* shouldn't drive the change. There's already enough that's out of their control.

The interesting thing about routine is that for the parent who's deployed, he usually remembers life at home through the filter of those routines. He remembers the rituals, the Friday dinners, and finds great comfort in the knowledge that no matter how crazy and dangerous things may be for him out in the field, back at home, things are going on just as normal.

Maintaining routines goes beyond the fun rituals. You should hold your kids to standards in all aspects of their lives. If Junior's expected to pick up his room, take out the trash, and empty the dishwasher as part of his daily tasks, then hold him to it. Don't cut him slack because mom or dad is deployed; he should keep up with his chores. Teach them that even though they may be sad and resentful that dad is gone, they still have responsibilities to themselves and to the family. The same thing goes for school.

While you should keep an eye on changes in behavior that can be attributed to the deployment, you're pretty savvy and can probably smell a con from a mile away. You know when your kids are playing you like a fiddle. You're not going to be doing them any favors by allowing them to use the deployment as an excuse for missed homework or bad grades. Be preemptive in dealing with academic problems. If grades start to slide and problems persist, get your children help with a tutor or extra time with a teacher.

As a "single parent," it's going to be difficult for you to attend all your kids' events and activities. You might want to schedule weekly calendar meetings where the family sits down and talks about what's coming up over the next week. Figure out who needs you where and when. It'll be easier for you to balance everything if you know up front what your kids' expectations are in terms of your presence at school events. Get it all down on a common calendar so that the events are de-conflicted.

You may be used to volunteering extensively in your kids' schools or with their after-school activities. You're not going to be able to maintain this same level of involvement while your spouse is gone because there will be more demands on your time. However, this doesn't mean that you have to forego volunteering altogether. If you're used to being the chaperone at the school events and can't make it now, perhaps you can call the food committee and see if you can donate refreshments instead. Flexibility in all you do is going to help you manage your kids' expectations while maintaining your sanity. Find out more about surviving a deployment in Chapter 16.

Communicating

Your kids will have a lot of emotions to deal with that they may not understand or be able to explain, and they may also ask you questions that you have a difficult time explaining to them. Both you and your children need to make some special efforts toward communication during this time, and these sections give you some ideas on how to best communicate with and understand the emotional ups and downs of each other.

Encouraging open communication

It may be difficult for your kids to articulate exactly how they're feeling. You're probably going to get frustrated that they're lashing out or are depressed and aren't sharing what they're going through with you. They may have problems understanding their feelings themselves, never mind sharing them with you. This might cause them some frustration. It's important to remember that they may not know how to help themselves.

Help your kids communicate to share some of what's going on inside them. If they're younger, they may express their feelings through pictures they draw. Older kids may find that journaling daily helps alleviate some of the stress. This type of exercise might help them express things that they have a problem saying out loud. The trick is to help your children find a medium that works for them. It's not so much about what you can read in the messages; it's more about what release your kids can get by getting some of their emotions down on paper.

In addition to helping your children deal with their stress and emotions over the deployment, encourage them to reach out and communicate with the deployed parent. They may be scared about dad's safety, but shutting him out or ignoring him is not the way to deal with this. They should maintain a line of communication even when they're separated. They should always feel like they have two parents they can turn to. One parent may not be as accessible, but they're certainly able to maintain the relationship through regular correspondence and phone calls.

The deployed servicemember should make extra efforts to stay in touch with each child. Everyone loves getting a letter personally addressed to them in the mail. While this is more time consuming than just sending a blanket e-mail, the extra effort is appreciated. It doesn't even have to be a great, long letter. Postcards or short notes are enough to let your kids know you care.

 You can help facilitate communication between your kids and your deployed spouse by putting together a little stationery kit for the deploying service-member. Include some stamps, cards, and maybe pre-addressed envelopes to make things easier to follow through.

Children are invariably going to experience some anxiety over a parent's absence. You can both help allay some of your children's fears by educating them before the deployment on where the servicemember is going and helping them understand a little more about the importance of the mission at hand. To give them a better idea of where dad is going, perhaps you want to show them the location on a map. Share with your kids as much as you think they can handle about what their dad is going to be doing and who he will be helping while he's away.

Communication during the pre-deployment period is just as important as during deployment. The children may have an easier time articulating their fears to the parent who's deploying because they don't want to compound the stress of the parent who's left behind. Don't underestimate the sophistication of your children's thought process or the depths of their consideration. Help them become more comfortable with the impending deployment by taking the time to sit down as a family and talk about what they can expect.

Explaining difficult topics

It can be difficult to explain to toddlers why daddy needs to go away. For young children, things are pretty cut and dry. They don't understand that daddy's out there serving the greater good. All they know is that their daddy is not at home. It's hard for them to understand why.

A few years ago, the *Sesame Street* Workshop, in collaboration with Wal-Mart, the Department of Defense, and other sponsors, debuted an interactive video series called *Talk, Listen and Connect.* One video in the series involves deployment. Toddlers may have a difficult time wrapping their minds around why a parent needs to be away from home for such a long period of time, but they may be more open to information when it's being presented by a trusted friend like Elmo.

This video helps children understand that their mom or dad is gone because they're doing something very important. It's a very sensitive treatment of the fears that children may have and lets them know that they're not in it alone. Their fears and feelings are expressed through the filter of Elmo dealing with his father's impending "business trip." Laced throughout are vignettes of real military children going through a deployment. There is also another companion video about homecomings that talks about the issues facing families during the reintegration period.

Most recently, the *Sesame Street* Workshop has also released a new video in the series that speaks about wounded warrior issues. In the video, the father of Elmo's friend, Rosita, comes back "changed." During his "business trip," his legs were hurt and he can't walk and now requires a wheelchair. His daughter's having a very difficult time adjusting to all the changes. This last video does deal with very sensitive issues, so you may want to preview it before sharing it with your kids because it will generate some questions. The videos serve as a tremendous resource for military families. You can download all the videos for free along with companion guides for parents and caregivers at www.sesameworkshop.org/initiatives/emotion/tlc.

For older children and teenagers, they tend to lean on their friends a bit more. Yet, sometimes, it doesn't seem like enough. If they usually hang out with kids whose parents may not have any connection to the military and may never have experienced a deployment, your kids may seek out opportunities to be around children going through the same things they are. Many Youth and Teen Centers on base have deployment support groups. If your installation doesn't have these types of programs, seek out other families in your same situation and invite them over to dinner. It'll help your kids to have the opportunity to hang out with other children going through the same thing.

Managing Anxiety

Just as the daily deluge of information can become somewhat overwhelming for you, it can have the same effect on your kids. Limit the amount of television news they are allowed to watch. They don't need to be bombarded by news of the current conflict. You should also be judicious about how much information you share with your children. Based on your child's age, determine how much information is enough and appropriate. It is absolutely possible to have too much information.

When your kids wonder about how to balance everything, they're going to look to you to set an example. Try to project some calm and evenness. Just as animals can smell fear from a mile away, your kids will be able to sense your anxiety, and if you're extremely stressed, they'll know and will react to it. While your children will try to live up to perceived (perhaps self-imposed) expectations and maybe swallow their own fears and anxiety to take care of you, that's not their job — they're kids and should be allowed to be kids. Find your support elsewhere (more about dealing with deployments in Chapter 16); your job is to be strong for your kids, not the other way around.

Sometimes, you get so involved with maintaining the day-to-day routine and surviving the deployment that you may forget to inject some fun into your and your children's lives. Halfway through the deployment, everyone's nerves may be a little frayed. If you start to get on each other's nerves, it might be time to play hookie. Get away from it all. Unplug and go see that movie your kids have been waiting for. Don't worry about the kids' homework — so what if it doesn't get done to their usual high standard for once. Forget about the e-mails you need to respond to and the phone messages you need to answer. Leave the electronic gadgets behind and go hang out with your kids. Long after the ill effects of the deployment have been forgotten, your kids will still remember the times when mom conspired with them to have some fun. Who says you have to be responsible 24/7? Sometimes, your kids need you to be a friend more than they need you to be a mom.

It doesn't take a rocket scientist to understand that the heightened state of anxiety during a year-long (or 15-month) deployment is difficult to maintain without some time outs. Find ways to celebrate your children's milestones. If your kids had an extraordinary day at school or at the track meet, celebrate by eating dessert before dinner. Or, let them order in their favorite meal. Maybe instead of doing chores all day Saturday, try to do a little during the week so you can have game night on Saturday. Invite other friends and their kids who may also have a loved one who's deployed. The kids will appreciate the opportunity to be around other kids who are going through the same thing they are. They won't have to worry about saying the wrong thing and can just relax and be themselves.

A great way for you to help your kids manage their anxiety is to listen to them and respect their fears. Don't belittle their feelings. Do your best to allay their fears, but don't be condescending and don't dwell on the issue. Find ways to fill their time with physical activities that will keep their mind off their fears for even a little while. Family walks, spending time at the community pool, sports camps, or lessons during breaks all fit the bill.

Staying Involved from a Distance

Don't let the deployed parent be "out of sight, out of mind" at your house. Keep the deployed parent in the loop. Share information about what's going on in your lives back home. Get the kids involved with writing letters and sending care packages. Maybe you can make a habit of picking out special school assignments that they're particularly proud of, such as an A+ on a particularly difficult quiz, a really nice picture they made in art class, or a report they wrote, and sending copies to dad. That's a great way to keep the deployed parent current on how the kids are doing.

There are also a number of organizations such as Connect and Join (www. connectandjoin.com) that provide secure Web sites where families can build and maintain family sites to keep in touch. This particular organization allows for multiple access passwords that can be shared with extended family members or friends. That way, you all have a secure Web portal where you can share pictures, calendars, and other projects. Information can be input by everyone, so dad can even share some of his insights or give input for class projects or assignments.

The deployed servicemember may miss some milestones by virtue of being far away from home, but there are ways to stay involved. Don't take the easy road and leave the responsibilities of gift giving, card buying, and acknowledgements to the spouse left at home. With a little preplanning and very little effort on your part, both parents can be involved in acknowledging the special occasions.

For children, the novelty of receiving a delivery of balloons or a cookie or fruit bouquet on their birthday from a parent far away is thrilling. Remember to send those birthday cards. The deployed parent can make an effort to send cards for no reason whatsoever. Knowing that they are special enough to rate a special effort is priceless to your kids. It's difficult enough for them while one parent's deployed. Find a way to maintain his presence in the home in small ways while he's gone.

For the toddler set, companies have popped up that produce likenesses of a deployed parent. Through a company called Flat daddies (`http://flatdaddies.com/`), you can request a life-size paper likeness of the deployed servicemember. There is also a company (`www.hugahero.com`) that puts the likeness of the parent on a soft fabric "doll." The dolls can go anywhere with the child, and some children find great solace in them.

Letting Kids be Kids

You're going to want your kids to behave like little angels. You're going to want to believe that your kids understand that mommy's nerves are frayed and they should be well-behaved so that they don't add to mommy's stress. Unfortunately, the reality is that your kids are going to act out — not always at the most opportune moments. It's up to you to react appropriately and help them through the emotional turmoil.

While kids may start out well behaved, at some point, they're going to get sick of being good and act out. Some may act irritable. Some may be angry or sullen. Some may even feel guilty. Younger children sometimes worry that daddy left because of something they did. They may feel that the deployment was a direct result of their bad behavior. Make sure they understand that this is not the case. You'll know best what your kids will respond to, but it's important for them to understand that whatever they're going through is a normal reaction. Validate their feelings. Let your kids know that it's okay regardless of what their feelings are regarding the deployment and separation.

Although there will be incredible demands on your time, try to find ways for your children to keep up with their extracurricular activities. It's important for them to maintain as much of their routine as possible. They should also have some escape from the day-to-day grind and worry associated with the deployment. Whether you rely on carpools, or cut back on the number of classes they take, do whatever you can to allow the kids to maintain as much of their regular schedules as possible.

Don't go overboard. When you're the only parent at home shouldering all the parenting responsibilities, this may not be the time to take on additional duties. Don't sign on for more activities unless you already have a plan in place to make it work.

Setting Realistic Expectations

Help your kids understand what they can expect when one of their parents is deployed. They're going to be a little apprehensive about what's going to happen while dad's away. They'll want to know how often they'll be able to talk to dad, what he'll be doing over there, and when he'll be back. Give them as much information as you think they can handle. Be very honest in the discussion and respect your kids enough not to be condescending. They're going to be justifiably concerned and you should be prepared to explain things until they're satisfied with the answers.

Your kids are also going to want to know how their normal routine is going to change. Discuss these changes before the deployment. As a single parent, you're not going to be able to maintain the same level of involvement that you can when there's another parent in the picture. You'll be doing it all. It's important that your kids understand this right off the bat and it should be both parents who have this discussion with them. Don't make it a one-sided discussion. Listen to their concerns and really hear what they're saying.

The deployment will go much smoother if you can get off to a strong start and manage expectations on all sides. You might be surprised to hear some of your kids' fears for your spouse. It's a big burden for a child to bear, so whatever you can do to take some of the load off their shoulders will help them weather the deployment that much better.

Looping in the Caregivers and Teachers

Childcare centers and schools often provide an anchoring effect for children whose parents are in the midst of deployment. While things are changing so much in their home life, it's nice for them to have an environment that stays the same. However, the anxieties and stress they feel may creep into their time at school. Your kids may be acting out in ways you may not be aware of.

Children in childcare facilities may be more irritable or short tempered. They may display less patience with other children and may even lash out uncharacteristically. At school, your kids' grades may slip because they can't concentrate or are stressed out. To be fair, you really need to give their caregivers and teachers a heads up. This shouldn't be confused with asking for special treatment. This is simply letting the people in your child's life know what's going on so that they can keep an eye out for any strange behavior. They may even be able to offer you some suggestions on how to keep your child focused or how to manage the demands on their time.

Some caregivers and teachers may be unfamiliar with the military and deployments. Take the time to educate them on what it means. It will be helpful to them to understand why the children in their care are behaving differently for some "unfathomable" reason.

Maintain a good line of communication with your children's caregivers and teachers. Make sure they have your contact information, and take the time to get theirs. Ask them if they have preferences in the way that they would like to be contacted. Perhaps they have office hours you can take advantage of.

You can't possibly hope to know what's going on with your child during work hours unless you develop those relationships with their teachers and administrators. They will become your best advocates for your children. Some teachers may even choose to be more pro-active in supporting their students who have a parent in the military. They may perhaps even make an effort to take pictures of events or special milestones during school hours so the pictures can be shared with the absent parent. Depending on the number of children in the classroom who are affected by deployments, they may even be more apt to bring elements of deployment into the classroom curriculum. They may even ask the class to help manufacture a welcome-home banner for returning servicemembers. Regardless of how involved they may or may not want to be, it's still very important to keep them in the loop.

Besides you, your kids' caregivers and teachers are the ones spending the most amount of time with your children. They will know (sometimes before you do) when there's something going on. Developing a relationship with them will help open up those lines of communication. You should consider them partners in your child's well-being.

Once you know when your spouse is coming home, you're going to want to pay your children's teacher and caregivers the courtesy of letting them know. This is especially the case if you have a family trip planned outside the cycle of a normal school break or holiday. If they're able to take a little time away, there will be homework to make up and you should make sure you have a plan of action in place to be less disruptive to the child's class and to the teacher.

Sharing Responsibilities

With one parent away for a time, there are going to be chores and responsibilities that will need to be redistributed. Let your kids know that they may be asked to help out around the house a little more. If dad usually walks the dog in the morning before he goes to work, then maybe Junior should accompany dad on those morning walks for a few weeks before the deployment. That way, when dad leaves, Junior's ready to step in and take care of walking the dog while dad's gone.

Your kids should be given chores that are age appropriate. Deployment should not have anything to do with them maintaining their chores. They should just be aware that while dad's gone, everyone may be asked to take on a couple more responsibilities. Work the changes in gradually so that the kids don't equate dad going away with having to do more work. That will only fuel the resentment.

While dad's gone, older children tend to step up to the plate and help out with their younger siblings. They may take on additional responsibilities that go beyond being mom's helper. When dad gets back, it's difficult to relinquish all those responsibilities and the authority that comes with them. You're going to have to be very careful to be sensitive to their feelings and not diminish their importance to the household. Reward them somehow for all their contributions (perhaps with an increased allowance), but remind them that now that they don't have to help so often with their siblings, they have more time for other things. Maybe because they had to step in and help out more often, they missed out on activities with their friends or classmates. Remind them that having dad come home is a good thing. It means more time for them to be with their friends. It doesn't mean that they're no longer needed.

Seeing the Light at the End of the Tunnel

Sometimes, it seems like the separations are interminable. Help your kids keep an eye on the prize — figure out a way to let them know that the deployment is not forever and that there is an end in sight.

Before he leaves, maybe he can show the kids on a calendar how long he'll be gone. Then every morning or evening, they can mark an X through the day that puts them one day closer to the end. Perhaps dad can write silly little notes to the kids. Put the notes in a large glass bowl, and let the kids pull one out every day. Not only are the notes a great way to get that little bit of encouragement or tidbit from dad every morning, when the notes are gone, daddy will be back. They can watch the level of notes in the bowl go lower and lower. The notes don't have to be long sentiments — just little reminders to the kids that there's another parent in the picture who cared enough to write a bowl full of notes for them.

Just because the deployment's supposed to be a year doesn't mean that the parent will be back in a year. Unfortunately, deployments have a way of extending, and being deployed beyond the initial return date is par for the course these days. Be preemptive and have some extra notes on hand. If dad's deployment is extended, add the notes to the bowl.

Look ahead past the deployment and plan a trip. Give the kids something to look forward to. Let the parent who's deployed contribute to the planning so that it really does become an anticipated family vacation. Keeping the kids focused on something positive channels their energy and helps the time pass.

Getting Away

You and the kids will need some kind of break during your servicemember's deployment. Whether you take small breaks by staying busy with volunteering and helping others or you take an actual family vacation, the following sections give you some ideas to make sure you get the break you need.

Taking some time off

Even though it seems like a deployment tends to take on a life of its own and sometimes runs an entire family's life, it's healthy to take some time off and not let the deployment run your life. There's nothing better at keeping children's minds off their own problems than volunteering and helping others. If you volunteered as a family before your spouse deployed, then maintain the tradition while he's gone. If volunteering as a family is new to you, then you might want to sit down with your kids and find things they may be interested in doing.

If you don't know where to start, check out America Supports You at www. americasupportsyou.mil to find organizations in your area that are already involved in some of the activities that you might be interested in supporting. Perhaps your kids would like to sponsor a Freedom Walk, or maybe they want to read to children at the hospital. Feed the homeless? Cook meals for families of wounded servicemembers? There's something out there for everyone.

Whether you plug into an existing charitable event being sponsored, or originate something on your own, you'll find that volunteering together will help you bond as a family and will achieve the dual purpose of keeping your kids occupied and letting them forget about their problems for a little while. There's no better cure for feeling sorry for yourself than by helping others. Teach your children the value of philanthropy early and it might help them keep everything else in their lives in perspective.

Looking forward to a family vacation

Is there a place your kids have always wanted to go? Perhaps Disney World? Perhaps they've always wanted to try skiing? Fortunately, there are a number of military discounts out there. With enough planning, you can put together an affordable family getaway. There are some advantages to getting away from the daily grind and the demands of well-meaning friends and extended family. Packing up and taking a little family getaway is a great way to get out and have some fun without any outside pressure or demands on your time.

Check out these resources for vacation planning:

- ✔ Perhaps your kids dream of breakfast with Snow White and Cinderella. And maybe the older siblings are dying to ride the new roller coasters. If so, a Florida vacation may be just what the doctor ordered. Shades of Green is a military recreational facility (resort) located on the grounds of Walt Disney World. It is steps away from the Magic Kingdom, is centrally located to all the parks, and is minutes away from downtown dining and shopping. There is something there for everyone, and with the special deals they run for returning OEF/OIF personnel and their families, it really is possible to have an affordable Disney vacation. Check out their Web site (www.shadesofgreen.org) for planning tools and information.

- ✔ In addition to information on Shades of Green, the U.S. Army Family and MWR Command Web site (www.armymwr.com) also includes information on the Hale Koa in Hawaii, the Dragon Hill Lodge in Korea, and the Edelweiss Lodge in Germany.

- ✔ Local installation MWR facilities are also a great place to look for vacation-planning resources. Perhaps you're looking more toward a cold weather location for your vacation. If your family's excited about hitting the slopes, you might want to think about starting your research at the MWR facility at the Air Force Academy. They run specials at the Keystone Resort that give military families access to condominiums and special deals. Check out www.rockymountainblue.com/.

- ✔ If you don't have time for a long vacation, you may want to just get away for a day or two. Anheuser Busch runs a Hero Salute program that allows currently serving servicemembers and their families a free day pass to any number of parks nationwide (www.herosalute.com/cavatx/overview.html).

- ✔ Perhaps you live far from any of these resort options and are looking for a vacation alternative that is within driving distance from your home. Then you might want to look into the Armed Forces Vacation Club (www.afvclub.com). This program specializes in condominium and vacation rental homes at discounted prices for active or retired military personnel.

These are all just starting points for you, but you get the idea. There are ways to plan a nice vacation on a budget. Let your kids decide where they want to go, with some input from both parents, and then you can do some legwork and find a vacation solution that works for your budget.

What the kids need to focus on is the fun planning aspect of the vacation. That way, when the conversations with dad out in the field start to get stilted, you can all fall back on talking about the upcoming vacation. Once you pick where you're going, help the kids find books and articles about the location that you can share with your spouse on the other end. That way, you're all on the same page in the planning process. Even though dad isn't around, you're all still working on a family plan together. Find these little ways to keep the parent who's deployed in the family mix. Don't fall victim to that "out of sight, out of mind" mentality. It's too easy for everyone to overcompensate for the parent who's gone by taking on extra responsibilities and leaving him out of the mix.

The added advantage of taking a family vacation at the end of a deployment or other extended separation is the opportunity to get away and get reconnected as a family. When a servicemember comes home, extended family members and friends will want to descend upon him and welcome him home as soon as possible. While understandable, it puts a crimp into any private family bonding opportunities. Don't miss out on this time together. Plan that vacation and get away. The time for big family reunions is after you get back.

Bringing Daddy Back into the Fold

When a parent returns from deployment, the closeness and familiarity is not necessarily going to automatically follow suit. For better or worse, the returning parent is a little bit of a stranger. When he left, the family dynamic shifted a little to accommodate the changes. Now that he's back, things have to move back around to bring him back into the fold.

Even under normal circumstances, kids can become confused. During one parent's absence, they have probably gotten used to the other parent doing everything for them. Now that dad's back, they may feel conflicted about having to choose between asking one parent over the other to help them. They will naturally default to the parent who was not deployed. Help your servicemember to understand this and to accept the children's feelings and the pace with which they let him back into their lives and their hearts.

Some of the reintegration issues can be mitigated by better preparation before the deployment. For example, if dad generally reads the kids a bedtime story, videotape dad reading bedtime stories that can be played for the kids at the appropriate time. That way, when dad comes back, and you're faced with the bedtime ritual of reading a story, the kids may more easily accept dad reading them the story because he's been doing it all along. Find ways to weave dad into the daily rituals even though he may be gone. The bigger presence he has in your children's life while he's away, the easier it will be for you all when he comes back.

For older children, maybe they can pick a book they want to read along with dad, so they have something to talk about while he's away. Encourage them to make dad a CD of favorite songs, and send the CDs along so that he can keep up with them. Keeping the connection with the older kids may be even more difficult than with the younger ones. Throughout the teen years, they're changing so rapidly. Before dad left, they may not have been interested in the opposite sex. By the time he gets back, they may already be dating. Or they may have hit other milestones such as being able to drive. They are too cool for words, so reconnecting with teenagers can be even more challenging than reconnecting with their younger siblings. Your servicemember needs to respect that teens need to do things on their own terms and in their own time.

An added complication to the reintegration period is that children may be a little timid because they don't know if mom or dad has changed. As silly as it sounds, they don't know if mom or dad still loves them the same way. They may worry that the parent has changed over the course of the deployment. Find a way to spend time with each child on a one-on-one basis doing something of their choosing. You can encourage your servicemember to do a couple of things to help alleviate that fear:

✔ Listen to them and pay them the undivided attention that they crave.

✔ Arrange a day that the servicemember spends with each child on an individual basis, allowing the children to plan the activities for the day.

Be aware that your children are going to feel conflicted about who they should be turning to, and you and your servicemember should make sure they understand that there's not a choice to be made. As far as you and the children are concerned, you're in it as a team unit.

Through the reintegration process, don't be surprised if your children express some fears about the next deployment. They may already be worried about daddy having to leave again.

Chapter 19

Keeping Connected with Your Loved One

*W*ith frequent deployments and extended separations, it can be quite challenging to maintain that connectivity between you and your service member. Fortunately, with today's technology, communicating across the miles is easier than ever. In this chapter, we take some time exploring the new technologies available to you as well as provide some suggestions on how to stay connected.

Communicating Securely

No one likes to think of this, but when your servicemember is deployed, you're very vulnerable, and no means of communication is entirely secure. Be careful what details you inadvertently reveal in your conversation or blog entries. Your general guidance should be, if you're not comfortable having a total stranger know certain details about your life, do not put them out there for anyone to read or hear. The following sections describe how to stay in touch with your spouse during deployment as well as encourage you to keep your communications private and secure.

Using the Internet

With the advent of technology, military families have started turning to the Web for support. Spouses, parents, and children are blogging online at an unprecedented rate. Sometimes that results in threats to *operational security* (OpSec). Not being cognizant of other people possibly eavesdropping, family members may inadvertently share too much information through casual conversation. It's a challenge for the services to allow troops and family members access to free and open communication lines while still maintaining OpSec.

Understanding that families will look for innovative ways to keep in touch, services have made efforts to build secure online forums for soldiers and families to communicate securely. The Army has established a Virtual Family Readiness Group (VFRG) to allow families and soldiers to go through a secure Web portal to communicate. Check out www.armyfrg.org.

The VFRG also allows the Army to push information out to families by updating the home page. This is especially convenient in reaching out to families who may be geographically remote from the installation or other families who do not self-identify themselves with the military and do not know where to look for resources.

Families have always journaled about their experiences and anxieties. Some things haven't changed. However, with today's technology, they're getting more sophisticated and taking their journaling to the Web. The blogosphere is literally replete with thousands of military-related blogs, and new ones come online every day. Blogs serve as a means for people to share anything from their innermost feelings to favorite resources and tools. For some people, it's a little like a voyeuristic view into someone's life. Some bloggers share very intimate details with their audience, while others are more circumspect.

Remember, blogs are out there for everyone to see. Be sure you don't share anything that you could regret others reading.

Making phone calls

Back in the day, servicemembers used to have to stand in line for hours to make morale calls to their families. When they finally made it to the front of the line, the calls were patched through the Pentagon operator and you never knew how long the connection would last. It was like playing roulette. The calls varied anywhere from a few minutes to ten minutes and frequently ended without any notice. You would be talking away and all of a sudden, the phone line would go dead and you were no longer connected. The phone call had ended unceremoniously. So, you'd find yourself starting each phone call with, "Hello, we love you, we miss you, stay safe, and we'll talk to you again soon." Back then, families were captive to other people's schedules and whims.

With today's technology, that is no longer the case. Through the use of satellite phones, even servicemembers in very remote areas are able to stay in touch with their families on a regular basis. For those not in remote areas that have access to the Internet, their options are endless. Free Internet telephone applications such as Skype make it possible for servicemembers and their families to connect on their timetables. They are no longer captive to high prices and crazy schedules. As far as you're concerned, all you need is a computer and Internet access. If you have video capability, you can even see your loved one during the calls. It's so much easier these days to stay connected.

Sharing a Piece of Home

When the servicemembers are so far away from home, it's easy to revert to the "out of sight, out of mind" mentality. Everyone gets caught up in their day-to-day routine and it's all too easy to collapse at the end of the day without giving a second thought to what extra tasks you can stuff into your day. This is when you should make the extra effort to show that you care, that you miss them, and that you are thinking of them.

Care packages are a great tangible way to express these feelings. In addition to breaking up the monotony of servicemembers' days, a care package is a sign that you care enough to take time out of your day to assemble a thoughtful package and then stand in line at the post office to send it. For servicemembers, it's also a great way to bring them a taste of home. Many of the things they miss from the states, they may not be able to get where they are. Keeping that in mind, there are some guidelines to follow when assembling your care packages:

✔ Don't send things that are contraband to that country. The post office will have a comprehensive list of what you can and can't send, but general guidelines of prohibited items could include alcohol, meat products, pornography, flammable items, weapons, fresh fruits, and vegetables.

✔ Chocolates are yummy, but if they're deployed to a forward location where it is exceedingly hot, you may want to forego the candy bars for gum or hard candies.

✔ Cookies are always popular, but as far as care packages go, not all recipes are created equal. Find cookies that will withstand a lot of jostling and that have a longer shelf life. Take care in packing them as well. Recycle tubular potato chip (Pringles) canisters — they become great containers for cradling cookies.

✔ Think of things they can't get where they are. Popular requests include bottles of Tabasco, plastic jars of peanut butter, Fluff, power bars, and Girl Scout cookies.

- Books help pass time. In addition to printed books, consider books on tape.

- For holiday care packages, you might think about including seasonal decorations. Again, be sensitive to the country, but at Christmastime, maybe sending along a little artificial Christmas tree with ornaments will give them a taste of home in the desert or wherever they may be.

- Packaging is very important in making sure everything arrives intact. Try to pack your items with enough padding to cushion them. Your box shouldn't rattle when you shake it. You shouldn't be sending things in glass containers, but if you're sending anything that could potentially break or spill, you might want to package it in a sealed plastic bag before adding it to the care package.

- It's always nice to send enough to share. Not everyone may have someone sending them care packages, and it's important to keep up everyone's morale. So bake a couple extra dozen cookies and send them along.

The United States Postal Service has a great Frequently Asked Questions page dealing with sending mail and care packages to the troops (www.usps.com/supportingourtroops/supportingfaqs.htm).

In addition to care packages, nothing shows you care more than a handwritten letter sent through the mail. Mail call may seem archaic in light of today's technology and e-mail, but that is far from the truth. E-mail is great, but it doesn't replace the appeal of snail mail. There's something priceless about receiving a letter written in your loved one's handwriting, knowing they took the time to sit down and put their thoughts down on paper for you. The same goes for notes and pictures written and drawn by children. Some emotions just can't be captured adequately in an e-mail. Take the time to write and send that letter. If you have kids, get them involved as well.

Celebrating Special Occasions

One of the most difficult aspects of military deployments is being separated from your loved ones during those special occasions and milestone moments. There's nothing worse than missing birthdays, holidays, and anniversaries with your loved ones. However, with some pre-planning, there's no reason your servicemember spouse should be left out of the loop. Keeping him involved with the kids is another topic altogether and is discussed at length in Chapter 18. For our purposes here, we will discuss how to stay connected with your spouse or better half.

You may think it's easy for your servicemember to send things home while he's deployed. A servicemember, with some planning, can cushion the blow of you having to spend birthdays and anniversaries alone by pre-arranging floral deliveries. By simply contacting a local florist before he deploys, picking out the arrangements, and writing notes, on those special days, your flowers will arrive on time. This doesn't just work with flowers. Any number of different gifts can be handled in the same manner.

And, as the spouse, you can return the favor. On the servicemember's birthday, why not send a birthday cake, some candles (if it's not too hot), festive paper plates, and napkins? Believe it or not, there are bakeries now that specialize in packaging cakes in a manner that makes them suitable for shipping over to the sandbox. Check out Web sites such as www.bakemeawish.com to send birthday cakes overseas. Or, if you don't want to go that route, send his favorite snack cake with some fun paper goods and other decorations. In this case, it really is the thought that counts.

For spouses and other family members left behind on the home front, a certain amount of pre-planning can help keep Mom or Dad in the loop and connected during special occasions and holidays. If Dad is the one who always reads "The Night Before Christmas" to the kids on Christmas Eve, then think about arranging a time for him to call when everyone else is together. With the help of a speaker phone, he can still be in the thick of things. If this solution doesn't work for you, why not videotape Dad reading the poem before he deploys? That way, on Christmas Eve, you can play the video; while it's not as good as Dad being there in person, it is a way for him to be involved on some level.

Staying Connected

It seems like every time you turn around, your kids have grown a few inches and developed totally different interests. When you talk about a parent deploying for months to over a year, it is challenging keeping them up to date on everything that's going on in a kid's life. Resist the temptation to take the easy route and do everything yourself. It takes some extra steps to keep your spouse looped in on how the kids are doing, but it's worth making the extra effort. It'll make the reintegration process that much easier when Mom or Dad comes home. So make the time to:

- Share the kids' calendars so that when the kids have an opportunity to speak to the deployed parent, the parent has a jumping-off point to know what was going on in their week.
- Make an effort to take lots of pictures and videos of the kids' various events. Share them frequently instead of waiting until they come home. That way, the deployed parent doesn't miss out on the little stories and events.
- Arrange for the kids to talk to the deployed parent frequently.

> ✔ Get the kids involved in putting together and sending care packages.
>
> ✔ The deployed parent should send the kids their own e-mails or mail, so the kids know they still have another parent they can talk to whenever they need to.

Find more information on supporting children through deployments in Chapter 18.

In addition to communicating with the children while deployed, it's important to keep the extended family in the loop. They will be concerned with the well-being of the deployed servicemember as well. Rather than having the ones left behind dealing with the multiple phone calls, it is helpful for the servicemember to send an e-mail update to the families. It's also nice for the servicemember to be receiving mail and e-mails from multiple sources.

Get the extended family involved in sending care packages and presents for special occasions. It's nice for the deployed servicemember to know that they're not losing a year out of their lives and that other people are thinking of them.

Managing Anxiety

When you are separated from your spouse and the news is broadcasting 24 hours a day from all corners of the earth, your imagination can start to run wild. Technology's a great thing, but sometimes enough is enough and you need to unplug. In the era of embedded journalists, we're often finding out about bombings and other incidents out in the field as soon as they've occurred. It is possible to become overstimulated.

To help manage anxiety, limit the amount of news you're exposed to. Trust that your spouse has the best training possible and that he will be fine. While he may be in danger only a portion of the time that he is away from you, it's easy for you to imagine that he's in danger 100 percent of the time that he is gone. All that can amount to quite a bit of stress. You're going to have to find ways to manage the anxiety, or you'll find yourself coming apart at the seams. Here a few ways help manage anxiety:

> ✔ **Exercise regularly.** Even if it's just a walk with a friend around the block, build some exercise into your routine to let off some steam.
>
> ✔ **Maintain healthy eating.** It's going to be tempting to not cook meals for one, but it's worth making the effort instead of eating out all the time. Find the spouse of another deployed servicemember and share meals.
>
> ✔ **Maintain healthy sleeping habits.** It's important to recharge your batteries every night.

✔ **Stay away from toxic people.** You'll recognize them — they're the ones that generate drama. They will drain your lifeblood — trust us when we say you do not have the time or energy for this. Do not empower them to take more of your attention than you're willing to give.

✔ **Have fun.** It's okay to have fun while your spouse is deployed or TDY. You don't have to do everything together. If you have an opportunity to take advantage of excursions or a little trip with another spouse and their kids, do it. It'll help pass the time and keep your mind occupied.

✔ **Get involved.** Don't spend days alone in the house by yourself. Before too long, the days will string together and become weeks. Without knowing it, you might have cut yourself off from the outside world. If you're not working outside the home, find volunteer opportunities that appeal to you or find other reasons to leave the house.

✔ **Remember that your spouse has the best training possible and that he is good at his job.** Have faith that he will be fine.

Part V:
Transitioning Out of the Military

"This option in the pension is a little tricky. You can start collecting benefits when you're 58 years old, as long as you <u>look</u> 58 years old."

In this part . . .

All good things must come to an end. When it comes time for the service member to look for that first job out of the military, the whole family feels the impact. This part will guide you to an easier transition from the military.

Chapter 20

Separating from Service

. . . .

In This Chapter

▶ Planning your separation

▶ Defining the ways members separate from service

▶ Evaluating financial impacts of transitions at different career stages

. . . .

Some people enter the military expecting to fulfill their initial commitment and nothing more. Others choose service as their career. For many families, military service has been a way of life for generations. Regardless of the reasons people choose to serve, they have even more reasons for why they choose to leave the service.

Your servicemember may discover that a career in the military is not for him. As a couple, you may decide that life in the military is not for your family. Transitions from service may occur at anytime throughout your servicemember's military career. For any person leaving the service, whatever the reason, planning ahead is essential.

In this chapter we discuss the essential pre-separation planning, the various characterizations of separation, and how these affect your family primarily from the financial perspective, such as access to veteran's benefits and military retirement benefits.

Preparing for Separation

The Department of Defense (DoD) recommends that you start your planning at least 12 months prior to separation and 24 months prior to retirement. In this section we focus on planning for separation from service. Check out Chapter 21 to find out more about planning for retirement from military service.

Transition assistance program

The DoD's Transition Assistance Program (TAP) is an outstanding resource to assist you and your servicemember in exploring all the options and opportunities for all types of employment (government and private sector) available, to answer questions, and to provide guidance and support through your transition from military service to civilian life.

Specifically, the TAP program consists of the following:

✔ Mandatory pre-separation counseling

✔ Department of Labor employment workshops

✔ Veteran's benefits briefings conducted by the VA

✔ Disabled Transition Assistance Program (DTAP)

Your servicemember must complete DD Form 2648 (Pre-separation Counseling Checklist) to begin the transition process, and then must make an appointment to see his local transition counselor. Transition counselors are available at your installation. Check with your Family Support Center for more information.

Transition assistance is available to your servicemember for up to 180 days after separation from active duty. Transition assistance counselors address the support available and help you with the stress of the drastic changes that are a natural part of the transition process.

Getting your records in order

It is absolutely essential that all of your servicemember's military records are accurate and complete before separating from service. Be sure to obtain and retain original, official copies of the following documents, and put them in a safe place:

✔ Service medical records

✔ Administrative/personnel file

- Performance evaluations

- Service-issued licenses or certifications

- DD Form 2586 (Verification of Military Experience and Training)

- Security clearances

- DD Form 214 (Certificate of Release or Discharge from Active Duty)

Veterans cannot obtain VA benefits without an original DD Form 214. Consider obtaining at least ten additional certified copies of this form.

If you discover or believe that there is an error on any of your official military documents, you should complete and file DD Form 149 (Application for Correction of Military or Naval Record). You can obtain this form at www.archives.gov/veterans/military-service-records/correcting-records.html.

Relocating

An important aspect of transitioning from the military is physically relocating your family. You should consult with your nearest Family Support Center and talk with a Relocation Assistance Program (RAP) representative. RAP reps can be an excellent source for relocation information and planning assistance. Relocation assistance specialists can assess your family's personal needs and circumstances and help plan a successful transition. RAP reps have access to extensive information about military and civilian communities worldwide, including housing directories, employment and education opportunities, wellness programs, and other family services available near military installations.

Employment education and training

Before separating from service, your servicemember should take advantage of the assistance and guidance available through your installation's Education Center. Counselors provide transitioning servicemembers assistance in assessing vocational interests and in helping to identify skills and interests and to clarify future career goals. They advise on continuing education programs and even help with paperwork. Some military training and experience may convert into college credit, and the education assistance counselors can help you through that process too.

The Department of Veterans Affairs also provides educational counseling after your servicemember leaves military service. The VA administers the Montgomery GI Bill program (www.gibill.va.gov) and provides assistance to Veterans enrolled in college degree programs, technical and vocational certificate programs, and on-the-job training and apprenticeship programs. However, all programs must be approved by the VA in advance, or they may not qualify for benefits. Refer to Chapter 11 for more information on the Montgomery GI Bill and the new Post-9/11 GI Bill.

Benefits must be used within ten years of separation from active duty.

Health insurance

One of the most important arrangements you need to make prior to separation is securing health insurance for your family. You may be fortunate enough to have a high-quality, affordable health insurance plan provided by your new civilian employer; however, commonly, coverage with your civilian employer doesn't begin immediately. You may need to buy private health insurance that covers you and your family between separation from service and the effective date of your civilian employer provided insurance.

The Transitional Assistance Management Program (TAMP) provides temporary health insurance coverage to certain separating members and their families. After TAMP coverage is exhausted, you may purchase extended healthcare coverage known as Continued Health Care Benefit Program (CHCBP), which is similar to TRICARE, and you can maintain coverage for up to 18 months. If you aren't eligible for TAMP, your family may still be eligible for CHCBP, but your veteran must apply within 60 days of separation.

If your servicemember is activated Guard or Reserve, or a Guard or Reserve veteran who served on active duty, your family may be eligible for TRICARE Reserve Select.

Check with your transition officer or your health benefits advisor at your medical treatment facility for assistance in exploring your healthcare options.

Pre-separation examinations

Prior to separation, servicemembers have the opportunity to receive thorough physical and psychological examinations and report any medical or psychological problems that they may currently have or have experienced in the past at any time during their service. They really should do this because one of the requirements for eligibility for VA disability benefits is that there is a record of problems, symptoms, treatments, and injuries during active military service. If your veteran develops a service-related disability and his service medical records reflect nothing and he had no pre-separation examination to confirm the presence of a medical or psychological problem, it's highly unlikely that the VA will award disability compensation.

So be sure that your servicemember reports all symptoms, problems, and concerns that he has experienced throughout his entire active service during his pre-separation examinations — if these concerns have not previously been addressed and/or documented. Make certain that the healthcare provider documents all of these details and that you obtain and maintain a complete copy of your military service medical records.

Life insurance

Servicemembers' Group Life Insurance (SGLI) continues to provide coverage for the initial 120 days after your separation. Refer to Chapter 7 for details on SGLI. You can convert your SGLI insurance coverage to the same amount of Veterans' Group Life Insurance (VGLI) and keep it indefinitely. VGLI is term life insurance that is renewable every five years, regardless of your veteran's health. VGLI can also be converted at any time into an individual whole life policy.

For many veterans, life insurance is available at a lower cost through other insurance companies than through VGLI. However, the guaranteed issue of VGLI is an extremely valuable benefit, if you're not insurable or highly rated. The VGLI rate table can be found at `www.insurance.va.gov/sgliSite/ VGLI/VGLIRatesAfter.htm`.

For a complete review of all veterans benefits, including VGLI, check out *Veterans Benefits For Dummies* (published by Wiley).

Retirement savings

If your servicemember contributed to his Thrift Savings Plan, you have several options upon separation:

- You can leave the money in the plan. Smart option!
- You can roll it over to an IRA account. Another smart option!
- You can roll it over to your new employer's retirement plan, if allowed by the employer. Yet another smart option!
- You can cash it out, pay all the taxes and penalties, and blow your retirement savings. Not recommended!

You don't have to do anything with your Thrift Savings Plan money until age $70\frac{1}{2}$. So if you don't know what you want to do with this money right now and you can't possibly even think about it with all of the other transitions you've got going on, revisit this at another time. Your contribution will be just fine accumulating interest and capital gains in your Thrift Savings Plan for a while longer.

Legal assistance

Okay — if you haven't taken advantage of your free military legal assistance services to have wills, healthcare directives, and powers of attorney forms updated in a while — do so now. These documents need to be revisited periodically. Life changes — so should your documents!

Also, you may find that you have legal questions or possibly problems related to your separation. Consult with the legal assistance officers at your installation for guidance.

Clarifying Voluntary versus Involuntarily Separation from Service

There are two categories of separation from the armed forces: punitive separations and administrative separations. And administrative separations are further subdivided: voluntary and involuntary. Although all of the categories may sound like a maze or Pentagon-eez, we break each category down in the following sections so that you understand what the categories mean and what they mean for your benefits.

You'll hear people using the terms *discharge* and *separation* while in the military, and they both mean the same thing. For the purpose of this chapter, we stick with the term *separation*.

Administrative separation

Administrative separations can be voluntary or involuntary. Examples of authorized reasons for a voluntary separation include a separation at the end of a commitment of service or early release for the following reasons:

- ✔ Further education
- ✔ Accept public office
- ✔ Hardship
- ✔ Pregnancy or childbirth
- ✔ Conscientious objection
- ✔ Immediate reenlistment
- ✔ Acceptance of another commission
- ✔ Becoming the sole surviving member of your family

All administrative discharges take into account the servicemember's conduct and performance to characterize the discharge status. Separation characterizations include:

- ✔ **Honorable:** Completely meets the standard of conduct and performance expected.
  - • Eligible for all veteran's benefits

✔ **General (Under Honorable Conditions):** A general discharge is not the same level as an honorable discharge. It means that the servicemember messed up, but their conduct wasn't serious enough to warrant the most severe or administrative discharge.

- *Not* eligible for the GI Bill unless they have more than one term of service and have an honorable discharge from that term

- Normally not allowed to reenlist

- Other restrictions may include eligibility for hire by veterans' service organizations and eligibility for programs like the SBA Patriot Express Loan

- Most other benefits, such as healthcare and VA Home Loans, are available

✔ **Under Other Than Honorable Conditions (OTH):** This separation is the worst form of administrative separation. The servicemember did not meet the expected conduct and/or performance required of military members. Members discharged under OTH characterization of service:

- Are not entitled to keep their uniforms

- Must repay any reenlistment bonuses they may have received

- Will not receive transportation assistance upon discharge

- Likely will be ineligible for all VA benefits (however, the VA will make its own determination)

✔ **Entry Level Separation (ELS):** A servicemember with less than 180 days of service may be discharged under the characterization of Entry Level Separation because the commander hasn't had enough time to adequately measure a person's conduct and performance — he isn't able to award Honorable, General, or OTH.

- Not eligible for any veteran's benefits

- Not allowed to reenlist

Punitive discharge

Punitive discharges are authorized punishments of a *court-martial*. This is *not* the way to separate from service. The two types of punitive discharges include:

✔ **Dishonorable discharge**

- The worst characterization possible

- Not entitled to any benefits

✔ **Bad-conduct discharge**

- Not entitled to any benefits

Considering Early Career Separation

Leaving military service after fulfilling his initial commitment enables your veteran to balance his desire to serve our country with his objectives to pursue a civilian career and lifestyle. He has earned valuable benefits that continue long past his military service, such as the Montgomery GI Bill, access to the discounts available through the exchanges, and the VA home loan. And his military experience can also be an outstanding launching pad into a civilian career.

However, from a financial standpoint, military service continues to become more valuable with time (see Figure 20-1 for a comparison). As your service-member achieves higher rank, he receives more pay and possibly additional benefits. You have the opportunity to save more money — letting the government subsidize your food, clothing, housing, and travel expenses. And the benefits of retiring with military retired pay are unmatched!

Rank	2008 MBP	2008 BAS (NT)	2008 Monthly BAH With Dependents (NT)		
			Atlanta	**Houston**	**Washington DC**
E-4 (over 4)	$2,048	$294	$1,107	$1,211	$1,718
E-7 (Over 12)	$3,443	$294	$1,377	$1,669	$2,167
O-3 (Over 4)	$4,546	$203	$1,509	$2,003	$2,357
O-5 (Over 20)	$7,212	$203	$1,823	$2,210	$2,745

Equivilent Civilian Salary Required to Replace Military Compensation

Rank	Atlanta	Houston	Washington DC
E-4 (over 4)	$44,355	$45,823	$52,981
E-7 (Over 12)	$64,904	$69,452	$76,060
O-3 (Over 4)	$81,944	$89,848	$95,512
O-5 (Over 20)	$118,969	$125,152	$133,712

Figure 20-1: Equivalent salary comparison.

Notes:
(1) This example includes only the three basic components of military compensation: monthly base pay, BAS and BAH
(2) It assumes a 15 percent tax bracket for enlisted ranks and a 25 percent tax bracket for officer ranks
(3) A separating (not retiring) servicemember would need to add another $3,000 (if single) or $7,000 (if married, with dependents) to cover medical costs

Keep in mind that separating from service is one of the most important and difficult decisions your spouse will make. The civilian lifestyle is so different from the community and lifestyle you experience in the service. There will be significant adjustment for all members of your family upon separation. And returning to the military job your servicemember had prior to separation may not be an option if he later changes his mind.

Leaving the military is a major change for you and your servicemember. Plan ahead. Consult with your transition counselors and work together.

Exploring Late Career Separation Issues

Transitioning from the military later in your spouse's career but before retirement is even more significant of a decision than early career separation. Your family has experienced a lot of the benefits of a military career, including travel, community, vocational training, and possibly completion of a college or advanced degree. But now you want to experience other things. The two of you may grow tired of being apart so frequently, having your partner miss out on major events in your children's lives, or putting your personal aspirations on the back burner to support your servicemember's career.

Leaving the service after several years but prior to retirement must be carefully evaluated. Your family is foregoing substantial military retirement pay, retiree healthcare, and many other financial benefits to make the transition prior to 20 years of service.

To illustrate the financial impact of walking away from your military retirement pay, review the example in Table 20-1.

Table 20-1	Cost of Lost Retirement Pay Benefit	
Subject	*Pre-retirement Separation*	*Military Retirement*
Years of Service at Transition	13	20
Age at Transition	32	39
Rank at Transition	E-6	E-7
Annual base pay	$37,260	$46,145
Military Retirement Benefit	$ 0	$23,072
Age at Mortality	84	84
Cost of Living Adjustment on Military Retirement Pay	n/a	3%/year

The estimated total missed opportunity value of military retirement pay is over $565,000. If you factor the opportunity value of seven additional years of service, which is required to qualify for the 50 percent retirement benefit, that comes out to over $90,000 per year.

Now when you consider career opportunities in the civilian workplace, keep in mind how much more money your family would have to earn each year to equal the value of your lost military retirement benefit.

Sometimes the transition is worth it for your family, your servicemember, and your personal objectives. But keep in mind the benefit you're walking away from. This example only illustrates the financial impact of your military retirement pay. We haven't even taken into account other military retiree benefits. But, you get the idea.

Seven years may seem like forever. But when you're 45 or 75, enjoying that monthly military retirement paycheck coming in like clockwork, you'll likely not regret your continued service.

Late career transitions from the military are difficult decisions to make. Although the most important things in life aren't financial, the financial implications of your separation decision should be thoroughly considered.

Chapter 21

Retiring from Service

· ·

In This Chapter

▶ Exploring military retirement benefits

▶ Planning your transition

▶ Evaluating your needs for additional income

· ·

A momentous occasion is drawing near — you and your spouse are considering military retirement. Military service has been your way of life for years. Significant, wonderful, and scary changes are just around the corner. Are you ready? In this chapter, we make sure that you are. We discuss essential pre-transition planning strategies and considerations and how these affect your family from the financial as well as the more personal perspectives.

Assessing the Financial Benefits of Retiring from the Military

Many of the benefits you know and love about military service continue on in some capacity even after retirement. These benefits include discounts through the commissaries and exchanges, legal assistance, Space-A travel, military lodging, and much more. In the following sections we highlight many of these "other" benefits, but focus our attention on the most significant financial benefits of military retirement — your retirement and medical benefits.

Military retired pay

If compound interest is the eighth wonder of the world, a retirement paycheck that keeps up with inflation and that is guaranteed for the rest of your life has got to be the ninth wonder of the world!

If your spouse entered service after August 1986, upon serving 15 years he will be — or already has been — offered the opportunity to choose from one of two different retirement plans. If you've already passed the 15-year mark, you've already made your election, by default or by choice.

- ✔ **Default** = High 36 Retirement System
- ✔ **Choice** = Career Status Bonus/REDUX System

If you've not made your decision about retirement plans, it is absolutely critical that you fully explore the pros and cons of both plans. Making the wrong decision could cost you a small fortune over the course of your retirement.

The basic pay that is used to calculate retirement benefits for members who entered service prior to September 8, 1980, is the final basic pay, rather than the average of the highest 36 months of basic pay.

Table 21-1 illustrates the major features of the two retirement plans. Under both plans the base pay used for the computation is the average of your highest 36 months of base pay. This base pay will likely come from your most recent three years.

Table 21-1	High 36 versus CSB/REDUX	
Feature	**High 36**	**CSB/REDUX**
Eligible earnings	Avg. highest 36 monthly base pays	Same
Multiplier	2.5 percent per year of service (minimum = 50 percent at 20 years; maximum = 75 percent at 30 years)	2.0 percent per year of service for the first 20 years, then 3.5 percent per year (minimum = 40 percent at 20 years; maximum = 75 percent at 30 years)
Cost-of-living adjustment	Consumer Price Index (CPI)	CPI minus 1 percent

CSB/REDUX

Based on Table 21-1 you're probably wondering why anyone would choose CSB/REDUX. Retiring with 20 years of service, you only get 40 percent of your base pay, versus 50 percent with the other plan, and you don't receive the full cost-of-living adjustment each year. So why would anyone choose CSB/REDUX? The answer — cash! A big chunk of immediate cash! $30,000 before tax to be exact — paid to you in year 15! Why put off 'til tomorrow what you can have today?

Take the cash! It'll save the government a lot of money if they can "buy" you out of your higher retirement benefit. But wait — you're supposed to choose the retirement plan that is going to be best for you and your family. It's not likely CSB/REDUX!

You may see comparisons that illustrate if you take your CBS/REDUX cash bonus and invest it *successfully* you can actually come out *about* the same as with the High 36 retirement plan. But, why take the *risk* involved in investing?

And besides, experience tells us that you're much more likely to spend that bonus money! And if you do — you're trading over $200,000 in retirement income for the price of a used Chevy.

Okay, okay, enough CBS/REDUX bashing. Let's discuss a legitimate reason why taking the Career Status Bonus *might* be in your best interest:

✔ You haven't saved a dime and you have the opportunity to buy your dream home. . . . Never mind — you can get a VA loan! You don't need CBS/REDUX for the down payment.

✔ You have a healthcare emergency. . . . That doesn't fly either. You have healthcare provided by the military.

✔ You use the money to obtain an advanced degree. This idea isn't a horrible one, it's just not necessary. Use your military benefits and government student loans if necessary. That'll be a better return on your investment.

✔ You have the opportunity to buy a business that is sure to make you a substantial amount of money that will more than offset the reduction in your retirement benefits. This reason sounds like a viable one. Maybe the CSB/REDUX cash benefit might be your better option. Whew . . . it took awhile, but we mustered up a potentially legitimate reason.

High 36 Retirement System

If you didn't elect the CSB/REDUX at your servicemember's 15-year anniversary, you're in the High 36 Retirement System. For most military families, that is the best option by far.

With the High 36 plan you'll receive 50 percent of the average of the highest 36 months of basic pay if your member elects to retire after 20 years of service. You receive an additional 2.5 percent per year for each year of service after 20, until you max out at a retirement benefit equal to 75 percent of your servicemember's base pay at 30 years of service.

You and your spouse are in your late 30s to early 50s and will receive a guaranteed paycheck for the rest of your servicemember's life, *and* it has a cost-of-living adjustment. This type of early retirement benefit, with the U.S. Government guarantee and inflation protection, can't be matched.

Most servicemembers transition from a career in the military to a subsequent career. With a military retirement equaling 50 to 75 percent of your base pay, your options for the next chapter of your life are virtually limitless. Speaking of the next chapter, in the next chapter of this book we delve into subsequent careers.

Survivor Benefit Plan

The above section on military retirement benefits applies while your service-member or veteran is living. In the event that your spouse predeceases you, the Survivor Benefit Plan (SBP) is available to insure that you will continue to receive military retirement benefits for the rest of your life. Without SBP, military retirement income stops when your veteran dies. With SBP you can continue to receive 55 percent of your spouse's military retirement benefits, adjusted annually for inflation, for the rest of your life.

While your spouse is on active duty, you're automatically protected under SBP at no cost to your family. Upon retirement, full basic SBP takes effect automatically, unless you elect a lower benefit or choose to opt out of the plan altogether. Your spouse can't reduce your benefit or opt out without your written consent.

At retirement you must pay premiums for SBP coverage. The premiums are withheld directly from your military retirement pay — before tax — which means Uncle Sam is also subsidizing the cost of your SBP premium. You may elect the amount of benefit you want up to 55 percent of your spouse's military retirement benefits. SBP premiums for spouse coverage are 6.5 percent of your chosen base amount.

For more information and to calculate your SBP premium, visit www.defenselink.mil/militarypay/survivor/sbp/index.html.

The government subsidizes the cost of coverage, so it's highly unlikely that you'd be able to purchase commercial life insurance that is truly comparable and more cost effective then SBP. On the surface the premiums might appear comparable; however, commercial life insurance policies:

✔ Are not guaranteed by the U.S. Government

✔ Are not a stream of income you can never outlive

✔ Rarely increase the benefit to keep pace with inflation

The concept of keeping pace with inflation may not sound like a big deal right now. But imagine your financial life if your spouse died shortly after retirement, or even in his eighties. With SBP you could receive cost-of-living adjusted monthly payments for decades. Table 21-2 illustrates the significance of cost-of-living adjustments (COLA) on your initial monthly benefit.

Table 21-2	Value of 4 percent COLA on SBP benefits		
Monthly Benefit	*Benefit Period*	*Total of Payments*	*Value*
$1,000	10 years	$147,000	$99,000
$1,000	25 years	$514,000	$189,000
$1,000	50 years	$1,909,000	$259,000
$1,500	10 years	$221,000	$148,000
$1,500	25 years	$771,000	$248,000
$1,500	50 years	$2,800,000	$380,000
$2,500	10 years	$368,000	$247,000
$2,500	25 years	$1,285,000	$947,000
$2,500	50 years	$4,773,000	$1,296,000

The "Value" column in Table 21-2 illustrates the amount of cash or life insurance proceeds that you would need to have at the time of your spouse's death to replace the benefit you could have received with the SBP plan. In some of these scenarios, buying life insurance looks like it could be a cheaper alternative than paying for the SBP premiums. The clincher is you've got to know exactly when you *and* your spouse are going to die to make sure that strategy would work.

Effective October 1, 2008, your SBP premiums are considered "paid-up" after 30 years and no additional premium payments are required, but you maintain coverage indefinitely. Contact your personnel counselor for details.

Medical Benefits

The other major financial benefit of military retirement is lifetime medical care. Most civilians are restricted in the types of jobs they can consider due to their need for quality medical insurance. And many civilians continue working well into their traditional retirement years, merely because they fear that healthcare costs could derail their financial security. Their fears are not unfounded. However, you and your veteran should not be limited by these concerns. We tell you in the following sections just what kind of healthcare benefits you can look forward to as well as how to make the most of those benefits.

Checking out your healthcare benefits

All the retired servicemembers, their spouses, and their dependents are eligible for TRICARE healthcare benefits. While your servicemember is under age 65, you must decide which TRICARE program is best for you and your eligible family members.

Don't forget to update your information in DEERS prior to retirement. Refer to Chapter 3 for details.

If your veteran is disabled, entitled to Medicare Part A, and enrolled in Medicare Part B, you are eligible for TRICARE for Life, rather than TRICARE Standard or Extra. However, you may prefer to keep coverage through TRICARE Prime to retain priority status at your Military Treatment Facility. (Refer to Chapter 6 for the specific details on TRICARE Prime, Standard, and Extra to determine which plan might be best for your family.)

For more information about TRICARE for Life, check out `www.military.com/benefits/tricare/tricare-for-life/tricare-for-life-and-dual-eligibility#8` or get a copy of *Veteran's Benefits For Dummies* (Wiley). For information on *all* TRICARE benefits, visit `www.tricare.mil`.

As the spouse of a military retiree, you and your dependent children are eligible for the TRICARE healthcare plans, pharmacy program, and dental health plans. These benefits alone are worth hundreds if not thousands of dollars each year.

Making the most of your military retiree benefits

Getting the most financial and personal benefit out of your military career involves a little ongoing effort on your part. In this chapter we highlight your military retiree benefits. Don't forget about all the benefits you've earned over the years. Keep informed and up to date by staying involved with your local military community, online groups and Web sites, and political organizations. See Chapter 14 for more information.

To maximize your retiree benefits you should plan ahead. If possible, start planning your transition 12 to 24 months prior to retirement. Your local installation has transition counselors available to answer questions and direct you to the resources you need.

Envisioning Life after the Military

You've spent most of your adulthood living wherever the military sent you. Moving is part of military life. But making the move from military to civilian life may be the most challenging transition yet. Your community, friends, coworkers, and neighbors are currently in the military or a part of the bigger military family.

Where you live after leaving the service will have a major impact on your lifestyle and your transition. You may want to relocate back to one of the areas where you were once stationed, or maybe a location you've visited on one of your Space-A adventures. Many families opt to live near a military installation for easy access to the exchanges, the Military Treatment Facility, and many of the other benefits available to retirees. But, it's much more than discounts on groceries and easy access to the MTF. It's the community — people with whom you share common experiences, patriotism, and esprit de corps.

Adjusting to the civilian world

It's going to be different, but maintaining connections with your active-duty and retired military friends will help immensely in your transition. Get involved with your civilian community just as you have each time you relocated to a new duty station. After all, you're an expert at transitions.

However, your servicemember may face more challenges. His job with the military is very well defined. He knows what to do, how to do it, when to do it, and to whom to report. There are systems and processes for everything. Your spouse may go bonkers with the lack of discipline, accountability, and just plain sloppiness frequently exhibited in our civilian workforce. Plus, for years he has been treated with respect and is known by his uniform and rank. Imagine how tough it may be when he is no longer referred to as Lieutenant Colonel Garrett Hoppin, but rather as "hey, mister."

Adjusting to significant change takes time, sometimes assistance, and often a village. Discuss any adjustment questions and concerns you have with your Transitions Counselor. You're not the first or only folks to go through this — it's normal. Surround yourselves with those you love and trust. Possibly the best village for you and your spouse is a military community. Stay connected physically and virtually as much as possible. Refer to Chapters 14 and 17 for additional resources to help you stay connected.

Evaluating your need for additional retirement savings

To determine if you need to save more — or how much more — answer the question, "How much money do we need to support our retirement lifestyle?" A quick method for answering this question follows:

1. **Start with your total current income (after-tax).**

2. **Add the amount of money you withdraw from your bank accounts or that you charge to credit cards to make ends meet each month.**

3. **Subtract the amount of long-term savings you are currently socking away each month. Include amounts that you're applying as additional debt repayments.**

4. **Subtract the costs of expenses that you won't have in retirement.**

    • Savings for retirement

    • Mortgage payment

    • Job-related expenses

    • Child(ren) expenses

5. **Add costs of new expenses that you will have in retirement.**

    • Relocating/housing

    • Traveling

    • Hobbies and leisure activities

6. **Total these items to arrive at the approximate amount of after-tax money you need to live on in retirement.**

Most retirees discover that they *need* 70 to 100 percent of what they are currently bringing in to enjoy their planned retirement lifestyle.

With your military retirement benefit replacing 50 to 75 percent of your base pay and Social Security providing another 20 to 30 percent of your income, you may find that you're in pretty good shape heading in to ultimate retirement.

If your servicemember served on active duty prior to 2001, there is a little-known extra earning credit available from the Social Security Administration. But you have to know to ask for it when you apply for your Social Security benefits! You'll need your DD Form 214 when applying.

Chapter 21: Retiring from Service 291

This earnings credit adds up to $1,200 per year to your creditable earnings that count toward your Social Security benefits. This amount is not chump change — it will amount to potentially tens of thousands of dollars in additional Social Security retirement benefits over your lifetime!

For more information, visit www.socialsecurity.gov/retire2/military.htm.

Supplementing your retirement income

Even with your military retirement benefit and Social Security, you'll likely desire additional cash flow to help you maintain your standard of living. Table 21-3 illustrates the amount of money you'll need to produce the cash flow to supplement your military retirement benefit and Social Security income.

Table 21-3	Capital Needed to Produce Monthly Retirement Income
Income Desired	*Capital Needed*
$500/month	$150,000
$1,000/month	$300,000
$2,000/month	$600,000

For each $1,000 per month in retirement income, you need to save at least this amount each month until age 65.

Current Age	Savings per Month
40	$315
45	$509
50	$867
55	$1,650

Strategizing the best ways to save for ultimate retirement

Given that you have guaranteed income for life, which has a cost-of-living adjustment for both of you (by securing SBP), and Social Security as well, the balance of your retirement nest egg could be invested for two primary purposes: first, for liquidity, and second, for growth.

Guaranteed streams of income are wonderful because you can never outlive that income. However, occasionally you'll find that you need a lump sum of money to replace a vehicle or make a repair on your home. You should have a readily accessible, cash reserve account (your liquid account) from which you can withdraw this money when it's needed. The Orange Savings account with ING Direct is a great option for this type of cash reserve account. There is no minimum deposit or balance required to open and maintain an account. The account is FDIC insured and pays a very competitive interest rate. For more information, visit www.INGDirect.com.

All of your military retirement income is taxable. The majority of your Social Security income will likely be taxable. To balance that out, the best way to save additionally for ultimate retirement is in a Roth IRA or Roth 401(k) plan. These retirement savings vehicles are the only ones that allow you to invest money in stocks, exchange-traded funds, and low-cost, no-commission mutual funds and never pay any tax on the earnings while they accumulate in the accounts and most importantly on the withdrawals you make during retirement. Although you don't get a tax deduction for contributing money to a Roth IRA or Roth 401(k), the earnings grow tax-deferred and all withdrawals from Roth accounts during retirement are 100 percent tax free!

If you don't make more than $159,000 for 2008, you can contribute to a Roth IRA account. You and your spouse can contribute up to $5,000 each in 2008. (Consult your tax professional for contribution amounts for years beyond 2008.) Invest your Roth IRA accounts with a low-cost, no-commission mutual fund company or discount broker. For additional tips on how to select the investments best for you, check out *Mutual Funds For Dummies* (Wiley).

Chapter 22

Exploring Subsequent Careers

*I*t makes little difference whether your spouse is retiring or separating from service. Nearly all veterans go on to subsequent careers after leaving the military. In this chapter we highlight the issues you and your spouse should consider and direct you to resources that can make this new chapter of your lives most rewarding.

Transitioning from the Military

Planning this transition a year or more in advance will help position your servicemember for the best and most appropriate outcome. Spend time exploring with your spouse what he will enjoy most for the next chapter of his working life. Through this process you'll discover his most passionate interests as he learns to translate his military experience and skills in the civilian world.

Planning for your next career

With time on your side and the right tools and guidance, your servicemember will transition into his new civilian job with confidence and enthusiasm. Career planning involves

✔ Assessing interests, preferences, skills, and strengths

✔ Addressing challenges or perceived shortcomings

✔ Organizing military records

- DD Form 2586 — Verification of Military Experience and Training

- Security Clearance

- Awards and commendations

✔ Obtaining proof of additional education

- College transcripts and diplomas

- Certificates and licenses

✔ Drafting resumes

✔ Securing references and letters of recommendation

After this groundwork, the job search can begin!

Assessing interests, preferences, skills, and strengths

Don't waste energy pursuing careers that you and your servicemember won't *love*. Invest time exploring the things that really matter to both of you. Address these questions separately and discuss them with your spouse:

✔ What are you passionate about? Interests and passions evolve over time. That's normal and expected. This is your opportunity to reinvent yourselves — so follow your passions.

✔ Does he prefer working with people, data and information, or things, machines, and equipment?

✔ Would he prefer a desk job in a traditional office environment, freelancing and working from home, or being outdoors and possibly traveling?

✔ How important is structure and routine in your partner's work life? Or do his passions lean more toward creative endeavors?

✔ Are you willing or do you want to relocate?

Military servicemembers have innate and acquired skills and strengths that are extremely desirable to civilian employers, including discipline, drive, appreciation for structure and procedures, ability to work well under pressure, strategic thinking, ability to work with or lead a team, and so on. In addition to the characteristics listed above, your servicemember also offers prior work experience and education, involvement in volunteer activities, and hobbies.

One of the toughest parts of transitioning to civilian life is converting experiences and training acquired through military service into words that civilians can relate to. Acronyms, military job codes, and titles don't compute. And you don't want your spouse to be perceived as someone who can't transition from the military way to a potential employer's culture. Military experiences and skills do translate into the civilian job market. It's mostly just a language barrier. You can help your spouse convert his military service history into a resume and language that all employers can comprehend. Military speak may be your first language at home, but get used to speaking without acronyms and jargon outside military circles.

A great resource for translating military job titles into civilian job titles can be found at www.military.com/Careers/Content?file=skills_leader.htm&area=Content.

Career assessment tools are available through local community colleges, the transitions office on your installation, and a number of online resources. Check out the career assessment tools at www.quintcareers.com/career_assessment.html.

Preparing for this transition

Just as you've come to expect, the military has processes and procedures for everything, including transitioning from service into a subsequent career. The best place to start your preparation is at the official Web site for the Transition Assistance Program: www.TurboTAP.org. You'll find a downloadable pre-separation guide for active-duty members and a transition guide for Guard and Reserve members. The guides are extremely thorough and they provide a great place to begin educating yourselves while providing structure to the process.

All transitioning servicemembers are required by law to receive pre-separation counseling to explain rights and benefits. Schedule your counseling meeting with your installation's personnel office or transition program manager at least six months prior to transition.

At this meeting, your servicemember will be given DD Form 2648, which *must* be completed prior to separation. DD Form 2648 — Pre-Separation Counseling Checklist — covers adjustments, education and training services, benefit programs, other assistance available, and your individual transition plan.

You can get more specific details of what's involved at the TAP Web site under www.transitionassistanceprogram.com/portal/transition/resources/Active_Duty_Presep_Guide.

Tapping into military and community benefits

The Transition Assistance Program (TAP) is much more than just the Web site mentioned above. TAP is available to assist separating and retiring servicemembers with job-search and related services during and up to 180 days following transition.

TAP also provides comprehensive three-day workshops at selected military installations around the country. Participants learn about current job market conditions, career decision-making, job searches, and presentation skills for their resume and interviews. You can also receive an evaluation of your servicemember's employability relative to the job market.

Transition Assistance Online is an outstanding resource (www.taonline. com/ticpages/). The program covers everything from how to cope with the stress of transitioning to how to respond to illegal employment interview questions. Get involved with TAP as soon as you know that a transition is imminent.

You can obtain a copy of the Transition Assistance Program manuals online at transition.military.com/reg/transition_center_ registration.do.

Transition assistance counselors on your installation stand ready, willing, and able to help with any of your questions related to transitioning. They can be one of your, if not your best, resources.

In addition to the Web sites already listed in this chapter, there are hundreds more that provide information to servicemembers, veterans, and their families about transitioning, resume writing, interviewing skills, job searches, and career fairs. The following is a selection of some the best:

- ✔ CareerOneStop: www.careeronestop.org
- ✔ COOL (Credentialing Opportunities On-Line): www.cool.army.mil and http://www.cool.navy.mil
- ✔ Department of Defense, Operation Transition Bulletin Board: www. dmdc.osd.mil/ot
- ✔ Military.com, Transition Center: transition.military.com/reg/ transition_center_registration.do
- ✔ Military Hire: www.militaryhire.com
- ✔ Military Job Zone: www.militaryjobzone.com
- ✔ Military Officers Association of America, Career Fairs: www.moaa.org
- ✔ Monster.com: www.monster.com (Search with key word *military* to find employers specifically looking for military experience.)
- ✔ National Hire Veterans committee: www.hirevetsfirst.gov
- ✔ Non-Commissioned Officers Association: www.ncoausa.org/ Enployment_VeteransEmployPG.html
- ✔ RecruitMilitary.com: www.recruitmilitary.com
- ✔ Transition Assistance Program official site: www.TubroTAP.org
- ✔ Transition Assistance Online: www.taonline.com

✔ U.S. Government's official job site: www.USAJobs.com

✔ Vets4Hire: www.destinygrp.com/destiny/index.jsp?cm_
mmc=redirect-_-vets4hire-_-na-_-na

✔ VetJobs.com: www.vetjobs.com

Check out section 3.3 of your TAP Participant Manual for great insights into how best to approach the job search process.

Too many people focus their job search primarily on want ads in the newspaper or on Internet postings. However, studies show that 80 percent of all jobs are filled without employer advertising. The number one way people find jobs is through networking. The TAP program provides information and resources that you can put to work immediately. In addition to the TAP resources and coaching, augment your job search with some of the online resources listed above.

Evaluating Employer Benefits

There are many similarities to military and civilian employer-provided benefits — presuming the civilian employer has benefits. In this section we compare and contrast civilian benefits with the military benefit programs with which you're familiar, and discuss how your civilian benefits will best coordinate with your military benefits. The overriding principle is to get you the best benefit coverage for the least amount of money. Sometimes you have to sacrifice some features to save money. Some features you can't afford to sacrifice. With the guidance provided in this section, you will have the information necessary to make those decisions that will best suit your family's needs and circumstances.

Fortunately, civilian benefits aren't typically as involved as your military benefits largely because you're just not going to run into that many types of employer-provided benefits in the civilian workplace. And those that are provided often have a cousin in the military. The following sections describe the most frequent civilian benefits used today. That doesn't mean that all employers offer these plans, but if they do, you'll have a better idea of what they mean to you.

Medical insurance

You likely have TRICARE Prime, Extra, or Standard coverage currently and you may be very familiar with these plans — at least the one your family is enrolled in.

TRICARE primary care plans:

- *TRICARE Standard* provides you with the greatest flexibility to choose healthcare providers, without a referral or pre-authorization, but it also costs the most. It is available worldwide. If you go out and buy healthcare insurance — and money is no object — this plan is for you.

- *TRICARE Extra* is more restrictive and less expensive. You pay the same annual deductible as those with Standard; however, your share of medical costs is 5 percent less. This plan is only available in the continental United States (CONUS). This is the military equivalent to a Preferred Provider Organization (PPO).

- *TRICARE Prime* is like a Health Maintenance Organization (HMO) and is geared toward preventative care. It is the least expensive option, but your choice of healthcare providers is limited. You pay nothing — or very little — under most circumstances.

Most civilian employers provide healthcare coverage to their employees. Larger companies are more likely to provide health insurance benefits. Those employers who do offer health insurance usually offer an HMO or PPO plan. These plans offer you no choice. On the other hand, with military healthcare you have to choose which plan is best for your family. The very large employers, and a few smaller companies, may give you the choice between an HMO or a PPO plan.

Unlike working for one of the Armed Forces, in the civilian world your spouse will be fortunate to find an employer that will pay for all of his health insurance, let alone the cost for your family's insurance.

Don't forget to factor this cost into your "after-transition" budget. Guess $250 per month for family coverage, unless you have actual details from your spouse's new employer. Also, be sure to add the cost of co-pays for each doctor visit. Using TRICARE Prime at the MTF is lookin' sweeter all the time. A new job where your family has to pay for health insurance can cost you thousands of dollars a year. Think about that when considering any job offer.

The employer typically pays all or the majority of the premium cost for employees. However, they generally do not pay much, if anything, toward the cost of your family's health insurance coverage.

As a veteran, you and your eligible family members may utilize your Military Treatment Facility if you elect to retain coverage through TRICARE Prime. Retaining your coverage could substantially reduce your healthcare costs if your new employer doesn't provide health insurance at all or doesn't pay for family coverage.

Prescription drug coverage

If your veteran's new employer provides health insurance, he or she generally will provide some type of prescription drug benefit. But that doesn't mean the prescriptions are necessarily free or even cheap. Depending on the drug you're taking, your co-pay may be a $4 to $20 order at best, or your prescription might not even be covered under your health insurance plan. These benefits vary greatly from plan to plan, so we can't really guess what type of plan or benefits may be available to your family through a civilian employer's plan.

Dental insurance

Dental insurance is a far less common employee benefit than medical insurance. Many employers will make the group insurance plan available to your family. However, you have to pay all of the premiums. On the other hand, some employers do pay for the cost of dental insurance for the employee only, your spouse, but not for your family. If you want family coverage that can be purchased through the employer's group plan, you have to pay all of the cost. Coverage may run your family about $35 per month.

Most dental insurance plans provide you with two cleanings and one set of bite-wing x-rays per year at no cost. Commonly, they also pay up to $75 for annual check-ups and half of most everything else, up to $1,000 per year. Check your plan for specific details. Some dental insurance plans can really be worth the cost for a family with kids with lots of cavities and a spouse who likes to play ice hockey.

Insurance should be purchased to cover risks that you can't afford to take on yourselves. Dental coverage doesn't usually fall into that category.

Vision benefits

Employer-provided vision benefits are even less common than dental benefits and are likely less important to you and your family. Many vision plans cost your family a few dollars per month, and for that cost you receive one eye exam per year and maybe discounts off glasses or contact lens.

This insurance is probably not worth the money.

Disability insurance — short term and long term

If you or your spouse became ill or injured and can't work or take care of your responsibilities to your family for a few weeks or much longer, what would you do? Hopefully you've got some savings in a cash reserve account — see Chapter 8. But, sooner or later even your cash reserves may run dry.

Disability income protection, also known as disability insurance, pays 60 to 70 percent of your salary if you can't work for a prolonged period of time. This protection is one of the most important types of insurance for the wage earners in the household. However, you only need disability insurance if you need that income. Now we're talking risk that most likely you can't afford to bear:

- ✔ **Short-term** disability: provides income replacement coverage if you become ill or injured and unable to work for more than seven days but less than six months. Frequently employers do not provide short-term disability insurance to their employees. We recommend that you self-insure — plan to use your cash reserve for additional income needed during this period of time.

- ✔ **Long-term** disability: provides income replacement coverage if you become ill or injured and unable to work for more than six months. Coverage ends at the later of age 65 or five years of disability.

If you and your spouse are dependent on both incomes, you both should have disability insurance. If your employer doesn't provide coverage as part of their employee benefit package, purchase commercial disability insurance coverage yourselves. Check out *Personal Finance Workbook For Dummies* (Wiley) for guidance on what to look for in a policy and where to find competitive coverage.

Long-term care insurance

You might think of long-term care insurance as *really* long-term disability insurance. Long-term care insurance pays for the healthcare that you may need at a nursing center or for professional healthcare in your home. It doesn't pay for hospitalization or doctor visits. Those expenses should be covered under your medical insurance. However, if you or your spouse develop a degenerative neurological disease or receive a spinal cord injury, long-term care insurance will pay for care in a nursing institution or possibly in your own home.

Most employers do not yet offer long-term care insurance to their employees. However, the federal government is a major employer of veterans, and long-term care insurance is a federal government employee benefit.

Consult Veteran's Benefits For Dummies (Wiley) for more information on your benefits available through the VA.

Life insurance

Life insurance is another one of those types of insurance that your family can't afford to be without. Don't skimp in this area. Coverage for fairly young, fairly healthy people is inexpensive. Having *enough* life insurance if the unthinkable occurs is invaluable!

Servicemembers Group Life Insurance (SGLI) is available to all active-duty servicemembers and members of the Guard and Reserve. Your service-member is automatically covered for $400,000 of death benefits. One of the major benefits of SGLI is the fact that servicemembers can convert to Veteran's Group Life Insurance (VGLI) — with no medical underwriting — upon transitioning from the military.

If your servicemember has health concerns upon transitioning from the military, this VGLI conversion benefit is a major deal! However, if your servicemember is healthy, they very likely he can obtain more cost-effective life insurance through other insurance companies.

Also, conversion from SGLI to VGLI *must* take place within 120 days of service if you want to avoid medical qualification!

Check out the following military friendly and very competitive life insurance companies:

- www.AFBA.com
- www.AAFMAA.com (Army and Air Force)
- www.navymutual.org (Navy and Marines)
- www.MOAA.org (officers)
- www.USAA.com
- www.USBA.com

While your new civilian employer may provide some life insurance benefit as part of your employee benefit package, the amount of death benefit is usually the lesser of one times your annual salary or $50,000.

You might have the option to purchase additional life insurance through your employer; however, most often you will be better off purchasing your life insurance directly from a commercial life insurance company. The cost is extremely competitive, and if you change jobs, you can't lose your life insurance. Plus, you probably need significantly more life insurance than your employer may provide. See Chapter 8 for help in calculating how much life insurance you need. Add this additional expense to your post-transition budget.

Retirement plans

Most civilian employers of any size offer their employees the opportunity to participate in a 401(k) plan or possibly a 403(b) plan. Both plans are very similar. You'll most likely have a 401(k) plan, so we focus our attention on the features and benefits of this type of retirement savings plan.

First of all, your military Thrift Savings Plan (TSP) is a 401(k) plan. All the money that you have withdrawn from your paycheck and invested in your TSP or any other 401(k) plan is a tax-deductible contribution. In other words, you don't have to pay income taxes on the wages that you direct to your 401(k) plan instead of receiving those wages in your net paycheck. Also, the earnings on your retirement account over the years grow tax deferred. You don't pay any taxes on money that you put into a 401(k) plan until you pull that money out. If you're 59½ years old or older, there is no premature distribution penalty. However, because you've not paid any tax on that money, 100 percent of the withdrawals from your 401(k) plan in retirement will be taxed as ordinary income.

The huge difference between your military TSP and a civilian employer-provided 401(k) plan is that your civilian employer may provide a matching contribution. A matching contribution is frequently equal to 25 to 50 percent of your contribution percentage up to a certain maximum each year. For example, your employer matches 50 percent of your contribution, up to a maximum of 6 percent of your salary, you put into your 401(k) plan.

Just for contributing to your own retirement account, you could receive 25 to 50 percent guaranteed return on your contribution — in the form of an employer-matching contribution. You can't get that kind of a guarantee on any other type of retirement plan investment. Don't walk away from *free* money. At a minimum, contribute up to the maximum amount your employer will match each year.

If your servicemember is retiring from service, you're likely extremely familiar with the military retirement benefit. With 20 years of service your spouse can retire with 50 percent of his basic pay guaranteed for the rest of his life. If he serves for 30 years or more the retirement pay is 75 percent of his basic pay. This type of retirement plan is known as a defined benefit plan. See Chapter 21 for more details.

Unfortunately, it is extremely uncommon to find defined benefit pension plans in the civilian workplace nowadays. A couple of generations ago pensions were common with large employers; however, most of those plans have gone away and have been replaced with the 401(k) plan. Many employers not only provide a matching contribution based on your participation in the plan, but they may also make profit-sharing contributions when the company has a particularly good year.

All of the money you contribute to your 401(k) plan is vested immediately. In other words, it's yours; you can take it with you if you leave employment. However, matching contributions and profit-sharing contributions are almost always tied to a vesting schedule. Commonly you become fully vested in your employer's contributions over a period of five years — 20 percent per year. So, if you don't plan on staying with an employer long, don't overestimate the value for the company's matching or profit-sharing contribution.

Health savings accounts

You can save up to $3,000 per year in a health savings account through your employer (if it offers one). Your contribution is tax deductible, the earnings on your account accumulate on a tax deferred basis, and if you use the money to pay for qualified medical expenses, no tax is due — ever. If you don't need the money or would just prefer to let it accumulate, you can use this savings to supplement your retirement income. Withdrawals from health savings accounts for retirement are taxed as ordinary income upon receipt.

Flexible spending plans

Many larger employers offer flexible spending plans, flex-accounts, or Section 125 plans, all just different names for the same thing. You can set aside money in your flexible spending plan to pay for unreimbursed healthcare expenses, such as co-pays on office visits, prescription drugs, and even over-the-counter medications, as well as childcare expenses.

Most plans allow you to withhold up to $5,000 per year before-tax from your salary for childcare expenses. However, that money can only be used to pay for childcare from a licensed childcare provider. In other words, you can pay for childcare pre-tax! This option could save you about $1,000 per year and is a substantial benefit to families with children in childcare.

In addition to the money you can sock away for childcare, you can also save an additional amount, generally about $2,500, for other qualified expenses such as medical co-pays, dental care, eyeglasses, and so on.

The money you save in your flexible spending account must be used or you lose it. This account requires thoughtful planning on your part, but if you know that you'll be spending a certain amount of money on childcare and/or healthcare expenses throughout the year, you might as well do so tax-free by utilizing your flexible spending account.

If you find out you have a little money left over in your account toward the end of the year, stock up on supplies you use such as contact lens solution, over-the-counter medication, and so on to make sure you don't leave any money on the table.

Paid vacations and holidays

Your servicemember has been on-call throughout his entire military career. In the civilian world he likely will *not* be on-call. He won't receive four weeks per year leave; rather, it's typical that he'll receive only two weeks paid vacation after one year of service. Many employers require that vacations be arranged far in advance, and these vacations are normally granted based on seniority. Often employers prefer, if not require, employees to take one-week vacations two times each year.

In addition to paid vacations, salaried employees are also paid when the employer is closed for a national holiday. If your spouse is paid by the hour, rather than paid a salary, and works on a national holiday, he'll generally receive one and a half to two times regular hourly pay.

Overtime

What a concept! If your servicemember takes a job where he is paid hourly, most employers pay time and a half for all hours in excess of 40 per week.

Education assistance

Some civilian employers provide full or partial reimbursement for college coursework or certificate programs directly related to your job or for enabling you to further develop skills that your employer deems beneficial.

Part VI:
The Part of Tens

The 5th Wave   By Rich Tennant

"My husband named the dog. Of course, he's in the military and I don't have the heart to tell the kids it's an acronym for Special Patrol Over The Hill Tactician."

In this part . . .

Every Dummies book includes a Part of Tens section that consists of chapters of top-ten lists with important information we think you should have. These are of course our subjective views of the top-ten in each of the categories. Take them in the spirit they're offered, a guide to the ten best and worst within the military community.

Chapter 23

Ten Best Benefits for Military Spouses

In This Chapter

▶ Making the most of the free assistance available to you

▶ Understanding your military benefits will save you money

▶ Maximizing your opportunities

Now that you know everything there is about being a military family, how about some inside gouge about the real ten best benefits for military spouses? Okay, so no one's ever going to be able to agree on the best benefits out there for spouses, so take this in the spirit in which it's offered — our opinion of the best benefits for military spouses.

Travel

With space-available flights at your disposal, you'd be silly not to take advantage of the travel opportunities. Just think about it, given enough time and flexibility, you can go almost anywhere on a dime. And all this with no luggage restrictions (okay, almost no luggage restrictions). With the airlines becoming more and more restrictive and air travel becoming tiresome, this is probably a good time to try military airlift.

Get acquainted with the regulations and the ins and outs of space-a travel and hit the road, or rather, take to the skies. It's always an adventure and sometimes it's the mishaps that are even more memorable and make for the best family anecdotes. If you have kids, this is a wonderful experience to share with them. Get them involved with researching the different locations and let them have some say in where you go. Remember also that space-a travel works best when you have more flexibility with your schedule and have the means to make alternative arrangements in case you're not able to catch a return trip back on military aircraft.

Education and Employment Assistance

If you're looking to go back to school and finish your degree, or start an advanced degree, look no further than your installation education office for a head start. They will know everything from degree programs to financial assistance available specifically for military spouses and dependents.

Perhaps you're not interested in going back to school and are looking for assistance to get back into the workforce, or find your first job. Well, look no further than the Family Support Center. There you can get assistance with your résumé and learn about job interviews and negotiating your employee benefits. Regardless of what stage in life you're at, the assistance available to servicemembers and their families is invaluable.

Healthcare

With medical costs skyrocketing out of sight, military healthcare remains one of the best benefits for currently serving military families, particularly if you are empanelled at a military treatment facility (MTF). Understanding your Tricare benefits and making the right choice for your family, in terms of Prime vs. Standard, ensures that as a military family your low healthcare costs are among the best in the nation.

Commissary/Exchange

Depending on where you live, shopping at the commissary and exchange can save you a significant amount of money. With the majority of military families living off of the installation, it may seem like a pain to make the extra effort and venture out to the installation to do your shopping, but the savings add up. On average at the commissary, you can save upwards of 30% from other grocery stores.

Shopping at the exchange affords you little benefits such as tax free shopping and the knowledge that all the proceeds go toward MWR funds. If you live in a cosmopolitan area, you might soon find that these quickly become some of your best benefits.

Family Support Centers

Wildly underutilized, your installation family support center should always be on the top of your go-to resources. With counselors on staff who can speak to every aspect of the military family experience from moves and transitions to employment counseling, there's no reason for you to start your information gathering anywhere else. A fair amount of money is invested in these centers to be able to provide you all this assistance for free, so take advantage of it.

Free Professional and Personal Development

Through the Family Support Centers, you have the opportunity to take any number of classes and continue to grow professionally and personally. There are classes on all aspects of financial readiness ranging from balancing a checkbook to understanding your military and financial benefits. In addition to the Family Support Center staff, subject matter experts are often brought in from the outside to augment the class offerings. If you have the time and are willing to learn, the opportunities are out there for you.

Free Support and Assistance

Remember that in addition to the resources you find on the installation, there are also other groups and organizations that support you outside of the military. Be informed about what's out there. The America Supports You Web site (www.americasupportsyou.mil) is a good place to start. This is an umbrella organization for the hundreds of groups seeking to help military families. Know to look for military specific resources. If you're looking for scholarships for military children, remember to also check a military scholarship finder such as the one found on www.moaa.org.

Discounts

Corporations have also banded together to provide discounts to service-members and their families. Military OneSource is a good starting point to find out more about the freebies and discounts available to you. Whenever you're planning a vacation, it would be foolish not to do your homework because there are free tickets to amusement parks for military families, as well as deeply discounted hotel rooms and other rentals.

Recreating Yourself Every Few Years

Some people lament that they have to move every two or three years, while others embrace it as an opportunity to start over each time. Don't like your house? No worries, you'll have a new one in a couple years. Don't like your job? Well, you can do anything for two or three years knowing that there's a light at the end of the tunnel. That idea might sound somewhat cavalier, and some people may chafe at having to leave a great area every few years. However, there is some comfort in the knowledge that if you're in a less than desirable situation, all you have to do is wait, and within a few years, you'll have the opportunity to recreate yourself. It's liberating knowing that you can try most anything because if it doesn't work out and that job is not what you had imagined it would be, you can start again in a few years.

Meeting Other Spouses

By far, the greatest personal benefit for military spouses has to be the opportunity to meet other military spouses. Even though the military throws people together, everyone comes from different backgrounds and the opportunity to learn from one another is one of the things that keeps military life interesting. Don't go into the military lifestyle girding yourself from the hurt of multiple good-byes by not taking the time or making the effort to get to know other military spouses. It's these friendships and bonds you'll make throughout a military career that'll make the whole experience that much more special.

Chapter 24

Ten Biggest Financial Military Benefits

In This Chapter
▶ Focusing on the benefits that matter most
▶ Maximizing the financial benefits of a military career

Y ou and your spouse have sacrificed a great deal to commit to a career of military service. The base pay isn't great; however, it's only a portion of your total compensation package. In this chapter we focus on all the major financial benefits of military service.

Retirement Benefits

Imagine receiving a guaranteed income for the rest of your lives. And it keeps pace with inflation. At the ripe old age of about 40, you and your spouse could bring in one half of your member's basic pay for the rest of your lives. You don't have to save any money. The U.S. government makes all the contributions for you. In addition to your military retirement, as early as age 62 you'll also qualify for Social Security retirement benefits.

There is not a better benefit plan available anywhere. Your spouse's retirement benefit is guaranteed by the U.S. government, has an annual cost-of-living adjustment, and they receive 50 percent of base pay after just 20 years of service and 75 percent after 30 years of service.

When you're 25 years old it's hard to think about what life is going to be like at age 40 or 50. It feels like a lifetime away. And a long-term career in the military is definitely not for everyone. If it might be for you, talk to your friends in your community who've been serving a while longer. Talk to folks who retired from service. Ask them if they have any regrets. And refer to Chapter 21 for a reminder about the financial cost of replacing a military retirement benefits.

Survivor Benefit Plan

The above section on military retirement benefits applies while your servicemember or veteran is living. In the event that your spouse predeceases you, the Survivor Benefit Plan (SBP) is available to insure that you will continue to receive military retirement benefits for the rest of your life. Without SBP, military retirement income stops when your veteran dies. With SBP you can continue to receive up to 55 percent of your spouse's military retirement benefits, adjusted annually for inflation, for the rest of your life.

At retirement you must pay premiums for SBP coverage. The premiums are withheld directly from your military retirement pay — before tax — which means Uncle Sam is also subsidizing the cost of your SBP premium. You may elect the amount of benefit you want up to 55 percent of your spouse's military retirement. SBP premiums for spouse coverage are 6.5 percent of your chosen base amount.

The government subsidizes the cost of coverage, so it's highly unlikely that you'd be able to purchase commercial life insurance that is truly comparable and more cost effective then SBP.

Healthcare

Less than 60 percent of the civilian workforce has medical insurance, and far fewer have dental, vision, or prescription drug coverage. Most civilians are restricted in the types of jobs they can consider due to their need for quality health insurance. When a civilian retires they almost never have employer-provided health insurance, and even if they do it's not guaranteed to be around throughout their retirement years.

Those employed in, or retired from, the armed forces and their families, have access to very affordable, quality healthcare, and insurance guaranteed for life by the U.S. government.

The value of your healthcare benefits alone is over $4,000 per year per person.

Housing

The military provides your servicemember with all their basic necessities; food, clothing, and shelter. Married servicemembers may be able to live on the installation. However, if you prefer to live off-base, or there isn't capacity on-base, the military provides you with the Basic Allowance for Housing, also known as BAH, to adjust for the additional costs of living off-base. The actual amount of BAH is based on the local rental housing market, your service-member's pay grade, and number of dependents.

Depending on where you live, this tax-free financial benefit is worth hundreds of dollars or more each month.

Education

A major financial benefit of military service is the opportunity to obtain a college education, specific vocational training, or an advanced or postgraduate degree — almost *all* paid for by the U.S. government!

The Montgomery GI Bill provides a very generous tax-free benefit to active-duty servicemembers and veterans. More than $38,000 per eligible service-member is available that can be used to pay for tuition, books, fees, and living expenses while earning a college degree or certification from a technical school. The Montgomery GI Bill can also be used for professional licensing or certification and on-the-job training programs. This benefit is paid directly to the student on a monthly basis.

Your servicemember's military career also provides them with on-the-job training, leadership skills, and opportunities for promotion. With each promotion they gain more skills, have more responsibility, and of course additional pay and benefits.

Travel

Join the service and see the world! There's a lot of truth to that statement if you want to make it happen. Your family can travel for free with the military's special travel benefits — but there's a little art and luck involved.

Space available flights, also known as, Space-A flights enable you, your servicemember, and family to take advantage of the unused seats on Department of Defense aircraft. Space-A flights can be of great value but you need to have some flexibility, know the rules, and do some research and plan ahead.

VA Loans

One home financing option that is available to you and your family but not available to your civilian counterparts is a VA loan. VA guaranteed loans have a number of advantages over other types of mortgages, specifically:

- ✔ No down payment is required.
- ✔ Your credit score can be lower than required for conventional loans.
- ✔ Interest rates are very competitive.
- ✔ No mortgage insurance is required.
- ✔ Fees for a VA guaranteed loan tend to be very low and are added into the loan so there are no out-of-pocket loan closing expenses.

VA loans are not issued by the Veterans Administration. They are *guaranteed* by the VA, but issued by traditional banks, savings and loans, and mortgage companies. The guarantee means that the lender is protected if you fail to repay your mortgage. Traditional lenders require a down payment of 20 percent, however due to the VA guarantee you can obtain a VA home loan with no down payment.

Servicemembers Group Life Insurance

Servicemembers Group Life Insurance (SGLI) is available to all active-duty servicemembers and members of the Guard and Reserve. Your servicemember is automatically covered for $400,000 of death benefits. The monthly cost for coverage is just $29 and automatically deducted from their pay before taxes.

One of the major benefits of SGLI is the fact that the premiums stay level for the duration of your servicemember's military career. Another very significant benefit of SGLI is the fact that servicemembers can convert to Veteran's Group Life Insurance — with no medical underwriting — upon transitioning from the military. If your servicemember has health concerns upon transitioning from a military this VGLI conversion benefit is a major deal.

Legal Assistance

Your Legal Assistance Center can assist you in answering questions about your legal rights and protections, as well as, draft wills, healthcare directives, and powers of attorney. Legal assistance attorneys can also answer questions and give advice about your income taxes or any other personal legal issue. All of this assistance is provided to you at no charge.

Family Support Center

Centers are available on all installations to assist in your transition and help you with any questions that you may have. The centers are staffed with people who've been through transitions, deployment, and reunions. They have spouses in the service and kids in the local schools. They are information central when it comes to what's going on in "town." The center staff can help you locate daycare, get you the scoop on schools, provide you with the run down on recreation programs to help the kids meet new friends, and fill you in on all the activities and events that you need to know about as a new member of the community.

The Family Support Center is command central for family support information, benefits, and programs, making it impossible to put a value on the services available from the Family Support Center. Take advantage of this resource on your military installation.

Chapter 25

Ten Worst Scams Against Servicemembers

In This Chapter

▶ Watching your back

▶ Recognizing schemes that are really scams

*W*ith all that you and your servicemember do for our country it's really disturbing to know that there are unscrupulous people out there who have marked you as an easy target. You're far from that. Check out some of the hottest scams against servicemembers in this chapter and tell your friends.

Sending Money to Injured Servicemembers

The American Red Cross reported that scam artists have been calling servicemember's families, claiming that they're with the Red Cross, asking for money to help their wounded servicemember.

The Red Cross does not call family members to share this kind of information. They only get involved if a family calls them. This kind of news would come from the branch of service or the servicemember's unit.

If you receive a legitimate call about your servicemember, the caller will provide you with an 800 number to use if you have any questions or concerns. This number is strictly used for casualty assistance officers and families.

If you are concerned about the legitimacy of a contact, call the rear detachment and talk with them immediately.

Protecting Your Privacy

You may receive an official looking email from your bank or credit card company asking you to verify information. Don't ever give out personal information to anyone you don't know. If this is a legitimate contact, the company should have the information they need. If in doubt — call the bank or credit card company directly and ask them about the call, email, or letter you received. It is probably fraudulent.

Scam artists collect private information about you and then use it to borrow money with no intention of ever paying it back, and leaving you to prove you didn't borrow the money yourself.

No one thinks identity theft will happen to them. However, it does happen about a million times a year and has become one of the fastest-growing crimes in America.

For more information on ways you can protect your privacy check out *Personal Finance Workbook For Dummies* (Wiley).

Repairing Your Credit

Nothing can "repair" your credit other than persistence and time. Don't waste your money on outfits that promise to fix your credit. They can't. The most positive thing that can come out of this is they might educate you on ways you can, with time, improve your own credit. Instead of paying one of these outfits $300 or whatever, pick up a copy of *Credit Repair Kit For Dummies* by Stephen R. Bucci (Wiley).

Falling for Get-Rich-Quick Schemes

Why is late night television filled with money making "gurus" hocking their secrets? If the guru could make millions the easy way with their "system" why would they sell all their secrets on expensive television airtime for just three easy payments of $59.95? It just isn't logical.

The only people getting rich are the marketers and the promoters. The old saying, "if it sounds too good to be true, it probably is" *is* true.

Don't be a victim of a great sales pitch. This would be a great way to get-poor-quick!

Outsmarting the SBP

There are plenty of financial advisors and insurance agents who will try to convince you that they can show you a way to get all the benefits of the Survivor Benefit Plan. They'll be trying to sell you life insurance — probably variable universal life insurance.

The SBP program has been drastically improved in recent years and it is extremely difficult, if not impossible to outperform the SBP. Refer to Chapter 21 for all the arguments.

Paying Too Much for Financial Advice

Beware of major financial services sales organizations who promote investment plans that require you to invest for 15 years into the same mutual fund. It's not that you shouldn't invest for 15 years. It's that you shouldn't buy these types of investments. They are extremely expensive.

These plans are structured this way to get around a law which sets the maximum commission on a mutual fund investment. Check out a press release on the Security and Exchange Commission's Web site http://www.sec.gov/news/press/2004-170.htm for details on a huge crack-down on deceptive sales practices used by one of the primary financial services companies who focuses on military families.

You can do better by spending time educating yourself about personal finance and investing principles. Check out *Personal Finance Workbook For Dummies* (Wiley) and *Mutual Funds For Dummies* (Wiley) for additional information.

Investing a Tax Shelter inside of a Tax Shelter

Financial advisors may suggest that you invest your retirement funds (tax shelter) or IRAs (tax shelter) into an annuity (another type of tax shelter). There is no legitimate reason for doing this. The only reason an annuity is being recommended in this case is to make more money off of you!

The Security and Exchange Commission has an article entitled Investor Tips: Variable Annuities What You Should Know at http://www.sec.gov/investor/pubs/varannty.htm.

Investing in the New, New Thing

You want to find the next Google. There's nothing wrong with day-dreaming about striking it rich with one grand-slam home-run. Just remember, Babe Ruth was the home-run king, and he was also the strike-out king. Swinging for the fences can leave you with nothing.

Don't gamble on the one hot, new thing that's going to change the world. Shocking as it may seem, those hot, new ideas come around constantly. Rather, diversify over several different types of investments. If one hits big, several do okay, and one strikes out, you're still in the game. Strive for consistent base hits.

Hedging Your Risks with Gold or Oil

In an uncertain economy many investment gurus tout the virtues of investing in gold, gold mining stocks, oil company stocks, and oil exploration. Gold is not worth anything by itself. It doesn't do anything, you can't eat it, and it doesn't earn anything. Gold mining stocks and oil exploration are extremely speculative types of investments.

If you're trying to minimize risk, don't subject yourself to unnecessary risks like these. Instead, invest in a low-cost, no-load index mutual fund, and you'll get some exposure to lots of different types of companies, including oil company stocks. Diversification is the best hedge against investment risks. For additional information check out *Investing in an Uncertain Economy For Dummies.*

Considering Payday Loans

Unfortunately, servicemembers and their families are prime targets for payday lenders. That's why the government had to step in and tell these outfits to back off our military personnel. Payday loan companies are extremely lucrative businesses — to own — not to borrow from. They are making a fortune off of people like you. Don't become their next victim.

Appendix

Military Acronyms

AA: Assembly Area

AAF: Army Airfield

AAFES: Army Air Force Exchange Service; also called BX

AAM: Army Achievement Medal; Air-to-Air Missile; Automated Acquisition Module

AAR: After-Action Review; Air-to-Air Receive; Air-to-Air Refueling; Aircraft Accident Report

AATFC: Air Assault Task Force Commander

AB: Air Base (overseas)

ABN: Airborne

AC: Aircraft Commander; Active Component; Alternating Current; Aircraft; Aircraft Carrier; Aircrew

ACC: Air Combat Command

ACE: Ammunition, Casualties, Equipment (a report given after contact); Armored Combat Earthmover

ACR: Armored Calvary Regiment

ACS: Army Community Service

ACSC: Air Command and Staff College

ACU: Army Combat Uniform; Assault Craft Unit; Annunciator Control Unit; Automatic Calling Unit; Administrative Control Unit

AD: Active Duty (the military member)

ADSC: Active Duty Service Commitment

AEF: Aerospace Expeditionary Force

AER: Army Emergency Relief

AETC: Air Education Training Command

AFAF: Air Force Assistance Fund (charity fund raising for AFAS)

AFAS: Air Force Aid Society

AFB: Air Force Base

AFI: Air Force Instruction (regulations)

AFIT: Air Force Institute of Technology

AFLC: Air Force Logistics Command

AFMC: Air Force Material Command

AFOQT: Air Force Officer Qualifying Test

AFSC: Air Force Specialty Code

AIT: Advanced Infantry Training; Advanced Individual Training (specialty training post); Automated Identification Technology

AJM: Assistant Jumpmaster

ALICE: All-Purpose Lightweight Individual Carrying Equipment

ALS: Airman's Leadership School

AMC: Air Mobility Command

AMF: Army Modular Force

AMN: Airman

AN: Army/Navy

ANCOC: Advanced Noncommissioned Officer Course; (pronounced *ay*-knock)

ANG: Air National Guard

AO: Accounts Office; Action Officer; Aircraft Officer; Aircraft Operator; Administration Officer; Air Officer; Area of Operations

AOC: Air and Space Operations Center; Air Operations Center; Army Operations Center; Area of Concentration

AOD: Administrative Officer of the Day

AOO: Area of Operations

AOR: Area of Responsibility; Allowance Overrides; Annual Operating Requirement; Area of Operations; Replenishment Oiler (underway replenishment)

APC: Armored Personnel Carrier; Acquisition Professional Community; Accelerated Provision Concepts; Account Processing Code; Activity Process Codes; Agency Program Coordinator; Air Project Coordinator; Aerial Port Commander; Assign Pre-programmed Conference; Air Program Coordinator; Approach Power Compensator; Approach Power Control; Approach Control; Assistant Project Coordinator

APFT: Army Physical Fitness Test

APO: Air Post Office

ARC: American Red Cross

ARCAM: Army Reserve Component Achievement Medal

ARCOM: Army Commendation Medal

ARFORGEN: Army Force Generation

ARNG: Army National Guard

ARSOF: Army Special Operations Forces

ASAP: As Soon As Possible

ASCC: Army Service Component Command

ASEP: Army Spouse Employment Partnership

ASOC: Air Support Operations Center

ASW: Anti Submarine Warfare

AT: Annual Tour

ATAM: Air-to-Air Missile

ATC: Air Traffic Control

AUTEC: Atlantic Undersea Test and Evaluation Center

AVF: All-Volunteer Force

AWC: Air Warfare Center

AWOL: Absent Without Leave

B/N: Bombardier/Navigator; the observer on a U.S. Air Force fighter bomber

BAH: Basic Allowance for Housing

BAQ: Basic Aircraft Qualification; Basic Allowance for Quarters

BAS: Basic Allowance for Subsistence

BC: Bradley Commander/Battalion Commander

BCD: Bad Conduct Discharge; Binary-Coded Decimal; Battlefield Coordination Detachment

BCNR: Board for Correction of Navy Records

BCT: Basic Combat Training; Brigade Combat Team; Best Conventional Technology

BDUs: Battle Dress Uniform; also called cammies (camouflage)

BEQ: Bachelor Enlisted Quarters

BLUF: Bottom Line Up Front (i.e., get to the point)

BMOC: Big Man on Campus (the General)

BMT: Basic Military Training

BN: Battalion; Basic Noncommissioned Officer Course

BOG: Beach Operations Group

BOQ: Bachelor Officers' Quarters

BPED: Basic Pay Entry Date

BRM: Basic Rifle Marksmanship

BSB: Base Support Battalion

BUMED: Bureau of Medicine and Surgery

BUPERS: Bureau of Naval Personnel

BX/PX: Base Exchange (AF); Post Exchange (Army)

C:IED: Counter: Improvised Explosive Device

CA: Civil Affairs

CAA: Career Advancement Account

CAB: Combat Aviation Brigade; Cabin; Centralized Accounting & Billing (Navy); Contract Adjustment Board; Cost Analysis Brief; Combat Action Badge

CAC: Common Access Card; Community Activity Center

CACO: Casualty Assistance Counseling Officer

CAO: Civil Affairs Operations

CAPE: Corrective Action through Physical Exercise

CAPEX: Capabilities Exercise

CAPT: Civil Affairs Planning Team

CATA: Civil Affairs Team Alpha

CAV: Cavalry (Armored Cavalry Regiment); Cavalry Fighting Vehicle

CBRND: Chemical-Biological-Radiological-Nuclear Defense

CC: Commander

CCA: Close Combat Attack

CCAF: Community College of the Air Force

CCF: First Sergeant

CCMSGT: Commander Chief Master Sergeant, formerly known as the Senior Enlisted Advisor (SEA)

CDC: Career Development Course

CDC: Child Development Center

CE: Civil Engineer

CENC: Commander-in-Chief

CENTCOM: Unites States Central Command (AFB MacDill, FL)

CEV: Combat Engineer Vehicle: the only tank type vehicle inside its own blast radius

CFC: Combined Federal Campaign (charity fundraising for multiple charities)

CHAMPU.S.: Civilian Health and Medical Program for the Uniformed Services

CHOPS: Chief of Operations

CI: Counter Intelligence

CIB: Combat Infantryman Badge; Combined Information Bureau; Controlled Image Base

CIF: Central Issue Facility

CIM: Civil Information Management

CINCLANTFLT: Commander in Chief, U.S. Atlantic Fleet

CINCPACFLT: Commander in Chief, U.S. Pacific Fleet

CINCU.S.NAVEUR: Commander in Chief, U.S. Naval Forces Europe

CJSOTF: Combined Joint Special Operations Task Force

CLS: Combat Life Saver

CMC: Command Master Chief

CMO: Civil Military Operations

CMOC: Civil Military Operations Center

CNET: Chief of Naval Education and Training

CNO: Chief of Naval Operations

CO: Commanding Officer

COA: Course of Action; Certificate of Achievement

COB: Close of Business; Chief of the Boat; Closing of Business

COIN: Counter Insurgency

COLA: Cost of Living Allowance

COMNAVYSEASYSCOM: Commander, Naval Sea Systems Command

COMSEC: Communications Security

COMSUBPAC: Commander, Submarine Force Pacific

CONU.S.: Continental United States (the contiguous 48 states)

COW: Chief of Watch

CP: Command Post; Counter Proliferation

CPO: Civilian Personnel Office; Chief Petty Officer

CQ: Change of Quarters

CRISTA: Counter Reconnaissance, Intelligence, Surveillance, and Target Acquisition

CSAR: Combat Search and Rescue

CSS: Commander's Support Staff

CSSAMO: Combat Service Support Automations Maintenance Office

CT: Counterterrorism

CTA: Common Table of Allowances

CVBG: Aircraft Carrier Battle Group

CWO: Chief Warrant Officer; Communications Watch Officer

D:NIF: Duties: Not Including Flying

DA: Department of the Army; Data Adapter; Aerospace Drift; Data Administrator; Direct Action; Directorate for Administration; Decision Agent; Developing Agency; Design Agent; Development Activity; Disbursing Advisory Notice; Drift Angle

DASO: Demonstration and Shakedown Operation

DCM: Distinguished Conduct Medal; Data Channel Multiplexer; Duty Chief of Mission; Data Communication Module

DD: Destroyer (Navy ship); Defense Department

DDP: Delta Dental Plan

DDS: Direct Deposit System

DECA: Defense Commissary Agency

DEERS: Defense Enrollment Eligibility Reporting System

DEMOB: Short for demobilization

DEROS: Date Estimated Return from Overseas

DFAC: Dining Facilities Administration Center

DFAS: Defense Finance and Accounting System

DIME: Diplomatic, Informational, Military, and Economic (forms of national power)

DITY: Do-It-Yourself move

DJMS: Defense Joint Military Pay System

DLA: Defense Logistics Agency; Dislocation Allowance

DO: Duty Officer

DOB: Date of Birth

DOD: Department of Defense

DON: Department of the Navy

DOR: Date of Rank

DOS: Date of Separation

DPP: Deferred Payment Plan

DS: Dependent Spouse

DSN: Defense Switched Network (worldwide telephone system)

DTG: Date Time Group

DZ: Drop Zone

DZSO: Drop Zone Safety Officer

DZST: Drop Zone Support Team

DZSTL: Drop Zone Support Team Officer

EAB: Emergency Air Breathing system

EAF: Expeditionary Aerospace Force

EAOS: Expiration of Active Obligated Service

EFMP: Exceptional Family Member Program

EFT: Electronic Funds Transfer

EOC: Emergency Operations Center

EOD: Explosive Ordinance Disposal

EOM: End of Month

EOOW: Engineering Officer of the Watch

EOY: End of Year

EPR: Enlisted Performance Report

EQUAL: Enlisted Quarterly Assignment Listing

ESC: Enlisted Spouses' Club

ETS: Expiration of Term of Service

EUCOM: Untied States European Command (Stuttgart-Vaihingen, Germany)

EWC: Enlisted Wives' Club (title being phased out in favor of ESC)

EXSUM: Executive Summary

EZ: Extraction Zone

FARP: Forward Arming and Refueling Point/Forward-Arming Replenishment Package

FBM: Fleet Ballistic Missile submarine

FEBA: Forward Edge of Battle Area

FERS: Federal Employees' Retirement System

FICA: Federal Insurance Contribution Act

FID: Foreign Internal Defense

FIT: Federal Income Tax

FITW: Federal Income Tax Withholding

FLT: Flight

FM: Family Member

FPO: Fleet Post Office

FRG: Family Readiness Group

FSA: Family Separation Allowance

FSC: Family Support Center; Family Service Center

FTX: Field Training Exercise

FY: Fiscal Year

FYI: For Your Information

FYTD: Fiscal Year to Date

GCM: Good Conduct Medal; General Court-Material; Guidance Section

GFOQ: General/Field Officers' Quarters

GMC: General Military Course

GMT: General Military Training

GOV: Government Owned Vehicle

GS: General Schedule (Civil Service worker)

GSU: Geographically Separated Unit

HA: Humanitarian Assistance

HAHO: High-Altitude High-Opening parachute technique (type of parachute jump, self-explanatory); also referred to as a stand-off infiltration technique

HALO: High-Altitude Low-Opening parachute technique (type of parachute jump, self-explanatory); High Altitude Learjet Observatory

HBCT: Heavy Brigade Combat Team

HDIP: Hazardous Duty Incentive Pay

HDR: Humanitarian Daily Ration

HHG: Household Goods

HOLA: Housing Overseas Living Allowance

HOR: Home of Record

HQ: Headquarters

HVT: High-Value Target

IAW: In Accordance With

IBCT: Infantry Brigade Combat Team

IDP: Imminent Danger Pay

IED: Improvised Explosive Device

IG: Inspector General

IO: Information Operations

IOBC: Infantry Officer Basic Course

IOTV: Improved Tactical Outer Vest

IPB: Intelligence Preparation of the Battlefield

IPI: Indigenous Populations and Institutions

IRR: Individual Ready Reserve

ITT: Information, Tours and Travel

JAAT: Joint Air Attack Team

JAG: Judge Advocate General (legal office)

JCMOTF: Joint Civil-Military Operations Task Force

JCS: Joint Chiefs of Staff

JETDS: Joint Electronics Type Designation

JFTR: Joint Federal Travel Regulation

JM: Jumpmaster

JMPI: Jumpmaster Personnel Inspection

JTF: Joint Task Force

KIA: Killed in Action

KISS: Keep it Simple, Sergeant

LES: Leave and Earning Statement

LPO: Leading Petty Officer

LRS: Long-Range Surveillance

LZ: Landing Zone

MASCAL: Mass Casualty (any large number of casualties produced in a short period of time that exceed support capabilities)

MBT: Main Battle Tank

MCCS: Marine Corps Community Services

MCFTB: Marine Corps Family Team Building

MCPON: Master Chief Petty Officer of the Navy

MCX: Marine Corps Exchange

MDMP: Military Decision Making Process

MEDCOM: Army Medical Command

MEDEVAC: Medical Evacuation (to an aid station or field hospital, usually by air ambulance)

MEPS: Military Entrance Processing Station

MIA: Missing in Action; missing in a battle situation, not known if alive or dead

MILSTD: Military Standard

MOAB: Officially, Massive Ordnance Air Blast (slang: Mother Of All)

MOB: Short for mobilization

MOS: Military Occupational Specialty; formal job classification, usually expressed as a number or number/letter combination (e.g., 11B Infantryman)

MP: Military Police

MPF: Military Personnel Flight

MRE: Meals, Ready to Eat

MSS: Mission Support Squadron

MTF: Military Treatment Facility, or base clinic/hospital

MWR: Morale, Welfare, and Recreation

NAF: Non-Appropriated Funds

NATO: North Atlantic Treaty Organization

NAVSEA: Naval Sea Systems Command

NCIS: Naval Criminal Investigations Service

NCO: Non-Commissioned Officer (an enlisted person with command responsibility; Corporal to Command Sergeant Major)

NCOIC: Non-Commissioned Officer in Charge

NEO: Non-combatant Evacuation Operations

NEX: Navy Exchange

NJP: Naval Judicial Punishments

NLT: Not Later Than

NMCRS: Navy-Marine Corps Relief Society

NPD: No Pay Due

NSSF: Naval Submarine Support Facility

O/A: On or About

O/I: Operations and Intelligence

O/O: Order of Operations, on orders

OBA: Oxygen Breathing Apparatus

OCONU.S.: Outside the Continental United States (overseas tour, includes Alaska & Hawaii)

OCR: Office (Officer) of Co-Responsibility

OCS: Officer Candidate School

ODA: Special Forces Operational Detachment: Alpha

OER: Officer Evaluation Report

OGA: Other Government Agency

OHA: Overseas Housing Allowance

OIC: Officer in Charge

OJT: On the Job Training

OLC: Oak-Leaf Cluster (signifying subsequent awards)

OOD: Officer Of the Deck

OP: Observation Post

OPNAV: Office of the Chief of Naval Operations

OPR: Office of Primary Responsibility; Officer Performance Report

OPSEC: Operational Security

OPTARTD: Operating Target

OPTEMPO: Operational Tempo

ORE: Operational Readiness Exercise

ORI: Operational Readiness Inspection

ORSE: Operational Reactor Safeguards Exam

OSC: Officers' Spouse Club

OSD: Office of the Secretary of Defense

OSI: Office of Special Investigations

OSUT: One-Station Unit Training

OTS: Officer Training School

OWC: Officers' Wives Club (title being phased out in favor of OSC)

PACAF: Pacific Air Forces

PAT: Process Action Team

PCA: Permanent Change of Assignment

PCC: Pre-combat checks; Done by team leaders prior to PCI's

PCI: Pre-combat inspection; an inspection of equipment before a mission

PCM: Primary Care Manager

PCS: Permanent Change of Station (reassignment to a different duty station)

PEBD: Pay Entry Base Data

PERSCOM: Personnel Command, short for United States Army Personnel Command; now known as HRC, or the Human Resources Command

PERSTEMPO: Personnel Tempo (refers to the unit workload level and number of developed days per year)

PFDR: Pathfinder

PFE: Promotion Fitness Exam

PFMP: Personal Financial Management Program

PI: Point of Impact

PIR: Parachute Infantry Regiment

PLDC: Primary Leadership Development Course

PME: Professional Military Education

PMI: Preventive Maintenance Inspection

POA: Power of Attorney

POC: Point of Contact

POG: Psychological Operations Group

POMPOC: Parachute Operations Mishap Prevention Orientation Course

POO: Point of Origin

POV: Privately-Owned Vehicle

POW: Prisoner of War; Privately-Owned Weapon

PRD: Projected Rotation Date

PRP: Personal Reliability Program

PSYOP: Psychological Operations

PT: Physical Training; plural (PTs) refers to the PT uniform

PX: Post Exchange; a multi-purpose store which usually includes a barber shop and a convenience store

QA: Quality Assurance

QTRS: Quarters (living area)

R&D: Research and Development

R&R: Rest and Relaxation

RADC: Regional Air Defense Commander

RAP: Relocation Assistance Program; also known as Relo

REG: Regulation

RGB: Ranger Battalion

RIF: Reduction in Force

RIO: Radar Intercept Officer, or "Rio"; an observer on a U.S. Naval Aviation two-seater fighter

ROE: Rules of Engagement

ROTC: Reserve Officer Training Corps

RPG: Rocket-Propelled Grenade

RRC: Ranger Reconnaissance Company

RSVP: Respond if you Please (expect yes or no)

RTB: Ranger Training Brigade

RTB: Return to Base

RTO: Radio Telephone Operator

SAM: Surface to Air Missile

SATCOM: Satellite Communications

SATO: Scheduled Airlines Ticket Office

SBCT: Stryker Brigade Combat Team

SBF: Support by Fire

SBP: Survivor Benefit Plan

SCA: Support to Civil Administration

SDO: Staff Duty Officer

SEA: Senior Enlisted Advisor, now known as the Command Chief Master Sergeant, CCMSGT

SEAL: Sea-Air-Land

SECDEF: Secretary of Defense

SF: Special Forces

SFODA: Special Forces Operation Detachment (Alpha)

SFQC: Special Forces Qualification Course, also known as simply the "Q course"

SGLI: Serviceman's Group Life Insurance

SITREP: Situational Report

SITW: State Income Tax Withholding

SKT: Skills and Knowledge Test

SLBM: Submarine Launched Ballistic Missile

SME: Subject Matter Expert

SO: Special Operations; Stability Operations

SOAC: U.S. Navy Submarine Officers Advanced Course

SOAR: Special Operations Aviation Regiment

SOBC: U.S. Navy Submarine Officers Basic Course

SOCOM: Special Operations Command

SOF: Special Operations Forces

SOMSUBLANT: Commander, Submarine Force Atlantic

SONAR: Sound Navigation and Ranging

SOP: Standard Operation Procedure

SORTIE: A flight or single flying mission

SOS: Squadron Officer's School

SOSCOM: Special Operations Support Command

SOSR: Suppress, Obscure, Secure, Reduce

SOY: Sailor of the Year

Space-A: Space-available (flights)

SRB: Selective Reenlistment Bonus

SSN, SSAN: Social Security Number

STAP: Spouse Tuition Aid Program

STEP: Stripes for Exceptional Performers

STRAC: Strategic Army Corps

STX: Situational Training Exercise

SUBGRU: Submarine Group

SUBORC: Submarine Rocket

SUBRON: Submarine Squadron

TA: Tuition Assistance (program for active duty members)

TAD: Temporary Additional Duty

TAFMSD: Total Active Federal Military Service Date; the date the servicemember came on active duty

TAP: Transition Assistance Program

TC: Tank Commander/Truck Commander

TDP: (Helicopter) Touch Down Point; used in HLZ Ops; TriCare Dental Plan

TDU: Trash Disposal Unit

TDY: Temporary Duty

TF: Task Force

THT: Tactical HUMINT Team

TIG: Time in Grade

TLA: Temporary Living Allowance

TLE: Temporary Lodging Expenses

TLF: Temporary Living Facility

TMO: Traffic Management Office

TO: Technical Order

TOA: Transfer of Authority

TOC: Tactical Operations Center

TOT: Time on Target

TPT: Tactical PSYOP Team

TRADOC: U.S. Army Training and Doctrine Command

TSP: Thrift Savings Plan

TTAD: Temporary Tour Active Duty

TYCOM: Type Commander

UA: Unit of Action; Unauthorized Absence

UCI: Unit Compliance Inspection

UCMJ: Uniform Code of Military Justice

UIC: Unit Identification Code

U.S.ACAPOC: United States Army Civil Affairs and Psychological Operations Command

U.S.AF: Untied States Air Force

U.S.AFE: United States Air Force- Europe

U.S.AFR: United States Air Force Reserves

U.S.AJFKSWCS: United States Army John F. Kennedy Special Warfare Center and School

U.S.AREUR: United States Army Europe (HQ: Heidelberg)

U.S.ASFC: United States Army Special Forces Command

U.S.ASOC: United States Army Special Operations Command

U.S.O: United Service Organization

UTA: Unit Training Assembly

UW: Unconventional Warfare

UXO: Unexploded Ordinance

V/R: Very Respectfully. The standard closure line on official mail/e-mail

V/STOL: Vertical/Short Takeoff and Landing

VA: Veteran's Administration

VAQ: Visiting Airman's Quarters

VBIED: Vehicle-Borne Improvised Explosive Device

VHA: Variable Housing Allowance

VIP: Very Important Person

VOQ: Visiting Officers Quarters

W2: Wage and Tax Statement

WAPS: Weighted Airman Promotion System

WG: Wag Grade (Civil Service worker)

WIC: Women, Infants, and Children's Program

WO: Warning Order

WSO: Weapon Systems Officer, or "Wizzo"; observer, navigator, or individual in control of weapon systems in a two-seater fighter

XILCO: Will Comply

XO: Executive Officer

YTD: Year to Date

ZULU/GMT: Greenwich Mean Time

Index

• N •

BUSINESS, CAREERS & PERSONAL FINANCE

Accounting For Dummies, 4th Edition*
978-0-470-24600-9

Bookkeeping Workbook For Dummies†
978-0-470-16983-4

Commodities For Dummies
978-0-470-04928-0

Doing Business in China For Dummies
978-0-470-04929-7

E-Mail Marketing For Dummies
978-0-470-19087-6

Job Interviews For Dummies, 3rd Edition*†
978-0-470-17748-8

Personal Finance Workbook For Dummies*†
978-0-470-09933-9

Real Estate License Exams For Dummies
978-0-7645-7623-2

Six Sigma For Dummies
978-0-7645-6798-8

Small Business Kit For Dummies, 2nd Edition*†
978-0-7645-5984-6

Telephone Sales For Dummies
978-0-470-16836-3

BUSINESS PRODUCTIVITY & MICROSOFT OFFICE

Access 2007 For Dummies
978-0-470-03649-5

Excel 2007 For Dummies
978-0-470-03737-9

Office 2007 For Dummies
978-0-470-00923-9

Outlook 2007 For Dummies
978-0-470-03830-7

PowerPoint 2007 For Dummies
978-0-470-04059-1

Project 2007 For Dummies
978-0-470-03651-8

QuickBooks 2008 For Dummies
978-0-470-18470-7

Quicken 2008 For Dummies
978-0-470-17473-9

Salesforce.com For Dummies, 2nd Edition
978-0-470-04893-1

Word 2007 For Dummies
978-0-470-03658-7

EDUCATION, HISTORY, REFERENCE & TEST PREPARATION

African American History For Dummies
978-0-7645-5469-8

Algebra For Dummies
978-0-7645-5325-7

Algebra Workbook For Dummies
978-0-7645-8467-1

Art History For Dummies
978-0-470-09910-0

ASVAB For Dummies, 2nd Edition
978-0-470-10671-6

British Military History For Dummies
978-0-470-03213-8

Calculus For Dummies
978-0-7645-2498-1

Canadian History For Dummies, 2nd Edition
978-0-470-83656-9

Geometry Workbook For Dummies
978-0-471-79940-5

The SAT I For Dummies, 6th Edition
978-0-7645-7193-0

Series 7 Exam For Dummies
978-0-470-09932-2

World History For Dummies
978-0-7645-5242-7

FOOD, GARDEN, HOBBIES & HOME

Bridge For Dummies, 2nd Edition
978-0-471-92426-5

Coin Collecting For Dummies, 2nd Edition
978-0-470-22275-1

Cooking Basics For Dummies, 3rd Edition
978-0-7645-7206-7

Drawing For Dummies
978-0-7645-5476-6

Etiquette For Dummies, 2nd Edition
978-0-470-10672-3

Gardening Basics For Dummies*†
978-0-470-03749-2

Knitting Patterns For Dummies
978-0-470-04556-5

Living Gluten-Free For Dummies†
978-0-471-77383-2

Painting Do-It-Yourself For Dummies
978-0-470-17533-0

HEALTH, SELF HELP, PARENTING & PETS

Anger Management For Dummies
978-0-470-03715-7

Anxiety & Depression Workbook For Dummies
978-0-7645-9793-0

Dieting For Dummies, 2nd Edition
978-0-7645-4149-0

Dog Training For Dummies, 2nd Edition
978-0-7645-8418-3

Horseback Riding For Dummies
978-0-470-09719-9

Infertility For Dummies†
978-0-470-11518-3

Meditation For Dummies with CD-ROM, 2nd Edition
978-0-471-77774-8

Post-Traumatic Stress Disorder For Dummies
978-0-470-04922-8

Puppies For Dummies, 2nd Edition
978-0-470-03717-1

Thyroid For Dummies, 2nd Edition†
978-0-471-78755-6

Type 1 Diabetes For Dummies*†
978-0-470-17811-9

* Separate Canadian edition also available
† Separate U.K. edition also available

INTERNET & DIGITAL MEDIA

AdWords For Dummies
978-0-470-15252-2

Blogging For Dummies, 2nd Edition
978-0-470-23017-6

Digital Photography All-in-One Desk Reference For Dummies, 3rd Edition
978-0-470-03743-0

Digital Photography For Dummies, 5th Edition
978-0-7645-9802-9

Digital SLR Cameras & Photography For Dummies, 2nd Edition
978-0-470-14927-0

eBay Business All-in-One Desk Reference For Dummies
978-0-7645-8438-1

eBay For Dummies, 5th Edition*
978-0-470-04529-9

eBay Listings That Sell For Dummies
978-0-471-78912-3

Facebook For Dummies
978-0-470-26273-3

The Internet For Dummies, 11th Edition
978-0-470-12174-0

Investing Online For Dummies, 5th Edition
978-0-7645-8456-5

iPod & iTunes For Dummies, 5th Edition
978-0-470-17474-6

MySpace For Dummies
978-0-470-09529-4

Podcasting For Dummies
978-0-471-74898-4

Search Engine Optimization For Dummies, 2nd Edition
978-0-471-97998-2

Second Life For Dummies
978-0-470-18025-9

Starting an eBay Business For Dummies, 3rd Edition†
978-0-470-14924-9

GRAPHICS, DESIGN & WEB DEVELOPMENT

Adobe Creative Suite 3 Design Premium All-in-One Desk Reference For Dummies
978-0-470-11724-8

Adobe Web Suite CS3 All-in-One Desk Reference For Dummies
978-0-470-12099-6

AutoCAD 2008 For Dummies
978-0-470-11650-0

Building a Web Site For Dummies, 3rd Edition
978-0-470-14928-7

Creating Web Pages All-in-One Desk Reference For Dummies, 3rd Edition
978-0-470-09629-1

Creating Web Pages For Dummies, 8th Edition
978-0-470-08030-6

Dreamweaver CS3 For Dummies
978-0-470-11490-2

Flash CS3 For Dummies
978-0-470-12100-9

Google SketchUp For Dummies
978-0-470-13744-4

InDesign CS3 For Dummies
978-0-470-11865-8

Photoshop CS3 All-in-One Desk Reference For Dummies
978-0-470-11195-6

Photoshop CS3 For Dummies
978-0-470-11193-2

Photoshop Elements 5 For Dummies
978-0-470-09810-3

SolidWorks For Dummies
978-0-7645-9555-4

Visio 2007 For Dummies
978-0-470-08983-5

Web Design For Dummies, 2nd Edition
978-0-471-78117-2

Web Sites Do-It-Yourself For Dummies
978-0-470-16903-2

Web Stores Do-It-Yourself For Dummies
978-0-470-17443-2

LANGUAGES, RELIGION & SPIRITUALITY

Arabic For Dummies
978-0-471-77270-5

Chinese For Dummies, Audio Set
978-0-470-12766-7

French For Dummies
978-0-7645-5193-2

German For Dummies
978-0-7645-5195-6

Hebrew For Dummies
978-0-7645-5489-6

Ingles Para Dummies
978-0-7645-5427-8

Italian For Dummies, Audio Set
978-0-470-09586-7

Italian Verbs For Dummies
978-0-471-77389-4

Japanese For Dummies
978-0-7645-5429-2

Latin For Dummies
978-0-7645-5431-5

Portuguese For Dummies
978-0-471-78738-9

Russian For Dummies
978-0-471-78001-4

Spanish Phrases For Dummies
978-0-7645-7204-3

Spanish For Dummies
978-0-7645-5194-9

Spanish For Dummies, Audio Set
978-0-470-09585-0

The Bible For Dummies
978-0-7645-5296-0

Catholicism For Dummies
978-0-7645-5391-2

The Historical Jesus For Dummies
978-0-470-16785-4

Islam For Dummies
978-0-7645-5503-9

Spirituality For Dummies, 2nd Edition
978-0-470-19142-2

NETWORKING AND PROGRAMMING

ASP.NET 3.5 For Dummies
978-0-470-19592-5

C# 2008 For Dummies
978-0-470-19109-5

Hacking For Dummies, 2nd Edition
978-0-470-05235-8

Home Networking For Dummies, 4th Edition
978-0-470-11806-1

Java For Dummies, 4th Edition
978-0-470-08716-9

Microsoft® SQL Server™ 2008 All-in-One Desk Reference For Dummies
978-0-470-17954-3

Networking All-in-One Desk Reference For Dummies, 2nd Edition
978-0-7645-9939-2

Networking For Dummies, 8th Edition
978-0-470-05620-2

SharePoint 2007 For Dummies
978-0-470-09941-4

Wireless Home Networking For Dummies, 2nd Edition
978-0-471-74940-0

OPERATING SYSTEMS & COMPUTER BASICS

iMac For Dummies, 5th Edition
978-0-7645-8458-9

Laptops For Dummies, 2nd Edition
978-0-470-05432-1

Linux For Dummies, 8th Edition
978-0-470-11649-4

MacBook For Dummies
978-0-470-04859-7

**Mac OS X Leopard All-in-One
Desk Reference For Dummies**
978-0-470-05434-5

Mac OS X Leopard For Dummies
978-0-470-05433-8

Macs For Dummies, 9th Edition
978-0-470-04849-8

PCs For Dummies, 11th Edition
978-0-470-13728-4

Windows® Home Server For Dummies
978-0-470-18592-6

Windows Server 2008 For Dummies
978-0-470-18043-3

**Windows Vista All-in-One
Desk Reference For Dummies**
978-0-471-74941-7

Windows Vista For Dummies
978-0-471-75421-3

Windows Vista Security For Dummies
978-0-470-11805-4

SPORTS, FITNESS & MUSIC

Coaching Hockey For Dummies
978-0-470-83685-9

Coaching Soccer For Dummies
978-0-471-77381-8

Fitness For Dummies, 3rd Edition
978-0-7645-7851-9

Football For Dummies, 3rd Edition
978-0-470-12536-6

GarageBand For Dummies
978-0-7645-7323-1

Golf For Dummies, 3rd Edition
978-0-471-76871-5

Guitar For Dummies, 2nd Edition
978-0-7645-9904-0

**Home Recording For Musicians
For Dummies, 2nd Edition**
978-0-7645-8884-6

**iPod & iTunes For Dummies,
5th Edition**
978-0-470-17474-6

Music Theory For Dummies
978-0-7645-7838-0

Stretching For Dummies
978-0-470-06741-3

Get smart @ dummies.com®

- Find a full list of Dummies titles
- Look into loads of FREE on-site articles
- Sign up for FREE eTips e-mailed to you weekly
- See what other products carry the Dummies name
- Shop directly from the Dummies bookstore
- Enter to win new prizes every month!

* Separate Canadian edition also available
† Separate U.K. edition also available

Available wherever books are sold. For more information or to order direct: U.S. customers visit www.dummies.com or call 1-877-762-2974.
U.K. customers visit www.wileyeurope.com or call (0) 1243 843291. Canadian customers visit www.wiley.ca or call 1-800-567-4797.